A *Citizen's* Guide to
POLITICS
IN AMERICA

How the System Works
&
How to Work the System

A *Citizen's* Guide to
POLITICS
IN AMERICA

··

How the System Works

&

How to Work the System

··

BARRY R. RUBIN

M.E. Sharpe
Armonk, New York
London, England

Library of Congress Cataloging-in-Publication Data

Rubin, Barry R., 1947–
A citizen's guide to politics in America : how the system works—and
how to work the system / Barry R. Rubin.
p.   cm.
Includes bibliographical references and index.
ISBN 0-7656-0028-5 (alk. paper : c).—
ISBN 0-7656-0029-3 (alk. paper : p)
1. Politics, Practical—United States.   2. Public opinion—United
States.   3. United States—Politics and government.   4. Political
participation—United States.   I. Title.
JK1726.R83   1997
323′.042′0973—DC20   96-46521
CIP
Printed in the United States of America

The paper used in this publication meets the minimum requirements of
American National Standard for Information Sciences—
Permanence of Paper for Printed Library Materials,
ANSI Z 39.48-1984.

∞

BM (c)   10   9   8   7   6   5   4   3   2   1
BM (p)   10   9   8   7   6   5   4   3   2   1

To my parents

Contents

Introduction

Politics isn't about candidates and elections, it's about solving public problems. How can we ensure that our water is safe to drink, that our schools provide quality education, that high-wage jobs do not migrate to other countries, that poor children do not go hungry, that excessive government regulation does not stifle job creation, and that crime and violence are reduced?

People have lost confidence in the ability of politicians, candidates, and the political process to solve these public problems. The public distrusts government in general and individual politicians in particular. Voters register as independents or seek out third-party candidates. They support term limits for "career politicians." They are tired of expensive, wasteful, government "solutions" that do not work and may even make problems worse.

But the problems will not go away, and the public does care. They may not like either candidate for Congress and may even stay home on election day, but they are concerned about the economy, the environment, health care, crime, and education, among other issues. The same public that opposes welfare supports helping families and children in need. Those who want lower taxes are willing to pay more if they get better schools and safer neighborhoods. People dislike government but demand police protection and clean water. They want to preserve endangered species, but not at the cost of their jobs.

And they are finding ways to make their voices heard. Increasingly, citizens, businesses, and interest groups are moving beyond the ballot box to change our public and private institutions. Occasionally, almost by accident, citizens discover the right levers to push—defeating the nomination of an unsuitable appointee or demanding and getting increased police protection. At the same time, businesses and interest groups are becoming more sophisticated in their efforts to shape public policy, using their resources to influence public opinion and persuade decision makers.

All of this is occurring in the midst of a reexamination of government and issues. Should public schools be run by private entities? Should welfare recipients lose their benefits if they have more children while on welfare? Should women and minorities have preference in hiring? Does government regulation protect workers and consumers, or does it unnecessarily restrict businesses and cost jobs? If there is a role for government in any of these areas, should it be at the federal, state, or local level?

How are these issues being addressed in our society? Who initiates change and how do they do it? What role do citizens, interest groups, and businesses play? The answers to these questions take on new significance in an era of electronic town halls, the Internet, 800 numbers, and slick television advertisements that sell issues to the public in the same way they sell candidates or toothpaste. It is also a time of radio call-in shows, fueled by continuous cable television coverage of Congress, that provide opportunities for citizens to make their views known to listeners across the country. And we all know that elected representatives scrutinize the polls and read their mail before taking a position. Whether it is health care, safe schools, clean air, abortion, gun control, property rights, or tort reform, America has entered a new age of issue campaigns.

Until recently, little effort has been devoted to understanding the forces at work in shaping the politics of issues. *A Citizen's Guide to Politics in America* is a comprehensive and practical guide to issue advocacy: how citizens, businesses, and interest groups influence the behavior of institutions such as government, businesses, and schools. It provides a systematic analysis of the political and social forces that underlie every effort to change the behavior of public and private institutions at the local, state, and national levels. It examines the way issue advocates harness those powerful forces that accomplish or frustrate change.

As a manual for issue advocates, from citizen activists to corporate issue managers who monitor and influence public policymaking, *A Citizen's Guide to Politics in America* takes the reader through the process of making change, from the germ of an idea to finding supporters, getting the word out, and building the critical mass of people, energy, and ideas necessary to make our society more responsive to the needs and desires of the public than it now is. This book combines a theoretical analysis of those forces with practical examples and guidelines for success drawn from recent issue campaigns.

A Citizen's Guide to Politics in America analyzes how public policy issues become ripe for action in our society at the local, state, and national levels, and how individuals as well as public and private institutions affect that process. It explores the key elements of all issue campaigns: the role of interest groups, the media, and other institutions in shaping issues; how coalitions are built and maintained to support issues; how the public arrives at a judgment about issues; how grassroots support is mobilized; the way information and lobbying are used to influence the outcome of issues; and citizen efforts to address issues directly, through state and local ballot initiatives.

A Citizen's Guide to Politics in America is dedicated to citizen advocates who, in the course of busy lives already full with careers and family and financial concerns, have made time to work for change. Their efforts have allowed the rest of us to draw the road map of the trails they have blazed. Here the experienced will gain greater insight and understanding into where they have been and where they want to go; the novice will find a guide through the hidden pathways of political power.

This book builds on the work of everyone, whether in citizen organizations, think tanks, academia, membership organizations, or business and industry, who wants the institutions of society to be responsive to their concerns. Only when more citizens master the tools of issue advocacy can we hope to find and implement lasting solutions to public problems, solutions that go beyond bumper-sticker slogans and transcend partisan politics.

A *Citizen's* Guide to
POLITICS
IN AMERICA

How the System Works

&

How to Work the System

1

Change Is in the Air

Myra Rosenbloom was a seventy-three-year-old woman from Bloomington, Indiana, whose husband died in a hospital that, to her surprise, had no physician on duty.[1] Spending six days and nights on a bench inside the Indiana state capitol, Mrs. Rosenbloom overcame objections from doctors and hospitals and convinced the state legislature to require hospitals to have a doctor on duty at all times.

Bill Gradison is a former member of Congress. He left Congress to become a highly paid lobbyist for the Health Insurance Association of America, and with the help of two television commercial "stars"—Harry and Louise—led a successful lobbying campaign to derail President Clinton's health-care-reform efforts in 1994.

Mrs. Rosenbloom and Mr. Gradison appear to have little in common. Mrs. Rosenbloom was an "ordinary citizen" who set out to right a wrong. She had no previous lobbying experience and knew little about the intricate legislative process she sought to influence. Mr. Gradison, in contrast, was an experienced legislator who was hired to lobby his old friends in Congress. But instead of relying on the time-honored, behind-the-scenes lobbying tactics that once dominated issue advocacy, Bill Gradison ironically tore a page from Myra Rosenbloom's book. He focused his lobbying resources on persuading and mobilizing ordinary citizens like Myra Rosenbloom.

Whether led by the likes of Mrs. Rosenbloom or Mr. Gradison, change happens whenever a small group of committed (and sometimes well-funded) individuals or organizations makes their voices heard loudly and clearly by their fellow citizens and by those in a position to accomplish change. From citizen activists circulating petitions and demonstrating at City Hall to support or oppose a new homeless shelter, to businesses and insurance companies seeking relief from government regulations or product liability lawsuits, individuals and interest groups are demanding change. To an extent largely unforseen by the political and legislative establishment, the public is taking an active and influential role in shaping the way issues are addressed at every level of government.

Citizens are responding spontaneously to the latest news coverage or C-SPAN broadcast of congressional hearings. And they are answering calls to action by interest groups or radio talk-show hosts, even the exhortations of that fictional couple "Harry and Louise" in their thirty-second issue advertisements. Citizen voices are amplified by the interest groups to which they belong and modulated by the sound of thousands of other interest groups.

Even Myra Rosenbloom did not act alone. She quickly found herself in the midst of a battle between the Indiana Hospital Association and the Disabled American Veterans. And Bill Gradison's voice was only one in a loud and angry debate dominated by the American Association of Retired Persons and the Pharmaceutical Research and Manufacturers Association, among other powerful interest groups.

This chapter examines the many roots and manifestations of the growing public dissatisfaction with government as usual that has led to an explosion of citizen and interest-group participation in public policymaking.

Everyone Has Something to Say

When President Clinton decided to nominate Zoe Baird as his first attorney general in 1993, Ralph Nader announced his opposition to her appointment. As general counsel of Aetna Insurance Company, Ms. Baird had spearheaded a campaign to limit corporate liability for legal wrongs. While the tort reform she had espoused later became a part of the House Republican's 1994 Contract with America, Nader's opposition did not resonate with the public. His numerous appearances on radio and television provoked no great outpouring of calls or letters to Congress. Few senators, who would have to approve Ms. Baird's nomination, raised any objections. Her confirmation as the nation's first female attorney general seemed assured.

Until, that is, the public learned that she and her law professor husband had failed to pay social security taxes for a nanny hired to care for her child. Failure to pay the required tax for a domestic worker is a relatively minor and widespread legal violation, but Ms. Baird's offer to make restitution and her belated apologies did not impress the public. She would be, after all, the nation's chief law enforcer; shouldn't she be above reproach?

Talk radio programs, led by the popular syndicated host Rush Limbaugh, emphasized her six-figure salary and her husband's position as a law professor to rouse public anger over her nomination. How could such a smart and well-connected woman be so negligent or so greedy? Public opposition to her nomination grew and fed upon itself, with talk radio providing a convenient forum for discussion and an outlet for hostility. If the public was unsure how to express its opposition, Mr. Limbaugh and others conveniently provided names, addresses, and phone numbers. Senate offices and the White House were flooded with telephone calls, faxes, e-mail messages, and even handwritten letters, expressing outrage over her nomination and urging that she not be confirmed. A chastened White House backed down.

What was most surprising about the public outpouring of opposition to Ms. Baird's nomination was the relatively modest nature of her transgression (although admittedly difficult for a prospective attorney general to explain) and the fact that she had not provoked the ire of an established and well-organized constituency. Her nomination was unlike President Clinton's plan to permit gays to serve openly in the military. That proposal had mobilized long-standing constituencies on either side of the issue (veterans, civil rights, and religious organizations, among others) who in turn activated their own alert networks and urged their members to communicate their views to the president and Congress.

Zoe Baird had struck a nerve in the body politic, and the public responded. Whether the public disliked or distrusted Ms. Baird because of her failure to pay the "nanny tax," or whether her nomination touched a deeper sense of unfairness or "politics as usual," it stimulated an angry and disgruntled public to take some small measure of control over its government.

People discovered the power to make their leaders listen to their views, and not just on election day. Politicians were learning the same thing. Zoe Baird's nomination would open the floodgates to public participation. In short order the public would make its voices heard on health-care reform, crime, the balanced budget, and even the North American Free Trade Agreement. The public was having its say on issues, and the politicians were paying attention.

Citizen Perot and the Contract with America

Just when it seemed that the public was ready to wash its hands of greedy politicians profiting from the savings and loan collapse or bowing to the onslaught of foreign lobbyists, Ross Perot emerged to tap a rich vein of public dissatisfaction with government policymaking. While he ultimately received only a small fraction of the popular vote in the 1992 presidential election, he identified and reinforced deep public concerns on a wide range of issues, including a profound distrust of "career politicians."

Ross Perot was not burdened with an established political party and its accompanying platform. Liberated from those constraints, he set out to talk issues with the American people. He did not rely on catchy slogans or take his cue from public opinion polls. Instead he tackled difficult, boring issues such as balancing the budget, restricting foreign lobbyists, and requiring trade to be free and fair. Perot believed they were the critical issues facing America, and he rolled up his sleeves and attacked them.

Perot appeared on television and radio to talk about dull, dusty issues. Sometimes he paid for the privilege; more often, the media competed for a few moments of his time. In the process, he helped stimulate a larger public debate about congressional term limits, the need for a balanced budget, and finally, after the election, approval of the North Atlantic Free Trade Agreement. Perot talked issues to the American people, and they responded. They listened, debated, voted, and made their voices heard.

Instinctively, Perot discovered a basic truth about American public life: people care deeply about issues, even ones they do not immediately grasp. Unburdened as he was by political parties and unconcerned by the effect of his "coattails" in a presidential election, Perot eschewed typical political rhetoric. He talked the public's language, addressing citizens' core concerns about jobs and family, and using words they understood. He changed the way the public learns about issues, the way politicians present them to the public, and the way the public reacts when it learns enough to care.

In many ways Perot inspired Newt Gingrich and the Contract with America. In 1994, Republican congressional candidates adopted their own political platform. But it was not replete with the usual platitudes and generalities of political party platforms that are meticulously negotiated and drafted and then promptly forgotten. Instead, the candidates pledged to take immediate action to reform Congress and to work for specific legislation to balance the budget, and address crime, welfare, litigation reform, and congressional term limits. They told the public in detail how they would solve America's problems. To great surprise, they proceeded to act on their platform and to try to fulfill their specific promises to the electorate. Politics would be changed forever.

"It's the Issue, Stupid"

The Contract with America did not have all the answers to America's problems. But it reflected the simple truth that Ross Perot also illustrated, that people may be skeptical of the motives of all politicians, but they care about issues that affect their neighborhood or family, their economic and physical security, their happiness and well-being. Should the local library be permitted to showcase books about alternative lifestyles? Will the plant down the street be allowed to emit toxic fumes? Will an employer be required to increase the minimum wage or pay for the cost of health insurance?

The public was fed up with crime in 1994. How did the politicians respond? They did what they do best. They argued.

But while politicians argued about gun control and "pork" masquerading as "midnight basketball," the public outrage at crime led to loud demands for passage of controversial and questionably effective "three strikes and you're out laws" at the state and federal levels. A public fed up with crime endorsed the death penalty, ignoring "expert" opinions that the death penalty was more costly and more trouble than it was worth. The politicians and the experts no longer had a monopoly on public policy.

Myra Rosenbloom was one individual fighting a lonely fight. She was, of course, the exception. Most Americans lack her dedication and determination. Instead, they join interest groups because they want to "hire" someone to advance their interests. An individual can create his or her own political agenda by joining groups that reflect the individual's concerns on public issues. Whatever the issue, there is always an interest group eager for members and money to advance its work: protecting health care for the elderly, repealing gun-control laws, supporting term limits or clean-air laws, opposing prayer in schools, and supporting abortion. Whether it is the American Association of Retired Persons or the National Federation of Independent Businesses, citizens and businesses are relying more on interest groups than politicians to represent them and advance their public policy concerns.

That is understandable because voters inevitably compromise on candidates, often choosing the lesser of two evils. After all, politicians must invariably appeal to the broadest possible group of voters: every legislative district contains people who are for and against the death penalty, gun control, abortion, the Endangered Species Act, and a tax on gas-guzzling automobiles. Voters must make compromises when they enter the polling place, for no voter will agree with any single candidate's stand on every issue. Interest groups, in contrast, are "pure" vehicles to help citizens make their voices heard.

Elected representatives still play an important public policymaking role, but now they must answer to the public and their interest groups, not just on election day, but every day they are in office, and on every issue they face.

"Harry and Louise"

Wherever presidential candidate Bill Clinton went in 1992 he seemed to find public support for health-care reform. Workers wanted health insurance and affordable medical care. People wanted to be able to change jobs without worrying about losing their health insurance or being denied coverage because of a "preexisting condition." Bill Clinton was taking his cue from the successful 1991 senatorial campaign of Harris Wofford in Pennsylvania, who appeared to have discovered the powerful public interest in health-care reform.

All that changed, however, after Bill Clinton was elected president in 1992 and began to devise a concrete proposal for reform. His proposal angered small and large businesses, insurance companies, doctors, hospitals, and drug manufacturers. It befuddled the public, whose early support for the concept of health insurance reform dissipated when the details of the Clinton proposal became clearer. Would individuals be forced to abandon their family doctors and be herded into health maintenance organizations? Would the quality of health care suffer? Would individuals pay more for less?

Credit for the swing in public opinion largely goes to "Harry and Louise," two fictional characters who appeared in issue advertisements created by Bill Gradison's health insurance clients. Using all the production values and persuasive powers that advertisers employ to sell consumer products through the mass media, Harry and Louise brought Madison Avenue to the selling of public policy. Instead of selling soap, they sold doubt about the president's health-care plan, and they did it very effectively. The commercials often aired in prime time; they attracted nearly as much attention on the evening news as Mr. Clinton.

The Harry and Louise advertisements marked the first real crossover from political campaigns to issue advertisements. Powerful interests were focusing attention on the public—the grassroots—instead of relying on traditional "under the Capitol dome" lobbying. The public was a full-fledged participant in public policymaking.

Now you can dial (202) 456–1111 and be in touch with the White House "comment line." You can use your touch-tone telephone to record your opinion on the latest issues. A summary of the responses is reportedly provided to the president, and the totals occasionally find their way into the media as reflections of public opinion. Or you can contact your senator through the Internet. Just point your web browser to http://www.senate.gov/senator/membmail.html.

The White House, with its comment line and Internet address and cadre of telephone and letter answerers, is not alone in soliciting and assessing public opinion. Issue advertisements that now routinely flood the mass media inevitably include a telephone number. The caller who indicates (by pushing the right combination of buttons) that he or she agrees with the position of the interest that paid for the advertisement can be directly put through to a senator or representative. A citizen sitting comfortably on the couch watching television can instantly be in touch with the right office on Capitol Hill. Advocacy was never so easy.

When the public responded by calling 800 numbers and communicating with its representatives, nearly every other interest quickly joined in with its own issue advertisements. Advertising blitzes directed to the public soon became commonplace on controversial issues, such as the North American Free Trade Agreement (NAFTA), tort law reform, and the balanced budget. A new era of issue advocacy was born.

The inability of President Clinton to persuade the public to support his health-care initiative (or to overcome the powerful efforts of reform opponents) was an early sign of a popular uprising. With media coverage of issues focusing in large part on daily assessments of public opinion, elected officials paid close attention to the polls and communications from their constituents before deciding what to say and how to vote.

This process, which is typical of electoral campaigns, was a relatively new phenomenon in issue campaigns. It raises anew an important question: are legislators elected to lead or merely to follow the current opinion of the majority of their constituents? This tension between representative and direct democracy is a continuing theme in this book, as it is in contemporary issue politics. It raises important questions, to which we return, about leadership and the willingness of elected officials to defy temporal public opinion in pursuit of the larger goal of identifying and implementing sound public policy.

"Vote Yes on Proposition 144"

When voters enter the polling booth, they are often asked to do more than choose between candidates for office. The rebirth of the ballot initiative is still more evidence of the public's dissatisfaction with the traditional ways government addresses issues.

Initiatives or referenda, now available in twenty-six states, allow citizens to gather signatures and place specific legislative proposals before the electorate for action. The public, acting as a citizen-legislature, can enact or repeal laws. Initiatives date back to 1904, but they have recently exploded on state ballots addressing issues such as gun control, homelessness, insurance reform, real estate tax, labeling products containing toxics, raising taxes on cigarettes and alcohol, the death penalty, school prayer, bottle deposit, abortion rights, gambling, term limits, permitting doctors to assist suicides, and campaign finance reform.

The recent rapid growth in the number and scope of initiatives dates to 1978, when California voters approved Proposition 13, which provided homeowners with relief from rising real estate taxes. The floodgates opened shortly thereafter, and citizens, businesses, and interest groups rediscovered the "direct democracy" tool of ballot initiatives. Any interest that did not believe it was getting a full and fair hearing by the legislature discovered that with enough time and resources it could bypass the legislature, taking the law "into its own hands." Understandably, the public responded enthusiastically to this opportunity to vote on issues it cares about; in some states ballot initiatives now draw more attention than candidates, particularly in off-year elections.

Citizens concerned with an unresponsive legislature had discovered a new tool to address important issues. Business interests often found their considerable campaign contributions to legislators of little use when the public acted as the legislature. But interests potentially affected by ballot initiatives soon became adept at mounting massive "Harry and Louise"-style advertising campaigns. Advertising and grassroots campaign professionals, often armed with considerable budgets, quickly lobbied the public, as they once did legislators. Everyone had suddenly discovered a new outlet for citizen anger and concern, and a new set of opportunities to shape public policies.

Everything Is on the Table

The Cold War is over, the Iron Curtain has rusted, and former enemies are friends in need of help. After forty years of fighting communism, Americans no longer fear nuclear annihilation.

But all the news is not good. For the first time since the dark days of the Great Depression and World War II, a generation of Americans are facing the prospect of not living as well as their parents. Government resources, whether to clean the air or pick up the trash, are suddenly and starkly limited. Individually and collectively, Americans can no longer have it all.

Legislators and the public now must make choices and accept the consequences of their choices. Lower property taxes, which are popular, might mean less money for local schools, which is unpopular. Incarcerating thrice-convicted felons for life is popular; raising taxes to build more prisons and hire more guards is not. Denying women welfare after a number of years or a number of children is popular; taking food out the mouths of their children is not. Cleaning up the air and the environment is popular; driving business costs up and jobs away is not.

As pressure mounts to balance our national and state budgets, and to reduce taxes in the process, important decisions must be made about which tasks government should not do. At the same time, questions are being raised about the efficacy of long-standing government programs: Are government solutions now part of the problem? Do affirmative action programs promote unfairness and inequality? Does welfare create need and dependency? Do endangered species laws protect owls over people? Do government regulations protect the public from dangerous drugs or delay the availability of life-saving medicines?

And if government action is appropriate, why should it be the federal government that takes the lead? Why not let the states (which are theoretically more responsive to public concerns) decide important issues that affect people's lives, such as education, health care, and the environment?

Traditional notions about government functions and national priorities are being reexamined. On issue after issue, a restless, anxious public is poised to make its voice heard. The next chapter begins the process of examining how issues are addressed and how the public's voice is heard.

2

The Anatomy of an Issue Campaign

Issue campaigns are not born, they are made. A successful issue advocate must do more than "manage" a predictable agenda of issues of concern to his or her constituency. Effective issue advocacy requires an active, ongoing analysis of issues and interest groups and their public and private activities. It also demands an understanding of the contemporary social, cultural, and political forces that shape how people view issues and the way government responds to them.

This chapter begins our analysis of issue campaigns, the people and processes that bring them to public attention, and the built-in resistances to addressing and resolving issues. It explores the many steps and cycles issues go through as they compete for public attention and gain momentum on local, state, and national public policy agendas. It describes tactics advocates use to analyze the dynamics of each issue and understand which individuals and interests are potentially affected by an issue. It takes a first look at determining who to influence, and how to influence them, to make change.

The Genesis of an Issue

Sometimes an issue arises out of Myra Rosenbloom's personal experience and sense of outrage. Other times, it is President Clinton, piggybacking on the success of Senator Harris Wofford, raising health-care reform. While it is easy to trace Mrs. Rosenbloom's actions to the unfortunate experience of her husband's death, it is more difficult to find the roots of health-care reform. Those roots are typically more eclectic and intertwined.

Senator Wofford's 1991 victory tapped into public concern about health-care costs and the availability of health insurance. But that was far from the first appearance of health-care reform on the national agenda. Its roots go back as far as Theodore Roosevelt's unsuccessful 1912 presidential candidacy during which he made national health insurance a campaign issue.[1] In 1937, President Franklin Roosevelt engineered passage of social security, which included very limited health-care insurance.

The mantle was taken up by President Johnson who, in 1965, signed Medicare and Medicaid into law. In 1969, President Nixon spoke of the "crisis" in health care but was unable to convince Congress to reform health insurance. President Carter attempted reform during his presidency, but his efforts came to naught.

But the presidents were not acting in a vacuum. Consumer organizations, unions, and senior citizens were active proponents of reform. So were businesses concerned with rising insurance costs that raised prices, siphoned profits, and made American products less competitive with those made in other countries. Doctors, hospitals, insurers, and small businesses were concerned that any health-care reform could affect them, sometimes negatively, sometimes positively, depending on the shape reform took.

Issues as different as Mrs. Rosenbloom's campaign to require Indiana hospitals to have attending physicians and President Clinton's efforts to reform the health-care delivery system will understandably follow different courses as they move through the political process toward resolution. Unlike a court case or even legislation, issues do not follow a prescribed track; rarely do two issues follow the same precise course. A full appreciation for the capacity of individuals and interests to make change requires us to understand what motivates Mrs. Rosenbloom and Mr. Gradison, and their allies and opponents, and to respect the inventiveness and creativity that each brings to issue advocacy.

While Mrs. Rosenbloom found the time and energy to convert her sense of outrage and desire to make change into a concerted issue campaign, most individuals face busy lives full of personal, financial, and family issues. They may care deeply about problems facing their community or their nation, but may not have time to work for change or an understanding of how they can be effective issue advocates. Many feel powerless, believing it impossible to "fight City Hall."

The small businessperson may face the same hurdles while trying to meet a payroll and deal with an unresponsive government licensing or regulatory system. Businesses would much rather be creating and market- ing products, planning advertising campaigns, and cutting expenses. But they cannot ignore the power of government to grant or deny benefits, and to create and solve problems. They just cannot afford to forecast sales without understanding—and trying to influence—government policies on minimum wages, mandatory recycling, and truth-in-advertising, among many others. Even Microsoft founder Bill Gates understands that his innovative corporation can suffer (or benefit) from government policies. Reluctantly, Microsoft diverted resources from new product development to issue advocacy: "I'm sorry that we have to have a Washington pres- ence," Gates announced.[2]

Change will inevitably run up against policy inertia. Citizens and their leaders are reluctant to try new and different solutions. The public may not have faith in social security, but it will likely be extremely reluctant to support privatizing social security. Health care costs too much and insurance may be difficult to get and keep, but the public is unwilling to embrace comprehensive reform and the possibility of dra- matic changes in health-care delivery. The preference for the "devil you know," and the fear of the unknown, pervades every effort at public policy innovation.

Despite these built-in resistances to change, change happens when citizens are sufficiently motivated and empowered to take action.

Issue Origins

Public and private events and experiences can stimulate individuals and organizations to work for change. A parent sends a child off to school for the first time and suddenly confronts schools that do not meet local fire codes; a small businessperson is sued by a large corpo- ration for the entire cost of cleaning up a toxic waste dump to which the small businessperson inadvertently contributed a small amount of waste; Lois Gibbs, the founder of the Citizen's Clearinghouse Against Hazardous Waste, discovers that her family's home is located on Love

Canal, one of the most notorious toxic waste sites in the nation; the parents of Stephanie Roper, brutally murdered in Maryland, form a committee to ensure that the rights of victims are adequately represented in criminal cases; a federal building explodes in Oklahoma City, and a president and a nation question hate speech and gun-carrying militias; a gunman opens fire in a crowded schoolyard in Sacramento, leading to a call for a ban on assault weapons; a doctor providing legal abortions is murdered by an abortion opponent, and a new debate arises on the need to protect clinics and lawful activities; young Adam Walsh disappears, and his father begins a national campaign to find missing children; Nicole Brown Simpson's murder draws public attention to domestic violence; an outbreak of disease caused by improperly labeled or handled meat at a Jack-in-the-Box restaurant leads to a reexamination of food labeling and preparation.

Issues can originate in the personal experiences of Lois Gibbs or Stephanie Roper. They can also begin as scientific or technical studies, such as an academic analysis of the effects of global warming, a federal government agency report about the health hazards of tobacco (even when inhaled by nonsmokers as "second-hand smoke"), or an environmental organization's survey of the extinction or endangerment of animal species. Reports can call attention to new problems or document the extent of acknowledged problems, such as childhood hunger or homelessness. Reports of increased crime can lead to calls for the death penalty or handgun control.

National or global political events can also compel society to address issues, such as the Iraqi invasion of Kuwait or nuclear proliferation or international terrorism. New technologies or scientific breakthroughs can lead to issues such as genetic engineering, surrogate parenting, or calls to restrict pornography and increase privacy on electronic computer networks.

Issues can arise from changing views of society or emerging values. Discrimination based on race or gender is no longer socially or legally acceptable. Now the public questions the wisdom of affirmative action, the need to bus children to integrate schools, whether to permit race-based scholarships, and the role of gays in the military. We no longer seem to have enough resources for everyone, so we question the need to provide universal medical care and education, even for legal immigrants and their children.

Most issues have multiple origins: government crime statistics reinforce individual concerns for public safety and are fueled by a single horrific and widely reported crime. The more different factors at work, the more likely an issue will attract broad and deep public attention.

Issue Catalysts

Issues need catalysts. Sometimes it takes only a single, persistent individual to draw significant attention to an issue. That person can be the "ordinary citizen" deciding to "adopt a cause"—Myra Rosenbloom or Lois Gibbs or homeless rights advocate Mitch Snyder. Or it can be a prominent individual who uses a public platform to advance an issue, such as former Surgeon General C. Everett Koop urging higher taxes on alcohol and tobacco, or changes in public behavior to curb AIDS; or former Education Secretary William Bennett campaigning against gangsta rap. Sometimes an issue is catalyzed by a popular or scholarly book, such as Upton Sinclair's *The Jungle* (safe food), Rachel Carson's *Silent Spring* (pesticide abuse), or Betty Friedan's *The Feminine Mystique* (women's rights).

For "ordinary citizens," making change is definitely an uphill battle, and one rarely engaged in alone. Most often, individuals band together in interest groups that act as issue catalysts. Interest groups, which we discuss in detail in chapter 3, are the main vehicle for small businesses or the elderly, for example, to raise and advance their interests. Interest groups have a sustained economic and political commitment to an issue that allows busy individuals to support efforts to make change without themselves becoming issue advocates. Individuals or businesses each make a small contribution to purchase the necessary resources and expertise to influence public policy.

The media (as we see in chapter 7) play a role in identifying issues and amplifying the voices that discuss them. While media investigations can raise important issues, such as Watergate, that is the exception rather than the rule. More often, the media publicize facts and events and draw attention to existing issues.

Political leaders can foster public consideration of an issue, such as Senator Dole's efforts to call attention to sex and violence in the entertainment industry. They generally serve as catalysts for issues already percolating up on our national agenda. So it was that President Clinton (and before him, Senator Wofford) took advantage of the public's concern with health insurance to raise the profile of the issue. And

Republican presidential candidate Steve Forbes used campaign advertisements and his own visibility to convert an economic idea—a flat tax system—into a national debate.

In a similar vein, House Speaker Newt Gingrich incorporated litigation reform into the Republican's 1994 Contract with America. But doctors, lawyers, insurers, large and small corporations, and academics and economists had been arguing about tort reform for years.[3] Manufacturers claimed that excessive jury awards stifled product innovation; doctors contended that rising malpractice claims forced them out of high-risk medical specialties, such as obstetrics, thereby limiting patient choices. Even before Speaker Gingrich took up the issue, Vice-President Dan Quayle championed it on the campaign trail in 1992.[4]

Sometimes the judiciary acts as an issue catalyst. Supreme Court decisions have catapulted to the top of our national agenda issues such as school desegregation, abortion rights, and flag burning. In each instance, the Supreme Court decided cases brought before it by individuals and organizations themselves seeking to make change. The Court interpreted the Constitution to find hitherto unrecognized rights to attend integrated schools, have an abortion, and burn the flag in protest. Each decision subsequently ignited a public debate.

Issues begin with a core group of committed supporters who care deeply and are willing and able to dedicate time and resources to making change. Their challenge is to nurture issues in a way that builds broad-based public support leading to public demand for action. In the next section we examine the process by which issues are advanced on public policy agendas.

The Life Cycle of an Issue

There is no single prescribed path for issues to take as they compete for public attention and move toward resolution. But there are some predictable stops issues make along the way. Whatever the issue and whoever raises it or advances it, an issue has a life cycle during which it emerges from dormancy (few issues are totally new species), germinates, grows, and comes to fruition. The speed with which issues progress through each stage varies, and it is often difficult to discern precisely where one stage ends and the next begins.

Issue advocates who identify and understand an issue early in its life cycle will have more and better opportunities to influence its course and its ultimate resolution. A basic principle of physics is that it is easier to change the course of a body in motion if you exert even a modest force on it early in its progress.

Corporate issue managers for large and small businesses are constantly on the lookout for emerging issues. In addition to monitoring ongoing and well-established issue campaigns that may affect their business, they establish "issue periscopes," systems that can alert them to the earliest stirrings of an issue. For example, a fast-food restaurant chain that opposed mandatory disclosure of the nutritional value of its products would have a much better chance of derailing legislation or regulation if it identified the issue before bills were introduced and hearings held and voluntarily made changes to accommodate at least some of the public's concerns.

Stage 1: Seeds Germinate

In the first stage of an issue campaign, the initial rumblings of an issue are heard, usually in many different geographic areas and social communities but without significant coordination among them. Individuals or businesses talk among themselves about an issue, as might academics and interest groups, but the issue rarely attracts the attention of the media or government officials.

Slowly, as neighbors or businesses talk with one another, informal "issue networks" arise of people and organizations concerned about an issue. An environmental network might be composed of local and state government officials, academics, journalists, interest-group leaders, business persons, and policy experts.

The issue can then be discussed with a larger public, either directly, at town meetings or trade conferences, or indirectly, through popular or specialized media coverage. In both instances, those concerned with an issue take every opportunity to raise it with those who might share their concerns. A businessperson might discuss it at a chamber of commerce meeting; a union member might mention it to a friend at church; an interest group might raise it in a coalition meeting.

In time, larger, more sophisticated issue networks develop, and existing ones begin to discuss the issue and test ideas. Not only does word spread, but the initial issue catalysts get crucial feedback about how others, less directly concerned and committed, view the issue. Issue networks help monitor and assess policy developments and provide a forum to discuss existing and potential solutions. They allow ideas to migrate across geographic, political, and other lines.

At this stage, issue advocates are more creative and forward looking than practical and solution oriented. An idea need not be comprehensive, nor must it necessarily be part of a coherent whole. Stage 1 allows issue catalysts to assess whether the issue is worth pursuing; whether resolution is possible; and the depth, breadth, and identity of potential support or opposition. Idea and issue clarification are of more importance at this stage than identifying specific targets or solutions.

Stage 2: Shoots Emerge and Put Down Roots

If Stage 1 reveals significant and widespread concern about an issue, and the energy and resources to pursue a resolution, the issue may continue its progress into Stage 2. The community of individuals and organizations interested in an issue broadens as several leaders emerge to speak out about an issue and stimulate discussion and analysis. This is the time to test and modify ideas, through workshops, conferences, and seminars that draw together citizens and experts to examine the problem and its solutions. The issue gains in legitimacy from serious public examination by policy experts and academics. Intensity builds and solutions and potential targets are explored. Trial balloons are often floated to gauge popular and political reaction.

In Stage 2 interest groups take positions on the issue and reach out in two directions: to educate and gain the support (or opposition) from their own members, and to attract broader public support (or opposition) through the media. Coalitions of interest groups are formed to advance the issue and coordinate and focus the work of the initial issue networks.

Issue catalysts probe public sentiment on the issue through polling and focus groups. They explore and test thematic approaches to putting forth the issue so that it will be received favorably and have the potential to attract the greatest number and broadest base of supporters. For example, what was once a campaign to require deposits on soft-drink containers is now reformulated as an effort to improve the community and conserve energy.

Different points of view emerge during Stage 2, as opposition grows and begins its own evolutionary process. Public debate increasingly includes opposition spokespeople who provide balance and perspective to the issue, creating additional challenges and difficulties for issue catalysts. Money is often raised during this stage to plan and execute a campaign and prepare for Stage 3.

Stage 3: Buds Form and Flowers Bloom

If sufficiently broad and deep support develops during Stage 2, the issue may advance to Stage 3, where the public debate intensifies. The range of potential solutions is narrowed as a specific proposal for action is formulated and endorsed or opposed.

Broad-based coalitions are formed to reach out for additional supporters, many of whom need considerable convincing before agreeing to join the campaign. At the same time, many different voices seek to be heard and have their positions accommodated on the issue. The media become the battleground as both sides marshal information and arguments to persuade the public and decision makers.

An active and well-organized opposition raises doubts and questions about the desirability and feasibility of the campaign's goals. "Unlikely" alliances draw together differing interest groups, causing opponents and weak supporters to reevaluate their positions.

A coordinated lobbying campaign targets the grassroots and decision makers in an effort to build and demonstrate public support. Information is adduced to persuade government officials and other decision makers, who are urged to assess their positions on the issue and choose sides. Newspapers editorialize and public opinion polls are taken and widely reported.

As resolution of the issue approaches, both sides consider compromise and alternative solutions. "Final" action occurs, and whether it is victory or defeat, both sides regroup and seek ways to continue to advance their positions.

Issue Dynamics

The first task of an issue advocate is to understand the issue and the dynamic forces that act upon it. For each issue, this means (1) *mapping the issue*, that is, understanding its ramifications, including who cares about it and why; and (2) *mapping the power*, identifying the key levers of power and how to pull them.

Issues are always more complex than they first appear. Each issue has its own dynamic: its effect on other existing or potential issues, and the nature and level of support or opposition it will likely engender from interest groups and the public.

Health-care reform appeared to be about providing insurance and medical care for those who could not afford it or whose health precluded getting coverage. It quickly became about the quality of care and an individual's ability to choose his or her doctor. The North American Free Trade Agreement began as an effort to increase trade and lower tariffs, but the public debate revolved around jobs, human rights, and the environment. The Endangered Species Act was passed to stop the destruction of plant and animal species, but the subsequent debate is about the wisdom of protecting every last spotted owl or snail darter, and whether doing so is worth the cost in lost jobs.

A simple example illustrates issue mapping and power mapping.

Mapping the Issue

Imagine that you head the local Downtown Retail Merchants' Association, representing small shopowners located in the downtown area of a small city of 50,000 people. Like many such cities, the downtown retail trade is struggling to compete against sprawling suburban malls. But your members have still another problem. The retailers have noticed a marked increase in the number of homeless people in the downtown area. Customer surveys reveal that aggressive panhandlers scare away customers and hurt business.

You raise the problem at the monthly luncheon meeting of the Downtown Retail Merchants' Association and ask for ideas. Everyone agrees that the presence of homeless people downtown deters shoppers. No one seems to know what to do about it until someone speaks up and suggests turning an abandoned school building several miles from downtown into a shelter or transitional home for the homeless. After much discussion, the association agrees to support an effort to convert the school into a shelter. They appoint you to raise the issue with the mayor.

You are pretty much a novice at issue advocacy (at least so far), but you do know the mayor, and he agrees to meet with you. The mayor, an old hand at issue politics, tells you that the idea sounds good to him, but he would like to know what other people in the city think about it: "I need to know who would support this project, who would oppose it, and why. And I'll need more information about how your proposal would affect the entire community."

Because you respect your old friend the mayor (and because you will need his support to achieve your goal), you agree to talk to citizens, community leaders, and other businesses and report back to him. Nevertheless, you still think your first instinct was right: who could oppose sheltering the homeless, making the downtown more attractive, and putting an empty, crumbling school building to use?

Plenty of people.

You discover that people in the residential neighborhood surrounding the abandoned school are opposed to "busing in undesirables from other parts of town." You suspect they are concerned about potentially declining property values. Parents and children's advocacy groups express concern for the safety of children who have to walk through the neighborhood to get to school or play in the adjacent playground. Someone raises the specter of child abuse.

To your surprise, a local church, already active in providing shelter for the homeless (and which you thought would welcome the help), opposes the idea. Church leaders explain that they know how to run a humane, caring, and religious-oriented shelter and are concerned with how the homeless will be treated in a city-run shelter. While they do not come out and say so, you suspect they might also be concerned about losing state and federal funding for their own shelter.

You approach the local police, who you believe are increasingly frustrated by the time and resources necessary to deal with the homeless people downtown. When you arrive for your meeting with the police commissioner, he informs you that your proposal will increase his department's costs by spreading out the need for patrols to the once-quiet neighborhood surrounding the old school building. After much discussion, he agrees to support your proposal, but only if your organization is willing to support increased funding to meet this new policing need. Of course, that might require higher taxes, which your members definitely will not like.

The police union, in contrast, supports your idea without qualification. Its members would rather patrol the suburban area in squad cars than the downtown area on foot. Besides, they believe your proposal will lead to more police being hired. Of course, that would also mean higher taxes.

Local doctors and hospitals object to spending money to convert the old school to a shelter, saying it is more of the same "warehousing of the homeless, when what they really need is more mental and physical health care." The school board, which you discover has no real plans for the building, is concerned that it will be sued if the homeless people sheltered there hurt themselves or others.

Local civil rights groups object to your idea as a form of punishment without trial, claiming you want to uproot the homeless (most of whom happen to be minorities in this community) and force them to live where it best suits you. Welfare reform groups think it provides too much help to the homeless, who, in their view, must be weaned away from government programs. Middle-class taxpayers who are struggling to make ends meet think it is unfair for them to have to work hard to pay the rent and buy food, when others get it free, and with the help of their own tax dollars.

Ah, but at least you have the business community on your side. Or so you think. While the downtown retail merchants, concerned with their own profits, clearly support you, larger businesses, and those located away from downtown, do not. They are concerned that if you "make things too comfortable for the homeless, they will flock to our community, giving us a bad image and lowering property values."

Mapping the Power

At this point you have learned more about the problems of the homeless and its effect on the community than you ever wanted to know. When you brief the association's members, they still want to pursue the issue, despite the substantial opposition you uncovered.

Your next step is to decide how to accomplish your goal. Who has the power to make the decisions you want made, and who has the power to convince them to support you? Your task is to assess and map the power structure.

First, where does the power lie? Can the elected school board or the appointed school commissioner convert the school into a homeless shelter? Or does the mayor or the City Council have that power? What about the zoning board? Or some combination of each of those officials? Once you have identified the key sources of power, you have to decide how to influence them.

It turns out that the key official is your friend the mayor. On your next visit with him, you proceed to answer his original question, explaining in detail which constituencies in the community care about the issue and why. The mayor has a worried look on his face and explains that with so much potential opposition he will have to "study the issue."

Since the mayor is obviously reluctant to support you, your job is to persuade him. You must identify the key constituencies the mayor cares about and how to influence them. If the mayor has the power to make this happen, then who has power over him?

The answer will turn out to be a surprising number of people inside the community and beyond. Perhaps it is a key labor or business leader whose support is valuable in an upcoming election. Or a City Council member or a campaign contributor. Or the editor of the local newspaper. Or the spiritual leader of the mayor's church. Or the mayor's wife. Or his doctor or lawyer. Or even the local state representative.

Your organization's members—the retail merchants—no doubt have many contacts with influential people in the community, people to whom the mayor listens. Can any of them be persuaded by you, or people who share your interest, to influence the mayor's decision on this issue? What is your next step?

In the following chapters we explore the component elements of an issue campaign. The next chapter examines the power of interest groups, including the sources of that power and ways to harness it.

3

Issues and Interest Groups

Americans are a society of joiners. People come together in organizations and clubs to share interests, learn skills, and make friends. Businesses join associations to share information, learn new technologies, and formulate strategic plans. State and local government officials create organizations to share resources, learn from others' experiences, and discuss mutual frustrations. When each of these efforts turns to influencing public policy, the organization becomes an interest group.

Interest groups are increasingly the mechanism of choice for individuals and organizations to make their voices heard on public policy issues. Individuals and organizations, who may not know enough about an issue or how to influence decision makers to participate effectively on their own, can hire an interest group to do the work for them.

Interest groups allow those who, individually, may have comparatively little at stake, to aggregate their stakes with others of similar size, thereby making it economically and politically feasible to attempt to influence policy. Using pooled resources, interest groups afford their members an opportunity to have a greater impact than they could have by acting separately.[1]

Inside Interest Groups

An interest group is an organized body of individuals or organizations (such as schools, businesses, state attorneys general, or churches) that attempts to influence public policy. The term *interest group* encompasses a broad diversity of formal and informal affinity groups and organizations. Some interest groups have a sustained presence and a long-term public policy vision, while others are created for a single, short-term purpose. Still others begin as social or fraternal organizations only to find themselves acting as interest groups when a shared public policy concern arises.

Veterans, seniors, union members, church members, lawyers, doctors, students, retailers, manufacturers—nearly everyone—is likely to find himself or herself a member of an interest group. And for every conceivable interest, citizens or businesses can find at least one interest group to represent them.

Interest groups pursue diverse policy agendas, such as civil liberties (for example, the American Civil Liberties Union), good government (Common Cause), consumer protection (Public Citizen), government regulations (Chamber of Commerce, Business Roundtable), and small business concerns (National Federation of Independent Businesses), or the rights of veterans (American Legion), seniors (American Association of Retired Persons), women (National Organization for Women), children (Children's Defense Fund), and minorities (National Association for the Advancement of Colored People).

Interest groups also represent libraries and librarians (American Library Association), artists and museums (American Arts Alliance), scientists (American Association for the Advancement of Science), chemical manufacturers (Chemical Manufacturers' Association), religious organizations (U.S. Catholic Conference), state legislators (National Conference of State Legislators), cities (National League of Cities), and nonprofit organizations (Independent Sector).

Many interest groups have dues-paying members who elect the organization's board of directors and help formulate policy and strategy. They have formal constituencies to which the elected or appointed leaders are answerable. Others ask only token contributions from their members, and in return give members little or no power in choosing the organization's leadership or policy priorities. They are accountable to a perspective or viewpoint, rather than to their membership.

President Clinton's 1994 effort to reform health care was the stage on which a vast diversity of interest groups sought to perform. The complicated dynamics of the issue included requirements that employers provide health insurance for their workers, potential restrictions on an individual's ability to choose his or her own doctor, the funding mechanism (taxes on alcohol and tobacco, so-called sin taxes), and restrictions on doctors' fees and prescription drug costs.

With so much at stake for so many, it is not surprising that more than 650 organizations and interest groups attempted to influence how, if at all, health-care reform would be accomplished. They represented the alcohol industry, hospitals, long-term-care facilities, pharmaceutical manufacturers and other health-care-related businesses, health-care providers, insurers, the tobacco industry, unions, large and small corporations not involved in providing health-care services, and those representing workers and citizens.

A random sampling of interest groups active on health-care reform provides insight into the nature and diversity of interest groups. They included the Alzheimer's Association, Beer Institute, California Abortion Rights Action League, Disabled American Veterans, Epilepsy Foundation of W. Central Florida, Food and Commercial Workers Union, Georgia Right to Life Committee, Hospital Council of Southern California, International Mass Retail Association, Juvenile Diabetes Foundation, Kentucky Medical Association, League of Women Voters, Medical Association of Georgia, National Association of Retail Druggists, Opticians Association of America, Pipe Tobacco Council, Republican National Committee, Self-Insurance Institute of America, Tennessee Association for Home Care, United Cerebral Palsy Association, Veterans of Foreign Wars, and the Wine Institute.[2]

The Interest-Group Explosion

As large as the above list is, it represents only a small fraction of the growing number of interest groups. And the number has been growing rapidly in recent years. Ten new interest groups were formed on average, per week, between 1970 and 1990.[3]

Why, when we elect and appoint dedicated public servants to make and implement public policy, does every conceivable interest feel the need to be represented by an interest group?

First, government, society, and the issues we face are becoming more complex. Trade, telecommunications, environment, and health care are just a few examples of areas where increased government and public examination of complicated issues has put large economic and other stakes at risk. The post–World War II growth in government, both at federal and state levels, has meant that more and more interests have had more and more at stake. It was natural to expect that with so much at stake, interest groups would arise to make sure each interest received its share.

Second, complex issues and a complex society create differing issue positions and a splintering of interest groups. At one time a single group could be relied on to advocate for the interests of the elderly or the business community; now, in this age of specialization, each sub-interest and subgroup is represented. Small businesses distinguish their positions from those of their larger colleagues, carving out distinct niches with a separate set of proposals and strategies. Doctors are no longer represented solely by the American Medical Association. Each specialty may have a separate perspective that it wants heard. And the American Medical Association certainly cannot speak for nurses or midwives or social workers, each of whom believes that its voice must be heard, distinct from those of other interest groups.

Even the slightest difference in views and perspectives seems sufficient to justify the creation of a "splinter" interest group. And interest groups compete with one another. Although interest groups are almost all some form of nonprofit entity, they compete for members, money, attention, credit, and glory. More members means more revenues, which can often lead to bigger organizations, more staffs, and larger offices. Interest-group creation has become an entrepreneurial activity, with specialists available to help in fund raising, membership development, and direct mail.

Third, government action and issue developments give rise to interest groups. The long struggle for minority and women's rights was led by numerous interest groups (which in turn spawned splinter groups and countergroups). The probusiness attitudes of the Eisenhower and Nixon administrations were fertile breeding ground for consumer interest groups. The subsequent rise of Ralph Nader and his network of powerful interest groups concerned with public health, safety, and the environment, coupled with the populist regulatory leanings of President Carter, led to the proliferation of business interest groups.[4] Health-care reform energized and mobilized many formal and informal organizations, which quickly realized that President Clinton's proposals required them to engage in interest-group activities to protect their own interests.

Fourth, as issues proliferate and become more complicated, election campaigns, with their reliance on sixty-second television commercials and the need to appeal to the broadest base of citizens, provide few opportunities for a full airing of issues. The arena of issue activity has thus shifted from campaigning to governing. Interest groups become essential if individuals and organizations are to have an effective voice in governing. At the same time, the business of government, both formal and informal, is increasingly being conducted in public. Interest groups eagerly take advantage of open deliberations, and the opportunities for public input they encourage. More interest groups have more ways to influence policymaking.

Fifth, while public problems have not diminished, there are fewer resources available to address them. Should money be spent on health care or the environment? On veterans or seniors? On worker safety or job creation? As we struggle to address these questions in an era demanding balanced budgets, interest groups seek to influence the outcome of our deliberations.

Finally, interest groups beget counterinterest groups. The rise of the American Association of Retired Persons as a powerful voice for senior citizens gave rise to Lead or Leave, an organization founded by two young people who wanted to make sure that the voices of their generation would be heard, as scarce federal resources are allocated between Medicare and college loans. The success of the environmental movement led to the Property Rights or Wise Use Movement, which seeks to balance preservation of the environment with the rights of landowners. Competing views of society and the role of government inevitably lead to interest groups espousing those views.

Why Members Join Interest Groups

Influencing Policy Is Only Part of the Reason

While some individuals and businesses join organizations primarily to advance a shared public policy agenda, many more join primarily for social, collegial, or other reasons. In fact, it is probably the rule, rather than the exception, that individuals or organizations join associations for reasons other than their desire to influence public policy. Yet just about any assemblage of individuals pursuing personal, community, or professional interests may, at one time or another, attempt to influence public policy as an interest group.

For example, in a local community, individuals and business may join an organization such as Friends of the Library, with the intent to raise money to buy additional books for the library, to provide volunteer services to aid the library staff, and to read to children in the library. Influencing public policy may be the furthest thing from the minds of most members when they join the organization.

But when the city proposes budget cuts that include closing libraries two days a week, the Friends of the Library may decide to fight the cuts. Members may talk to their business colleagues, neighbors, and library patrons, urging them to contact the City Council and the mayor to express their support for the library. They may testify before the City Council and speak to the media about the effect the cuts will have on the community and its children. They may even argue among themselves about the desirability of raising property taxes to pay for library services. The members of Friends of the Library, who were initially motivated by their concerns for literacy and the community's children, now find themselves part of an interest group attempting to influence public policy.

The Retail Merchants' Association we encountered in the last chapter was likely formed to help its members promote the downtown business district, coordinate advertising and promotion, and make business and social contacts. Yet, as we saw, they were easily mobilized into action when public policy changes could advance their interests.

So it is that lawyers may join the American Bar Association (or doctors the American Medical Association) for an opportunity to keep abreast of current professional developments or even to take advantage of group life insurance discounts. They may have a greater or lesser interest in their organizations' ongoing lobbying efforts on tort law reform.

Individuals often find themselves part of an organization that engages in interest-group activity, without being aware of, or interested in, that activity. For example, people may join the American Automobile Association to get services such as maps or hotel discounts or roadside assistance, without regard to (or even knowledge of) the fact that the organization lobbies local, state, and federal governments on transportation policy issues. Indeed, some members may actually disagree with the organization's positions, taken in the name of its members, on issues such as the need for more roads or lower gasoline taxes.

Similarly, senior citizens may join the American Association of

Retired Persons (AARP) for group health insurance benefits or discounts on travel, rather than out of any desire to protect the integrity
and funding of the social security and Medicare programs.[5] But AARP
is an active participant in public policy debates, often choosing sides
between Republican and Democratic health-care reform and other policy initiatives. When it attempts to influence public policy, it does so in
the interest of its more than 32 million members. It is inconceivable,
however, that they all could support AARP's public policy positions or
even be aware of them.[6]

Many individuals and organizations share interests and seek to advance those interests without belonging to any formal interest group.
Informal, unorganized interest groups have arisen around issues such
as the balanced budget amendment, the crime bill, and the opposition
to the nomination of Zoe Baird. Often fostered by talk radio hosts such
as Rush Limbaugh, or public figures such as Ross Perot, individuals do
not formally join together in an interest group. They may act in concert
only on one issue, although much of their activity parallels that of
recognized interest groups. These shifting and temporary interests are
potential interest groups but typically lack the means and wherewithal
to sustain themselves beyond the particular issue around which they
first mobilized. Or they are short-lived, unorganized interest groups:
"Citizens to Oppose Zoe Baird as Attorney General." They are gone as
soon as their objective is achieved or the battle is lost.

When organizations engage in interest-group activity and attempt to
influence policy, they implicitly or explicitly do so on behalf of their
members. But have the members joined the interest group because they
care about an issue or because they get other benefits? The effectiveness of these organizations may depend on the reasons why members
join and their level of commitment to their interest-group activities.

How Policy Change Benefits Interest-Group Members

We have seen that most members join organizations, even interest
groups, for reasons that have nothing to do with changing public policy. In this section we discuss the benefits individuals and organizations receive when they join interest groups and attempt to affect
public policy and how those benefits affect the interest group's power
and credibility. (In chapter 10 we explore how interest groups mobilize
their members and the public to influence policy.)

Sometimes members receive a direct and tangible benefit from policy changes. Other times, the benefit is indirect and intangible, and individual members receive nearly the same benefits as every other citizen. The public policy benefits interest-group members receive fall along a continuum, from personal benefits to the benefits of an improved society in which they and others can live.

Direct Benefits

Most businesses join interest groups to obtain or protect financial or other benefits. The Retail Merchants' Association urged the mayor to transform the old school building into a homeless shelter to increase its members' sales and profits. With equal fervor, residents living near the old school building opposed the shelter, seeking to protect the value of their property. In the process of building their campaign, the association would, of course, argue that the homeless people and the entire community would benefit from the shelter. And the neighboring community would argue that relocating the homeless to a new neighborhood—their neighborhood—would violate the civil rights of the homeless.

Looking back at our list of organizations lobbying on health-care reform, and focusing on their efforts to influence public policy on health care, it is easy to identify the groups seeking direct benefits for their members. They include the Wine and Beer Institutes (opposing higher taxes on alcoholic beverages to pay for health-care reform) and the Kentucky Medical Association (opposing limits on doctors' fees and measures that would require doctors to participate in health maintenance organizations). The members of those organizations had a direct financial and personal stake in the outcome of the health-care-reform proposal.

The Food and Commercial Workers' Union, another interest group that participated in health-care reform, lobbied to ensure that its members would not be forced to pay more for fewer health benefits and that those workers not already insured would be covered. In so doing, the union was protecting and advancing the direct financial interests of its members. Of course, like the Kentucky Medical Association, the Food and Commercial Workers' Union engages in a broad spectrum of interest-group activities, including many that do not directly benefit their members' financial interests, such as lobbying for child nutrition programs.

Indirect Benefits

Frequently, the benefits interest-group members derive are less direct and tangible. They may come in the form of benefits to the larger community to which members belong. For example, members of a neighborhood or community-based organization may band together to preserve the historic or peaceful character of their neighborhood or to convince the city to fix potholes in the road or improve the city school system. Some individual members will obviously gain more direct benefits than others, such as those with children in school.

Members who dislike driving on crowded highways may benefit indirectly from successful lobbying by an organization to which they belong, such as the American Automobile Association, for new and wider roads. Sailing club members, who are frequent users of the water, will benefit if their interest group succeeds in convincing the government to stop dumping waste in the river. Members of a local gun club—or the National Rifle Association—will benefit if they remain free to buy and shoot guns without additional governmental restrictions.

Three organizations that lobbied on health-care reform typify still another form of indirect benefit to members. The Alzheimer's Association, Disabled American Veterans, and Epilepsy Foundation of W. Central Florida all attempted to influence the outcome of the health-care-reform debate to ensure that the constituency they represented (their members) received the best possible treatment under any revised health-care system. As such, the members might receive a range of benefits, including lower health-care costs, portability of health-care insurance despite preexisting conditions, and an assurance that the quality of care at veterans' hospitals would not decrease.

At the same time, benefits received by all Alzheimer's patients or all veterans do produce benefits to society as a whole, just as better schools and more educated workers benefit everyone, not just affected students and their parents. That moves our analysis further along the continuum of benefits members receive from changing public policy.

Societal Benefits

A safer, healthier, and fairer society benefits everyone, not just those individuals who join organizations and work toward those goals. Interest groups may argue for better education, child nutrition, or job opportunities, not because those benefits will inure to any individual member, but because they will help everyone. Environmental interest groups, which can claim tens of millions of members, seek to ensure that nature and species are preserved for future generations and that water is safe to drink and air is safe to breathe.

Two organizations that sought to influence health-care reform occupy this end of the continuum. The Georgia Right to Life Committee and the California Abortion Rights Action League represent opposing sides of the abortion debate. The Georgia Right to Life Committee wants to eliminate abortion, believing it to be morally wrong; in their view, our society should not permit abortions. The California Abortion Rights Action League, in contrast, believes our society should not interfere with a woman's decision whether or not to have an abortion. Both organizations seek to conform public policy to their societal visions. Members join either of these organizations primarily to advance their view of society and the future, rather than to obtain benefits for themselves.

As should be clear by now, there are few bright lines and clear distinctions in the type and amount of benefits members receive. While all citizens benefit from a cleaner Chesapeake Bay, boaters and swimmers who use the bay frequently obviously benefit to a greater extent than others who do not. Society in general obviously benefits from fair treatment of veterans and adequate health care for those who served in the military, but those who actually did serve and need health care will benefit most directly.

Women's and minority rights organizations raise similar analytical challenges. When young women join an abortion rights organization to ensure that they can have an abortion, if they choose, aren't they seeking a benefit for themselves? When minority rights activists urge that affirmative action programs be expanded or that the civil rights laws be more strictly enforced, aren't they receiving a benefit from their efforts? Are the benefits to the individual members in each of those instances merely incidental and subordinate to the members' visions of a better, more just society? What if a man joins an abortion rights organization or a white woman joins a minority rights organization?

It is not crucial that advocates be able to place every interest group and the benefits to its members at a precise point on the continuum. What matters is that they be able to assess (and use to their advantage) the way the benefits to members affect the interest group's power and authority as it attempts to influence public policy debates.

For example, large corporate interests may argue for limits on the government's clean-air requirements, claiming that jobs and economic opportunities will be lost if environmental regulations are not relaxed. The unstated, but well understood, consequences of relaxing the regulations will be increased profits for the corporations, their stockholders, and employees.

That does not necessarily mean that those business interests do not have a powerful or meritorious argument, only that an analysis of the merits of the argument should include the reasons why it is being made and the benefits individuals or organizations would receive from the policy change. In this instance, the businesses are trying to make their argument from a broader, more appealing "public interest" perspective (falling near the right end of the continuum), rather than a narrower "special interest" perspective (nearer the left side of the continuum). They understand instinctively that in our democracy we are constantly concerned with finding and implementing solutions that serve the broader public interest, rather than benefit narrow economic or other interests, and that arguments based on the former are more persuasive than those based on the latter.

In the next section we look at what makes interest groups effective policy advocates and explore the distinction between public and special interest groups.

How Interest Groups Influence Policy

Sources of Interest-Group Power

Interest groups derive their influence from three sources: their grassroots political power, the contribution they make to the public debate, and the values inherent in their interest and position.

- *Grassroots Political Power.* The voters are the ultimate source of power in our representative democracy. Members of Congress—or city councilors—are accountable to the people who elect them. Before taking a position on any issue, a responsible legislator will want to know how many people care about the issue, why they care, and how deeply they care. All things being equal, the more people interest groups represent, and the more committed to the issue those members are, the more effective the interest group will be.

Interest-group power can be more political than grassroots, relying on lobbying connections and access to decision makers.

- *Contribution to the Debate.* An interest group can be effective if it has the necessary issue advocacy skills. Can it build broad-based coalitions with significant public appeal? Does an interest group have solid, persuasive information that will help decision makers and the public make up their minds? Does it have effective spokespeople who can use the media to communicate their message? (A handgun-control organization with few members and little money can still be influential if it has an effective spokesperson such as James Brady.) Does it have the money and resources to get its message out? Finally, "contribution" can come in the form of financial support to candidates from well-heeled interest groups and their members.

- *Values.* With little grassroots power and no money for campaign contributions or television commercials, an interest group can still succeed if it represents an important interest or value. An environmental organization arguing for preservation of an endangered species, a children's rights group seeking expanded child immunization programs, or a small business organization seeking relief from government red tape so its members can get on with the work of creating jobs, all depend for their effectiveness on the values they represent: justice, fairness, opportunity, equality, compassion. They seek to promote policy changes that will advance those and other societal values, reminding decision makers of the broader "public interest."

But as we saw in the last section, it is necessary to look behind the way an interest articulates its concerns to determine how it and its members will benefit from policy changes.

To appreciate how these factors contribute to interest-group effectiveness, imagine that you approach a distinguished senator in your state legislature as a representative of your hitherto unknown (to the senator) interest group. You, on behalf of the members of the Mom and Pop Store Owners' Association, are asking the senator to oppose legislation requiring a five-cent deposit on all glass containers. How will the senator determine how much weight to assess to your views? What will she want to know?

After you introduce yourself and make a brief presentation, the conversation could go something like this:

Senator: How many members do you have?

You: [Hmm, she's trying to figure out my group's grassroots power. She wants to know whether we have a million members or a thousand, and she'll probably make some initial judgment about how much attention to pay to us based upon the number. Oh, well.] One hundred.

Senator: I see. Well, who are they?

You: [I'm sure she doesn't want their names, but with only a hundred I could almost recite them from memory. No, she probably wants to know what interest we share. Are we union members, concerned parents, or environmentalists? From that, she'll try to determine how important and powerful we are.] Our members are small business people who own and operate convenience stores in your Senate district.

Senator: Very good. Now tell me why they care about whether or not we require a five-cent deposit on soft-drink bottles.

You: [Because it's going to cost us business, of course. That's the reason every retailer in the state opposes the bottle bill. It's the same reason all the large soft-drink manufacturers oppose it. If people have to pay a nickel more per bottle up front and then drag the bottles back to the store, well they might just switch to water or homemade iced tea or something. But she's heard all that before from the big boys with the campaign contributions and the expensive lobbyists. What can make our organization more effective than them?] Our members are small business people, individual entrepreneurs. As you know, small businesses are the source of most new job creation in the state and in your district. This bill would affect us much more than the big chain stores. We depend much more than they do on the sale of bottled drinks for our profits. If this bill passes, everyone agrees that sales will go down.

And what happens when bottles break in our stores, as they always do? We'll get stuck having to pay the deposit out of our pockets. The large chain stores can absorb the breakage out of petty cash, but we'll really suffer. Like many small businesses, our members are just managing to make ends meet. If this bill passes, we might even have to lay off workers. Just take a look at this study of the effect of the bill on our members. Is that what you want?

Senator: Well, you've given me a lot to think about. I see that it means more than just profits to your members, although I know they're concerned that they'll lose some money. But it also could hurt jobs and the value we put on small businesses. No one, least of all me, wants to put the small business person out of business. I'll get back to you on this.

As you leave, you deposit on the senator's desk studies and charts prepared for you by a leading economist demonstrating the harmful impact of this proposal. You think you had a pretty good afternoon.

Representing the Public's Interest

Every interest wants to portray itself as acting in the broad public interest, rather than in its own narrow self-interest. Oil companies view their exploration in Alaska as providing oil to heat our homes and power our automobiles, not as despoiling the environment. Ralph Nader's Public Citizen organization views allowing consumers to sue manufacturers for product-related injuries as redressing wrongs and eliminating defective products, not as unduly burdening legitimate businesses with frivolous lawsuits.

Public policy debates should be about finding and implementing solutions to provide the greatest benefit for the greatest number, not rewarding noisy, well-funded interest groups concerned with acquiring benefits for their members. That is why the Mom and Pop Store Owners' Association argues that the bottle-deposit bill will cost jobs and hurt the economy, rather than decrease its members' profits. It is the same strategy the American Medical Association used to help defeat health-care reform, arguing that patients should be allowed to choose their own doctor. And it is the favored tactic of the Wine Institute in opposing higher wine taxes, claiming that wine has been shown to be healthful in moderation and that a tax on wine is regressive and unfair to those on the lower rungs of the economic ladder.

But who truly speaks for the public's interest? Apart from whatever economic interests stand to gain from the collection, processing, and recycling of returned bottles, who speaks for the broader interest of conserving energy and resources and eliminating roadside litter? Who represents low-wage workers whose employers do not provide health insurance and are unable to afford it on their own?

Interest groups that organize themselves to advocate for a better society do so in the "public interest." Their members receive only the most indirect and intangible benefits from their efforts. Where do public interest groups derive their authority to speak for the public? On what basis does their own legitimacy rest? Are these interest groups themselves models of participatory democracy?

There are no easy answers to these questions, in part because different interest groups operate in different ways. While many small, community-based organizations take positions only after their membership decides that doing so is in the public interest, many more are large bureaucracies with thousands of members who operate more as corporations than as democracies. To be sure, some large public interest organizations allow their members to elect their directors, but most do not. Some survey their members before taking a public policy position, but most rely on a professional staff or unelected board to formulate policy positions.

Often these groups, with public health, consumer protection, environmental, or economic matters on their agenda, require little or no financial or other commitment from their members. Individuals may join the organization primarily to subscribe to its newsletter (or, as we have seen, to get maps or discounts) and find themselves described as one of the organization's many thousand members when a board of directors they did not elect and an executive director they did not appoint decide to seek a public policy change on which they were not consulted.

Most public interest organizations are supported by membership dues or contributions from the public or foundations (some of which may themselves represent narrow economic interests). Others are funded, in part, by economic interests that stand to benefit if the public interest group's position is adopted. It would not be surprising to discover, for example, that environmental organizations supporting a bottle bill received financial support from recyclers and others whose profits would increase if the bill were adopted.

How do these organizational and decision-making structures add to or detract from the effectiveness of public interest organizations? How much does it matter who funds a public interest organization or why they fund it? How does a public interest organization balance the public's interest in a bottle bill that will reduce litter and conserve resources against the public's interest in fostering small businesses and the jobs they create? How do public interest organizations decide what is in the public interest? And is there always a single, definable public interest?

These are important questions to be considered in the formulation of public policy, as decision makers increasingly look beneath the surface of competing interest groups to try to determine where the public interest really lies. We continue our search for answers in chapter 10.

Do Interest Groups Foster Democracy or Imperil It?

Interest groups can be a powerful force to permit citizens and businesses to have an ongoing and effective voice in public policymaking. They can permit more, and a more diverse range of, individuals and organizations to have their voices heard in an active, sustained, and thoughtful way, including voices that might otherwise be lost in the noisy clamor of public debate. Interest groups can educate their members, the general public, and decision makers about issues, public policy, and the views of their members.

Interest groups have been a traditional source of countervailing power.[7] They can act as checks or balances on the activities of government, powerful institutions, and each other. Consumer interest groups try to hold elected and appointed government officials accountable for protecting the broad consumer interest as they see it, while business and industry groups try to ensure that government actions and excessive regulation do not choke off business activity. Interest groups representing minority interests (seniors or ethnic minorities) try to ensure that those unpopular interests get a full and fair hearing and that issues of concern to them are raised and discussed.

What some organizations do not have in grassroots numbers or resources, they can make up through the importance society places on the values inherent in their position. Others, with many resources, can compensate for a lack of grassroots power or a relative lack of importance of the values they advocate with campaign contributions, public education programs, and grassroots mobilization.

To work effectively as counterweights, however, there must be some rough balance between the interest groups. The proliferation of interest groups has provided some element of that balance. For every conceivable interest group there appears to be an interest group willing and eager to take a contrary position. The resulting "balance of power" among interest groups has had important effects, both positive and negative, on the process of government and citizens' participation in it.

First, as Jonathan Rauch terms it, we have seen "demosclerosis," a slow hardening of our political arteries caused by the proliferation of interest groups. Elected and appointed leaders cannot act without hearing from interested groups on every conceivable side of the issue, each seeking to shape the final outcome. Can our leaders rise above the din caused by those who seek some benefit from their decisions and instead learn to lead, even when to do so involves making unpopular decisions or defying powerful interest groups? Or will we endure a process that seems to respond best to the loudest, most powerful voices, amplified by the most effective interest groups? Where does that leave those without the time, resources, or inclination to join an interest group?

Second, do interest groups, by educating the public about issues and allowing them to be represented in the corridors of power, foster public participation in policymaking, or do they turn off cynical citizens who view interest groups primarily as campaign contributors and power brokers? Do individuals or small businesspersons believe interest groups enable their voices to be heard and heeded in policy discussions such as health-care reform? Has a broad segment of the public turned to interest groups to represent their interests in public policymaking because they are distrustful of political parties, which must necessarily cast a wide net for support? Does that imply an increasing selfishness, as individuals and businesses are concerned with increasing their own share of the pie, possibly at the expense of others?

Do more interest and subinterest groups give citizens confidence that decision makers will hear all sides of an issue before they resolve it, or do citizens see interest groups, perhaps including those to which they themselves belong, as contributing to government gridlock?

Is the proliferation of interest-group advocacy a symptom of what is wrong with American politics or part of the cure?

Are interest groups, as James Madison believed, inherently "selfish, narrow, and bad"? Or are they, in their modern incarnations, the most effective way individuals and organizations can make their voices heard in a large and diverse society?

We return to these questions in the course of this book.

4

Targets of Opportunity: Issue Arenas

The diversity of our society and the proliferation of interests and interest groups is matched only by the number of forums or arenas where issues can be raised. More, and more complex, government has led to the creation of more regulatory and administrative agencies, more legislative committees, and increased involvement of the courts in making and reviewing public policy. This multiplicity of "decision points" has created "many more doors at which influence might knock and enter."[1]

While many issues are addressed by federal legislation, many more are dealt with by state laws or city or county ordinances. And the number of laws and ordinances passed by every jurisdiction within the United States is dwarfed by the volume of rules and regulations adopted by elected and appointed administrators. The courts, at all levels of government, are interpreting laws and making policies that affect every issue. Finally, corporate and institutional activities shape issues.

In this chapter we explore the interrelationship of the branches and levels of government, how each addresses issues and presents different opportunities and different threats to issue advocates. We also examine the advantages and disadvantages of addressing issues in each forum, including the skills necessary to be effective in each. In chapter 9, we take a closer look at specific strategies to influence decision makers in each arena.

To illustrate the many places an issue can be raised, we begin with an in-depth look at the opportunities tobacco-control advocates have to raise and advance their issue and the threats presented for tobacco companies.

Places to Go and People to Persuade

When the surgeon general announced in 1964 that smoking caused cancer, health advocates launched an intensive campaign to restrict tobacco companies' advertising and promotion and to increase public awareness of the harms caused by tobacco. The 1964 report led to federal law requiring the familiar warning labels on cigarettes (since strengthened).[2] Health advocates recognized, however, that much work remained to be done and that federally mandated warning labels were only one small step in a long process to change public policy on tobacco sales, promotion, and use.

Imagine you are a persistent antismoking advocate (or a stubborn tobacco company). How and where can you influence (or must you defend) tobacco policies?

- *Federal Legislation.* Cigarette-package warning labels were the first legislative victory in the war against tobacco. Higher federal excise taxes on cigarettes, which are established by federal law, could decrease cigarette use, particularly among youth. Federal laws could ban or restrict cigarette advertising and promotion.
- *Federal Rules and Administrative Decisions.* The U.S. Congress presents a single, focused target for legislation. But the many and winding corridors of the administrative or executive branch of government—the bureaucracy —present numerous other potential targets for smoking control advocates. For example, the Federal Trade Commission, which has the power to ban or restrict "unfair" advertising, could decide that cartoon character advertising, such as Camel's "Joe Camel," unfairly target underage smokers.

   The Environmental Protection Agency could decide that so-called second-hand smoke (smoke inhaled by nonsmokers) is a dangerous carcinogen, leading to restrictions on smoking and tobacco use. The Occupational Safety and Health Administration could prohibit smoking in the workplace because it creates health hazards. The National Park Service could prohibit tobacco companies from using federal park lands to promote their products, through events such as the Virginia Slims Tennis Tournament, which was formerly held in at least one federally controlled park, Washington, D.C.'s Rock Creek Park. The federal government, through its landlord, the General Services Administration, could ban smoking in federal office buildings to protect the health of its workers.

The National Cancer Institute and the National Institutes of Health could expand (and publicize) their research on the connection between smoking and health. The surgeon general could issue further reports and warnings about the dangers of smoking.

Because these important administrative functions are within the discretion of appointed government officials, tobacco-control advocates can attempt to influence the president and agency heads to appoint officials sympathetic to their cause, by suggesting candidates and participating in the Senate confirmation process for high-level government officials.

- *Federal (and State) Court Cases.* Can tobacco companies be held legally responsible for the harm caused by the products they sell, just as any manufacturer of a dangerous product? Smokers and their estates have filed numerous lawsuits in federal and state courts seeking damages for the harm caused them by their use of widely advertised and promoted cigarette products. One obstacle to smokers' winning has been the cigarette-package warning labels required by federal law, but many lawsuits are still being filed and litigated. If one or more lawsuits succeeds, the potential damages could be so large that cigarette companies could be forced to restrict their advertising and promotion, or even to abandon the sale of cigarettes entirely (just as A.H. Robbins abandoned the Dalkon shield, and Manville the manufacture of asbestos, when courts held them liable for damages caused by their products).

More recently, states, led by Florida and Massachusetts, sued tobacco companies seeking reimbursement for state Medicaid funds expended on patients whose diseases were caused by using tobacco products. Because the states are suing, rather than individual smokers, the tobacco companies may not be able to mount

a defense based on smokers' understanding and accepting the
risks of smoking after reading the warning labels.[3]

- *State Legislation.* States can levy excise taxes on the sale of tobacco
  in addition to those imposed by the federal government. Increasing
  state taxes, either through the traditional legislative process or
  through a ballot initiative, could further reduce tobacco use, particularly among young people. An initiative approved by California
  voters in 1988 raised the state excise tax on tobacco products and
  designated part of that money for antitobacco advertisements. States
  can also enact "clean indoor air laws," which ban or restrict smoking
  in public places, such as restaurants or hotels.

- *State Administrative Action.* Many state agencies have authority
  similar to their federal counterparts but limited to the state's borders. For example, state health departments and attorneys general
  are responsible for protecting public health and policing unfair
  and deceptive advertising within the state. State agencies could
  adopt administrative bans or restrictions on smoking in state buildings or in public places as a means to protect worker or public
  safety.

  States also manage large pension funds on behalf of their employees. They could influence the behavior of tobacco companies whose
  stock they own, or sell their ownership stakes entirely, in an effort to
  send a public message of disapproval to tobacco companies.

- *Local Ordinances.* Counties, cities, and even towns can restrict or
  eliminate smoking in public places. They can prohibit billboard
  advertising for tobacco products and even ban the sale of tobacco
  products through vending machines, which are likely to be used
  by underage smokers. A county zoning board or liquor control
  authority could deny the necessary permits or license to a bar or
  liquor store that illegally sold cigarettes to minors.

- *Local Administrative Action.* The local police could increase their
  enforcement of laws against cigarettes sales to minors. Local school
  boards could aggressively prohibit smoking on school property and
  include nonsmoking education in public school curriculums.

- *Corporate and Institutional Behavior.* Many large and powerful
  institutions play, or have the potential to play, an important role in
  tobacco control. Universities, like state governments, can eliminate tobacco company stock from their endowment portfolios or
  use their considerable stock holdings to change company policies.

Medical societies, such as the American Medical Association or its state affiliates, could encourage doctors to list smoking as the cause of death on death certificates, rather than the effects of smoking, such as lung cancer or heart failure. Interest groups, such as seniors or religious organizations, could place tobacco control on their own issue agendas and join antismoking coalitions.

Restaurants, hotels, and other businesses could restrict or eliminate smoking on their premises. Grocery stores and restaurants could eliminate (or closely supervise) the sale of cigarettes through vending machines.

Tobacco companies, which are the indirect target of nearly all the public policy initiatives described in this section, could also be direct targets of tobacco-control activities. Consumer boycotts could be organized of nontobacco products, such as the Nabisco products of cigarette manufacturer RJR Nabisco.

- *Individual Behavior.* Persuading individuals not to smoke is at the root of antismoking activities. But issue advocacy is about influencing public policy, rather than individual behavior. We will therefore not address efforts to persuade people not to smoke, except when those efforts involve changing governmental or institutional behavior, such as through warning labels or government-sponsored antismoking campaigns.
- *Global Government.* All politics may be local, but most issues are now global. Tobacco companies are developing new markets outside the United States, particularly in Asian countries with few restrictions on smoking or warnings on cigarettes. At the same time, increased global trade and the General Agreement on Tariffs and Trade (GATT) has led to the creation of the World Trade Organization with jurisdiction over government-created trade barriers. Could the WTO decide that Canadian restrictions on cigarette packaging and labeling, designed to reduce their appeal to minors and others, are an improper restriction on trade and are therefore invalid under GATT?

Influencing Corporate Behavior: Alternatives to Influencing Governmental Policy

Imagine you are concerned that the widespread use of styrofoam packaging by the fast-food industry damages the environment. Or that tuna companies condone the needless killing of dolphins in the course of catching tuna. Or that a large international oil company intends to sink an offshore oil rig in the North Sea.

In each instance, those who seek to change corporate practices have several targets from which to choose. The most obvious first choice might seem to be governmental action: law or regulation at the federal, state, or even local level. But governments may be powerless to control fishing in international waters or subject to pressure from powerful economic interests to continue the manufacture and use of styrofoam, or supportive of sinking the oil rig offshore instead of disposing it on land. Issue advocates may instead turn their attention toward directly influencing corporate behavior.

Persuading businesses or corporations to change their policies requires different skills and strategies from influencing elected and appointed officials, who are generally responsive to the constituents they represent. In chapter 9 we discuss in detail the process of influencing—lobbying—corporations and other institutions. For now, we recognize that influencing corporations requires exposing their actions in ways that can cause them economic harm, either directly through consumer boycotts or indirectly, by embarrassing or shaming a corporation, thereby debasing its image and influencing its corporate bottom line.

The States and the Federal Government: Our Uneasy Federal System

- One state requires a two week waiting period between the time an individual seeks to purchase a gun and the time he or she is permitted to do so. Another state has no waiting period at all. When Congress passed the Brady bill in 1993, it mandated a five-day waiting period before a gun purchase. State laws that require longer waiting periods can continue in force; more lenient ones cannot.
- Federal regulations require used car dealers to disclose any applicable warranties or announce that the car is sold "as is." For some states that is not enough; they give their citizens the right to get their money back if the car they buy is a "lemon."
- Federal law requires pesticides to be approved by the U.S. Environmental Protection Agency before they can be sold. Some state

laws place further restrictions on how and when pesticides can be used, and by whom.

- A consumer product containing a dangerous chemical can be sold in one state with no warning on its label. In California the same product cannot be sold without a warning that it contains ingredients shown to cause birth defects.

Those are but a few examples of our complex federal system at work. The Constitution gives Congress the power to legislate on matters that affect interstate commerce, but it also preserves states' rights to legislate on most matters that are not exclusively the province of the federal government. The result is "cooperative federalism," a system of complementary, and potentially overlapping, jurisdiction between the states and the federal government.

Supreme Court Justice Louis Brandeis wrote in a 1932 opinion that "it is one of the happy incidents of the federal system that a single courageous state may, if its citizens choose, serve as a laboratory, and try novel social and economic experiments without risk to the country."[4] The states have eagerly taken advantage of the wide latitude afforded them.

Oregon and Hawaii have experimented with universal health insurance coverage and rationing of health care; Maryland prohibits the sale of certain forms of handgun ammunition and requires photo identification cards for gun licensees; the District of Columbia prohibits its elected officials from obtaining campaign contributions in excess of $100 from any one individual; California requires the labeling of hazardous products and limits the number of terms in office for its elected state officials.

Despite Brandeis's lofty pronouncement (or perhaps because of it), tensions have arisen between the states and the federal government. In our complex society people and goods frequently move between states. Should we have as much uniformity as possible in our laws so that individuals and businesses can have one set of requirements with which to comply? Or is it more appropriate to allow each state (or local government) to decide what is best for its citizens?

These questions took on new significance after the 1994 congressional elections. On every issue, Congress began asking itself two questions. First, is federal action necessary or is the matter more appropriately left to the states? Second, if federal action is necessary, should the states still have authority to act on the same issue?

Who Rules the Road? The Federal Government versus the States

During the oil crisis of the 1970s, the federal government required that states limit speeds on most highways to fifty-five miles per hour. Slower traffic saved energy and, not incidentally, lives. By 1995, times had changed.

Proponents of states' rights, who had gained the upper hand in the 1994 congressional elections, argued that the federal government had grown too big, too expensive, and too inefficient at the expense of both the private sector and state and local governments. Many believed that excessive government regulation of business had stifled entrepreneurship and cost the economy jobs and money. This belief provided a rationale for reducing the role of government and streamlining its operations, particularly at the federal level.

Shouldn't the states and localities, which are closer to the people than Congress and federal bureaucrats, make as many decisions as possible affecting people and their lives? Could federal officials possibly know—or care—as much about the average citizens (and their problems) as their state and local officials do? More than sixty years after the New Deal had greatly expanded the role of the federal government, the tide of government appeared to be turning back to the states.

The debate quickly became one of states' rights, with many relying on the Tenth Amendment to the U.S. Constitution—reserving to the states those powers not delegated to the federal government—for the proposition that our federal system required (perhaps at its constitutional core) less intrusion by the federal government into the affairs of states and localities.

But some level of government still has to set speed limits or decide what goes into school lunches or how long to pay compensation to the unemployed. Nowhere was this issue presented more starkly than in the 1995 highway bill. States' rights proponents argued that it made little sense to set a national speed limit of fifty-five miles per hour. After all, states and roads differ; why should the federal government set uniform limits for all states, and why does the federal government know better than the individual states what limit to set? The answer, according to Congress and the highway bill, was that the federal government does not know better. The fifty-five-mile-per-hour federal speed limit was abolished.[5]

Consumer organizations, insurance companies, and highway safety advocates argued that the fifty-five-mile-per-hour speed limit saved lives, and that raising it to seventy or seventy-five or eliminating it entirely (as Montana subsequently did) would inevitably cost lives. It was difficult for states' rights advocates to argue that the laws of physics did not apply to highway crashes, that higher speeds would result in fewer deadly accidents. But it was even more difficult for those who favored the national fifty-five-mile-per-hour speed limit to contend that individual states have less regard for their citizens' safety than the federal government.

The demise of the national speed limit was hailed as a victory for states' rights. But the same highway bill required states to lower the blood alcohol threshold for drivers under the age of twenty-one, to .02 percent, and to enforce their drunk-driving laws strictly. Logic and consistency would require allowing each state to decide for itself what level of blood alcohol constitutes impaired driving, and how many of its limited police resources to spend in enforcing its drunk-driving laws.

But logic and consistency do not always prevail in congressional lawmaking. States' rights often fall to political expediency. For example, federal tort reform would limit the authority of state courts to award injured persons damages for injuries caused by defective products. Tort law reform was included in the Contract with America and espoused by many who also supported states' rights.

Federal programs that return money to the states traditionally required that the money be spent for specific purposes. The 104th Congress reflected a growing states' rights consensus that most program decisions should be made at the state, rather than the federal, level: federal money should flow to the states as "block grants," with only general restrictions on their use. States would decide how best to care for their needy and educate their children. At least in theory.

In practice, welfare reform legislation drafted by the same states' rights advocates in the 104th Congress would leave it to the states to decide who is eligible for welfare, how much they will receive, and what conditions to place on its receipt. But many supporters of block grants—avid states' righters—sought to require teenage welfare recipient mothers to stay home or attend school; others sought to prevent states from giving welfare to women who had more children while on welfare.[6]

If more power to the states and less to the federal government is not a consistent theme, at least it is a persistent one. It surfaces in another guise in opposition to "unfunded mandates"—federal requirements imposed on states for which the states, not the federal government, must pay. States object that time and again the federal government sets standards and requires states and localities to meet environmental, health, education, and other goals, but fails to provide funds to carry out those activities.

The Brady bill, for example, requires states to conduct a background check on all prospective gun purchasers, but it does not give states money to perform the checks. Legislation signed by the president in 1995 (which was part of the Contract with America) requires disclosure and accounting of all such federal unfunded mandates imposed on the states.

Opposition to unfunded mandates, like other states' rights arguments, presents additional opportunities (or obstacles) for issue advocates who seek (or oppose) federal solutions to public problems. It is no longer enough to establish that a federal law can solve a problem; now it is necessary to explain why a federal, rather than a state or local, solution is appropriate, and who will pay for any requirements federal laws or regulations impose on the states. With limited federal resources, it should theoretically no longer be possible for Congress to "pass the buck" to the states on health, environment, public safety, and other issues.[7]

For example, there is general agreement that drinking water should be clean and pure. But who should decide how clean is clean? Why not allow each state to determine the permissible level of contaminants in its citizens' drinking water just as it decides how fast they can drive? How and why are those decisions so different that one must be made by the federal government and the other left to each state's discretion? And if Congress establishes federal drinking water standards, in apparent contravention of states' rights, should it be required to pay the states to comply with the national standard?

When Congress enacted the Family and Medical Leave Act of 1993,[8] it required employers to provide a period of unpaid leave for family or medical needs. Had the same bill arisen in 1995, it would not have been enough for leave proponents to persuade Congress that family and medical leave was good public policy. They would have had to answer a more difficult question: why should not each state have the right to decide whether or not to require employers to provide family and medical leave, and how much leave to provide? And since the 1993 law even applies to states in their capacity as employers, are not each state's costs in implementing the law for their state government employees an "unfunded mandate" imposed on the states by the federal government?

Finally, by the time Congress passed the Family and Medical Leave Act, several states had already passed laws requiring some form of family and medical leave for employers within their borders. How should the federal law deal with differing state laws? The answer was to supersede—or preempt—any state (or local) laws that provided fewer family and medical leave rights, but to allow state (or local) governments to enact (or continue to enforce) laws that provided greater rights. But that is not always the case.

Preempting Protections

The relationship between federal and state lawmaking is an uneasy one. While the federal government purports to respect the rights of states to act as Brandeis's "laboratories of democracy," it often asserts its power to regulate in many issue areas, at the same time "preempting"—taking away—state authority in those areas.

In the late 1960s and 1970s, the federal government was widely viewed as the key protector of consumers, public health, safety, and the environment. New federal agencies such as the Consumer Product Safety Commission and the Environmental Protection Agency were created, and moribund agencies such as the Federal Trade Commission and the Federal Communications Commission were given new life and a new mission to protect the public interest. While this new commitment fluctuated somewhat with Republican and Democratic administrations, it was not until Ronald Reagan became president in 1980 that the regulatory pendulum took a huge swing in the direction of less regulation and more reliance on free market forces.

What caused the Federal Trade Commission, a government agency derided in the early 1960s as the "little old lady of Pennsylvania Avenue" for its do-nothing approach to consumer protection, to become so activist that it earned criticism in the late 1970s as "the national nanny?"[9] Nothing more than a shift in governmental and regulatory philosophies, a shift that also marks the relationship between state and federal regulatory policies.

Instead of consumer or public protection, the watchwords of the Reagan and Bush years became "regulatory relief" and "regulatory reform." The economy, under that view, was being hobbled by unnecessary regulatory burdens placed on business and industry. If the private sector were free of those burdens, it would do what it does best: create jobs and wealth. That philosophy, grounded in Adam Smith, led to an era of deregulation, where federal agencies were either stripped of their public protection mandates or led by individuals who believed that government governs best that governs least.[10] Federal agencies across the board set about to relax regulations designed for public protection and to ease their enforcement of them.

Whatever forces swept first Ronald Reagan and then George Bush into power, they did not include a public dissatisfied with high levels of worker and environmental safety, consumer protection, or public health enforcement. So when the federal government relaxed public protections in all those areas, it fell to state and local governments—legislatures and regulators—to fill the gaps.

State attorneys general began enforcing their own antitrust and consumer protections laws, attempting to stop mergers and deceptive practices that the federal government no longer found objectionable. Localities (Minneapolis, for one) banned shipments of styrofoam packaging—"peanuts"—as an environmental hazard. California led the way in requiring labeling of cancer-causing products. If the federal government would not pass laws (or enforce existing ones) to protect consumers against deceptive credit practices or air pollutants, state lawmakers and administrators stood ready to fill the void.

The regulatory pendulum had acquired a new dimension. Instead of swinging away from federal regulation toward deregulation, it was now swinging toward activist state regulation as a replacement for federal inaction.

This new dimension did not escape the notice of the business community that had supported Reagan and Bush's deregulatory policies. In fact the pendulum threatened to hit the business community squarely in the back of the head on the downswing. Where business once faced action at one concentrated level of government—the federal level—it suddenly confronted a proliferation of issue arenas. Fifty states and innumerable cities, towns, and counties all threatened to fill the regulatory void. Even if regulation could be curbed at the state level, there was no guarantee that it could be stopped in every city and county in a state.

How, then, could business groups complete the deregulatory process? Indeed, how could they avoid making the situation worse: replacing single, albeit disliked, federal standards with a myriad of patchwork, inconsistent state and local laws with which they were forced to comply? The answer lay in Congress's power to preempt state and local laws. And, as if that were not enough, in the power of states to preempt local laws.

Preemption derives from the Supremacy Clause of the U.S. Constitution, Article VI, Clause 2, which makes federal laws the supreme law of the land.[11] State laws that contradict or interfere with federal laws are preempted or invalidated. Preemption is necessary when inconsistent state and local laws make compliance with federal laws impossible, or when state laws threaten to frustrate the goals of federal law. For example, the federal civil rights laws of the 1960s and 1970s, including those protecting every citizen's right to vote and to obtain public accommodations, preempted state laws that permitted discrimination by race. The overriding federal interest took precedence over state and local laws.

But Congress has the *power* to preempt state laws, as a matter of discretion, even when preemption is not necessary to accomplish a federal goal. That means preemption can be just another step in the process of deregulation, one that can invalidate public health, safety, and consumer ordinances and laws passed at state and local levels of government.

Congress chose that route in the 1965 Federal Cigarette Labeling Act, 15 U.S.C. 1334(b). The law mandates the familiar health warnings on cigarette packages. But it also provides that "no requirement or prohibition based on smoking and health shall be imposed under State law with respect to the advertising or promotion of any cigarettes" labeled in conformity with the federal law. Courts have even held that state common-law damage suits, based on inadequate labeling or advertising that fails to disclose the health hazards of smoking, were preempted by the federal law, even though the federal law never expressly mentioned private tort suits.

"Discretionary preemption" can be an important strategy for issue advocates seeking to replace numerous existing or potential state or local laws with a single federal standard. The possibility that fifty states would mandate fifty different warning labels was a powerful incentive for cigarette manufacturers to accept a relatively weak, federally mandated warning label as long as state and local regulators could not add their own, more stringent warnings.

Businesses support modest federal regulatory schemes as long as federal laws or regulations also preempt state and local laws. They frame their preemption arguments in terms of the desirability of a single set of nationally uniform laws and regulations, citing the costs and burdens of excessive and duplicative regulation, especially in an economy dominated by the free flow of goods across state borders. Consumer interest groups, in contrast, champion the need for the flexibility and responsiveness that come from preserving state action. States differ from one another, they argue (parroting many of the same arguments of the states' rights advocates), and each reflects different political wills and judgments about the kinds of protections their citizens deserve. States are often more flexible and responsive than the federal government in attacking emerging problems, finding imaginative solutions to existing problems, bringing new technology to bear to solve old and new problems, and experimenting with solutions that are more progressive than federal laws or regulations, they contend.

At the same time, there are real costs to even the best-intended laws and rules. More warning labels or clean-air regulations can cost businesses money and sales, which translate into lost jobs and profits.

Is this a principled debate about state versus federal regulation, or are proponents and opponents of government regulation merely couching their arguments in terms of "cooperative federalism," "states' rights," "national uniformity," and "regulatory burden" in a search for an issue arena they perceive will be most amenable to their position? There is ample evidence that the latter is the case.[12] One commentator notes that "federalism and the 'genius of the states' are almost always invoked more as tactics than as principles. Indeed, liberals and conservatives have shifted to and fro on federalism, depending on their needs at a given moment."[13]

One possible approach that has been adopted in several federal statutes, such as the Family and Medical Leave Act, is to permit states to add protections to those imposed under federal law. Congress allowed states to pass laws granting greater rights to employees than those afforded under the federal law. But it did not have to do so. Congress could have adopted a single, federal standard for family and medical leave and then legislated that no state could pass any law on the subject, even one granting greater rights than the federal law.

Similarly, the Clean Air Act Amendments of 1970[14] states that "nothing in this Act shall preclude or deny the right of any State or political subdivision thereof to adopt or enforce any standard or limitation ... except that ... [it] may not adopt or enforce any emission standard or limitation which is less stringent than the [federal] standard or limitation." Federal law establishes a floor, rather than a ceiling, for public protection. States are free to build on that floor and add extra protections for their citizens.

The Nutrition Labeling and Education Act of 1994 takes this approach one step further. It recognizes that the federal law, which mandates disclosure of the nutrition content of food sold at retail stores, addresses the vast majority of public health concerns and accommodates the legitimate interests of businesses seeking relief from the burden of complying with fifty different state labeling laws for the same product. The act preempts state laws, but gives states the right to petition the federal government for permission to add additional labeling requirements. It is then up to the Food and Drug Administration to decide whether the state petitions raise legitimate concerns that deserve to be addressed by additional label disclosures.

Federal preemption of state laws has become just another battleground in the struggle between the forces of regulation and deregulation. Preemption is fundamentally a tool to control the level of government at which an issue is addressed. The choice will likely depend more on the direction of the regulatory pendulum than on principles of federalism.

Beyond Legislation: Implementing the Law

For every page of federal laws there are dozens of pages of regulations and administrative interpretations of the law. For every legislator (every member of Congress or state legislature) there are thousands of bureaucrats busily writing regulations and implementing the laws those legislators pass. These bureaucrats toil in the executive or administrative branch of government and are in many ways the source of the greatest power in any government. It is no surprise, therefore, that issue advocates devote considerable attention to influencing and persuading them. But what do bureaucrats do? They, and the agencies and departments and offices for which they work, interpret, enforce, and administer the law.

The thousand daily decisions bureaucrats make administering laws can cause issue advocates more consternation—and require more time and attention—than the legislative process. Hard-fought legislative successes can turn into pyrrhic victories in the hands of an unfriendly or unresponsive bureaucracy. Indeed, issue advocates who win legislative battles barely have time to pop the champagne corks before they must turn their attention to how the law, for which they fought so hard, will be implemented. Or those who thought they had tamed the legislative process may learn that the executive branch has implemented policy changes that accomplish the goals they sought to avoid. As one commentator observed: "Nothing in law ever seems finally settled because there is always one more stop in the process where both winners and losers may try to negotiate different terms."[15]

At the federal level, bureaucrats set criteria for determining who is eligible for social security disability benefits; they decide whether federally funded clinics can advise pregnant women on the availability of abortions; they establish the permissible level of pollutants industries can release into the air and water; they decide how many vegetables constitute an adequate school lunch; they decide who gets college loans; and they determine whether interest rates go up or down.

At the state or local level, they decide whether to permit a zoning variance in a residential neighborhood; they choose the books to buy for the library and what textbooks to use in the public schools; they decide when and where to build public housing; they provide safe drinking water; and they decide who is eligible for welfare and how much they receive.

In these and a myriad of other actions, bureaucrats are exercising their discretion.

Administrators Exercise Discretion

> Where law ends tyranny begins.
> —Inscription on the pediment of the Department of Justice, Washington, D.C.
> (quoting William Pitt)

> Where law ends, discretion begins.
> —Administrative Law Professor Kenneth Culp Davis

A police officer clocks a driver going five miles an hour over the speed limit. He takes no action. Another officer arrests a man for possessing a small amount of marijuana, but the prosecutor decides to drop the charges because the amount is too small, the case is too weak, and the courts are too crowded. The Federal Trade Commission decides not to act on complaints of deceptive advertising, despite its power to outlaw "unfair or deceptive acts or practices," since the transgressions are relatively minor and it must use its limited resources where they can do the most good.

The state highway commission decides whether and where to build a new road after examining transportation needs and several possible routes for the highway. The local water and sewer department decides whether to grant a permit for a new housing complex. The state hospital board decides whether to approve construction of a new medical facility. The liquor licensing board decides whether to grant a new restaurant a liquor license.

In all these instances, and in many more, administrators or bureaucrats are doing precisely what they should do. They are exercising discretion. Administrative agencies do the hard work of governing, making difficult decisions about how to apply the solutions mandated by laws to particular individuals and situations. Law enforcement agencies, both criminal (the police) and civil (the Federal Trade Commission) make necessary decisions about how best to use their limited resources. Other bureaucracies decide the details of how to distribute government benefits and meet public needs.

Legislatures create administrative agencies precisely because laws cannot address every conceivable situation. Agencies are needed to determine the facts, interpret and apply the law, and decide what is appropriate in the circumstances after the facts and law are known. Congress could attempt to describe each and every business practice considered "unfair or deceptive" or it could create an agency, the Federal Trade Commission, and empower it to make those decisions in an evolving business and social climate. In some cases, lawmakers have little choice but to delegate authority to agencies within broad limits. Congress can require workplaces to be safe or disabled workers to receive social security payments, but how could it possibly establish detailed standards applicable to every workplace or every injured worker?

Administrative agencies derive their power from delegations of authority from the legislative or executive branch of government. The Supreme Court has long held that our federal Constitution permits Congress to delegate the power to make binding, legislative-type determinations to administrative agencies and departments.[16]

Administrative discretion becomes important for issue advocates when, as often happens, bureaucrats can choose one of several permissible ways to implement or interpret the laws entrusted to them. For example, in 1988 the secretary of health and human services in the Bush administration announced that federally funded clinics could not counsel pregnant women about the availability of abortion, even if the clinics did not use federal funds for counseling. The secretary had been delegated broad powers by Congress under the 1970 Public Health Service Act to issue rules implementing the act's prohibition against using federal funds for programs where abortion is used as a method of family planning.

Abortion rights activists, women's groups, civil libertarians, and others were outraged by the way the secretary exercised his discretion under the 1970 law. In their view, he had improperly infringed on the ability of women to receive proper care and medical advice from their physicians in situations where no federal funds were being used to provide (or even discuss the possibility of) abortions.

The secretary's opponents took their case to the Supreme Court, which upheld the secretary's action as a permissible exercise of his discretion to interpret and implement the law.[17]

The secretary's 1988 rule thus stood as the law of the land. At least until 1993, when President Clinton's election led to the appointment of a new secretary of health and human services, who promptly reversed the 1988 rule. Two different bureaucrats had exercised their discretion in two different ways, either of which was legally proper.

Congress and the Courts Limit Discretion

Administrative discretion may be broad, but it is far from absolute. First, administrative action is limited to the authority afforded the agency by the legislative branch. By contrast, Congress is limited in its lawmaking activities only by the Constitution.

Second, agencies afford the public opportunities to make their views known to, and considered by, the agency. Congressional committees may choose to hold public hearings on legislation, but they need not do so, and they are free to ignore all the witnesses and all the evidence presented to them.

Third, agency actions, as we saw in the last section, can be reviewed by the courts to ensure the actions comply with all applicable laws and procedures. When Congress passes a law, it can be challenged in court only on the grounds that it violates the Constitution.

The main vehicle to control agency discretion at the federal level is the Administrative Procedure Act.[18] That law requires agencies to make most decisions in the open and to afford the public meaningful opportunities to comment on proposed agency actions. It also allows those who disagree with agency decisions to ask courts to invalidate them if they are not in accordance with applicable law and procedure or if they are not solidly grounded on the facts and the law.

These limitations on administrative discretion reflect the fact that agencies exercise broad powers, yet are only indirectly accountable to the public, through the presidential appointment and Senate confirmation of a small number of officials.

Although agencies often make decisions on a case-by-case basis, many agencies can exercise their discretionary powers by issuing rules or regulations. These "minilaws" codify administrative interpretations and establish clear guidelines for bureaucrats and the public. The FTC, for example, supplements its individual investigations and law enforcement proceedings with numerous rules or regulations spelling out in detail which practices are legal and which are not in the sale or marketing of such products and services as eyeglasses, funerals, insulation, used cars, mobile homes, health spas, and extension ladders.[19]

The broad policy discretion afforded bureaucrats provides issue advocates good reasons to attempt to influence how laws are enforced and administered. And the processes of administrative decision making—the requirement that, for the most part, it be open to the public and subject to judicial review—provide advocates important tools to accomplish that goal. In chapter 9 we discuss tactics to influence the legislative and the administrative process.

Courts of Last Resort: "Taking" the Policy Initiative

The courts are most often the last resort of those who seek to influence public policy. Litigation is costly and time-consuming; appeals can drag on for years, and tangible results are often hard to achieve. Yet the federal and state courts provide critical outlets—safety valves—for issue advocates who are unable to get a full and fair hearing before the administrative or legislative branch of government.

The doors of the courthouse are open to all. Legislatures are accountable only to the electorate and only at the ballot box. Bureaucracies can be slow and unresponsive. But advocates who seek redress in the courts are guaranteed a hearing by an impartial arbiter who will decide the case on its merits.

The courts are the prime arena for vindicating rights, particularly minority or unpopular rights. Issues such as equal rights for gays and lesbians or allowing women to attend all-male state colleges are likely to be unpopular, and their advocates may be unable to build the necessary legislative or grassroots support to achieve a legislative victory. The courts, in contrast, are unconcerned with popular support or public opinion polls. Their only duty is to determine if the Constitution or other laws entitle the plaintiff to prevail.

While courts can, at least in theory, only vindicate existing rights, important public policy issues, such as the prohibition against segregated public schools or the legal right of women to obtain abortions in the first trimester of pregnancy, have been addressed by the courts. In both cases, it is unlikely that there would have been sufficient political will to accomplish the same goals. Indeed, the Supreme Court's 1954 decision in *Brown v. Board of Education*,[20] abolishing separate but equal education, was so unpopular that federal troops were required to enforce the decision. The Supreme Court properly did not concern itself with how southern states would respond when it required that schools be integrated. It did not, nor should it have, considered the social or political consequences of its decision. The Court's only concern was the Constitution.

Litigation can advance an issue, even when the plaintiff loses. It can provide a forum for a public airing of an issue or a problem, such as educational inadequacies or racial segregation. It can be used to stimulate or shape public opinion, as when litigation demonstrates the failure of a state's foster care or public housing programs.

Litigation can hold business and industry accountable for defective products. While there is considerable controversy over tort litigation and the need for reform, private damage suits (along with punitive damages designed to change the conduct of the malfeasor, not just to compensate the injured party) can prod manufacturers to make safer products, and government agencies to enforce the law. For example, when fast-food restaurants were held responsible by the courts for selling dangerously undercooked meat products that caused illness and even death among children, the court decisions prodded restaurants to adopt safer cooking techniques and government agencies to strengthen health inspections and label warnings to protect the public.[21]

Organized litigation groups use the courts to advance public policy on a range of issues: administration of government programs to benefit the poor and the hungry (requiring states to establish programs to implement federal nutrition guidelines); or vindicating the rights of children (requiring states to spend equal amounts per pupil on schools, regardless of the tax base in the school district), women (attempting to establish equal pay for equal work as a legal standard), or the handicapped (requiring school districts to provide adequate educational facilities regardless of costs). Traditionally, public policy litigation was dominated by public interest organizations espousing a "liberal" perspective and urging more government action. Today, free-market and "conservative" interest groups are using litigation to advance their own public policy goals.[22]

But by far the largest number of lawsuits seek to influence government and business environmental policies.[23] For example, owners of oceanfront property contend that laws designed to protect environmentally sensitive wetland areas should not be able to limit what landowners can do with their existing property.[24] Because of the overwhelming public interest in protecting wetland areas for the future (as weighed against the narrow interests of the landowners in further developing their properties), political bodies, particularly state legislatures, have not been sympathetic to the concerns of the landowners.

The landowners took their unpopular cause to the courts, where they hoped to find a more favorable forum. They contended that it was perfectly appropriate for Congress or a state legislature to pass environmental laws that restricted the use of their property as long as they were compensated for the restrictions placed on the use of their property. The government, they argued, had "taken" their property, and under the Fifth Amendment to the U.S. Constitution (and state constitutions), they had the right to be compensated for that "taking."

The "takings" argument received scant support in legislatures, particularly when made by businesses who wanted to be compensated for the costs of complying with federal clean-air and clean-water laws.

After all, how could the federal or state government ever enforce environmental or health laws if it had to pay companies not to pollute or landowners not to destroy an endangered species' habitat? The costs of compensating every property owner for every environmental law or rule that restricted the use of that property would be enormous. Rather than compensate the property owners, lawmakers would have little choice but to roll back environmental protections.

While courts have largely upheld environmental and zoning restrictions, rejecting the property owner's arguments,[25] they have begun to outline areas where government regulatory actions might constitute a taking of private property that would require compensation. The only question for the court is whether the property owners' constitutional rights have been violated.

This is but one illustration of issue advocates with an "unpopular" cause choosing a favorable, albeit costly, forum to address an issue. After the 1992 presidential election (but before the 1994 congressional elections), property rights advocates correctly determined that the regulatory pendulum had swung against them. Activist agency heads and a Democratic-controlled Congress would likely be unfavorable forums in which to have their issue addressed. At the same time, thanks to twelve years of judicial nominations by the Reagan and Bush administrations, the federal courts had become more conservative and therefore more likely to be sympathetic to arguments based on protecting private property rights.

The long and expensive takings litigation has yet to resolve this issue, but it has brought public and legislative attention to it. Congress now considers compensating private property owners for restrictions placed on the use of their property. Local zoning and planning boards must now pause to determine whether their actions require compensating affected property owners.

Not only does the regulatory pendulum swing between federal and state government, it swings within and between the different branches of government. An issue advocate must carefully assess the likely receptiveness of each branch and level of government when deciding how and where to advance an issue.

5

Understanding and Influencing Public Opinion

Question: "Some people say the 1975 Public Affairs Act should be repealed. Do you agree or disagree that it should be repealed?"

Agree:	24%
Disagree:	19%
No Opinion:	57%

Just another sampling of public opinion? Not quite. There is no 1975 Public Affairs Act. There was no such act in 1975 when the poll was originally conducted, nor in 1995, when a telephone survey "updated" the original results.[1]

Public policy in our representative democracy is not decided by academic experts or political leaders working in seclusion. It is determined instead in the crucible of public debate and discussion, through a process by which competing interests are heard and their arguments accepted or rejected in the search for the "best" possible policy decisions. And the ultimate decision is up to the voters.

Unfortunately, there are no easy or reliable ways to gauge public sentiment. Individuals do not make up their minds on issues in a systematic, predictable way. Different populations and subpopulations—men, women, seniors, labor union members, urban dwellers, Hispanics—may have different views for different reasons. Their opinions are the product of incomplete and often misleading information transmitted and received by formal and informal means, from personal discussions between friends and neighbors to mass media and the Internet.

Public opinion may be inconsistent—supporting lower taxes and higher pay for teachers. Or it may be based on erroneous assumptions or incomplete data, such as the level of individual welfare payments or the number of children living in poverty. Or it may change for no apparent reason, sometimes fueled by seemingly meaningless or irrelevant events.

Politicians know that all power rests in the electorate. Candidates and elected officials, with one eye always on reelection, constantly attempt to assess the way the public views the important issues of the day. They conduct polls and focus groups, meet with constituents, read the letters to the editor column in the local newspaper, and keep their ears to the ground in their state or district—all in an effort to get (and stay) in touch with the electorate. They are careful not to stray too far from the views of a majority of their constituents and to measure the impact of positions they take on their chances for election or reelection.

Consider the dilemma of an elected official faced with making a difficult decision on a controversial issue. No doubt she brings to the issue a personal preference. Might she change her view if a significant segment of the public disagrees with her? Or might she persist in trying to explain her view and persuade the electorate to see things her way? Whatever decision she makes will depend on how she assesses and interprets public opinion. How will she know whether the public supports her? How will she know whether she truly represents the views of her constituents?

At the same time as candidates and elected officials are trying to craft issue positions that meet with public approval, issue advocates are trying just as hard to understand public opinion and shape it in their own image.

What is public opinion? How do we measure it? How do we influence it? As the example of the 1975 Public Affairs Act demonstrates, the answers to these questions are far from obvious.

This chapter examines the meaning of public opinion, its importance to issue advocacy, and the techniques to assess it. Chapter 6 discusses how information can be used to influence public opinion. Chapter 7 analyzes the role of the media and how issue advocates can use the media to transmit their message and shape public opinion. The following chapters look at strategies to persuade the public and influence decision makers.

Taking the Public's Pulse

Public opinion moves and shifts in response to changing information and perceptions. The challenge for issue advocates is to supply the information that shifts public opinion in their favor. But before they can influence public opinion, they must first understand it.

Understanding Society

Public opinion is not formulated in a vacuum. Whatever the issue—crime, welfare, health care, the environment, international trade—the public begins with a set of assumptions and understandings. Individuals arrive at an opinion about an issue by combining their own preferences, prejudices, misconceptions, and personal and family backgrounds with their perceptions of society and its problems.

For example, health insurance may not have been a particularly important concern for many people when most employers offered adequate coverage with modest employee contributions. But as corporations "downsized" and even long-time employees began to worry about losing their jobs (or feared that new employers would not provide adequate coverage, particularly for family members with preexisting medical conditions), health-care reform became more urgent.

Similar insecurities in the workforce, and the decline in the availability of corporate pensions, lead many people to be concerned about the stability of social security and Medicare. Tough economic times and an antitax mood make people less eager to support welfare programs and more worried about their own jobs and their children's economic future. The dissolution of the Soviet Union prompts people to question the need to send troops to Bosnia when America's safety is unthreatened.

Such basic conclusions about people's core values and concerns do not come as much from public opinion data on specific issues as from a broader understanding of the economic, social, cultural, and political forces at work in our country. An individual's opinion about crime is shaped by his personal and neighborhood experiences, the movies he sees, the books he reads, the music he hears, and the news he watches.

It is also a product of how he feels about the economy, race relations, welfare, education, the environment, and teenage pregnancy.

That is why issue advocates begin their understanding of public opinion by striving to understand society. To learn about America and its problems, they are voracious readers of national and local newspapers, magazines, journals, and books. They monitor the media, not so much to learn about events, but to see what the media are telling people about events. They listen carefully for reliable gauges of public sentiment, from radio talk-show callers to instant opinion polls. Do people really believe in UFOs? Are they afraid to walk in their own neighborhoods after dark? Do young people believe they will not live as well as their parents?

Advocates look everywhere for insights into America. What is the public reading, watching, and listening to? What books consistently make the "best seller" list? Why were so many people fascinated by the O.J. Simpson trial and so sharply divided on the verdict? Why do people join militias? What accounts for the popularity of gangsta rap?

Advocates begin each issue campaign with a base of knowledge and understanding about contemporary America. Public opinion data can reveal only so much; the start of a campaign is too late to learn that the public fears losing a job more than an endangered species. Understanding society enables advocates to put issues into context and craft campaigns that resonate with public concerns. At the least, advocates will know which questions to ask, and have a context in which to interpret the answers.

Polling the Public

Every newspaper and magazine seems to include at least one survey or poll. Numbers are cited on how many Americans support aid to Russia or drink coffee for breakfast. Americans have a view on everything, no matter how trivial, and an abiding curiosity about the habits and opinions of their fellow citizens.

In this section we explore what advocates can and cannot learn from public opinion polls or surveys. In the next section we examine focus groups and how they can be used to develop issue advocacy campaigns.

If you want to know what your neighbor thinks about an issue, you can ask her. You invite her in for coffee and share your thoughts and discuss hers. If her answers seem hesitant or confusing, you ask for an explanation. If they seem to reflect a faulty understanding of the issue, you supply needed information or correct misperceptions. An hour later you have a good idea of what she believes, why she believes it, and how strongly held her beliefs are.

Polls or surveys are attempts to replicate and expand that process in order to obtain a dependable measure of public sentiment.[2] They differ in two important ways, however, from your neighborly conversation.

First, polls cannot solicit everyone's views. The best they can do is sample public opinion, drawing on a limited number of carefully chosen individuals whose opinions can be expected, with some degree of scientific precision, to represent those of the larger public.

Second, polls are limited in the questions they can ask and the time and effort they can devote to getting a response. Someone has to decide which questions to ask, how to phrase the questions, and how to record ambiguous answers.

Polling is a sophisticated science, part mathematical probability, part sociology. In theory, polls allow issue advocates to obtain statistically reliable measurements of public opinion. The best polls provide more than just numbers. They give issue advocates insight into the breadth and depth of public sentiment.

For example, on the surface a poll may reveal that 63 percent of the public (with an acceptable margin of error) favors welfare reform. Beneath the surface, the poll yields information about the characteristics of welfare reform supporters. Poll results can show different levels of support among men and women or among different age groups or political party members. By seeking information about other personal characteristics, polls can cross-tabulate data to determine the average income of welfare reform supporters or their views on other, possibly related issues, such as crime. Armed with detailed information about the identity of likely supporters or opponents, issue advocates can craft campaigns to mobilize and persuade targeted individuals and groups.

Polls can be purposely misleading, of course. They can use "loaded questions" or phraseology designed to elicit a particular response. They can then be released to the media or used by a decision maker to justify a predetermined position. Even the best-intended polls can be flawed, such as by using samples that are too small or are not randomly selected.

And all polls or surveys have their limitations. They begin with a series of written questions that inevitably reflect at least some biases or preconceived ideas. Poll takers are concerned with getting answers to questions, not probing responses, and even when open-ended responses are permitted, they are rarely encouraged. The poll takers simply do not know (or care) enough about welfare reform to engage the respondents in a meaningful discussion.

Despite the best efforts of poll takers and analyzers, polls have a distressing habit of gyrating wildly. Just examine a graph of any year's data showing public satisfaction with the president—any president. Are they accurate reflections of the public's opinion? If so, what causes such rapid and seemingly erratic movements? What is the public really thinking when it answers yes or no to a particular question? To find out, advocates need to use an additional tool to assess public opinion: the focus group.

Focusing Attention

However carefully crafted, polls boil down to one person asking another person a series of questions. They are fine for taking a snapshot of public sentiment. But issue advocates who seek to change public opinion need to learn how and why the public forms its opinions. What is behind the answers? What assumptions are people making when they support or oppose welfare reform?[3] Why do individuals hold the opinions they do? How strongly do they feel about them? What, if anything, would change their minds? How well do people really understand an issue as complex as crime or welfare? When they say there is a "crisis" in health care, what do they mean?

Focus groups enable issue advocates to probe public understanding of an issue and the assumptions and possible perceptions that go into formulating public opinion. If a poll or survey is a black-and-white snapshot of public opinion, then a focus group is a moving picture, complete with color and action.

A focus group is a structured group interview where carefully chosen individuals (selected, perhaps, because initial polls indicate they share demographic or other characteristics that make them important targets for an issue campaign) are asked questions, and their responses are probed. Free and frank discussion among focus-group participants can reveal the real reasons behind the often "quick and dirty" opinions people express in response to polls.

An experienced focus-group leader can ask follow-up questions to assess the breadth and depth of support or opposition to an issue. The interviewer can encourage a discussion to allow participants to explain the reasons behind their answers. He or she can explore initial reactions by deliberately raising second thoughts and creating doubts.

Focus groups are excellent testing grounds for issue campaigns (just as they are for more traditional product advertisements). Individuals can share—and explain—their reactions to proposed campaigns. Advocates can learn, for example, that the reason people may react negatively to a campaign has nothing to do with the merits of the issue. Instead, they may dislike or distrust the campaign's proponents or their issue advertisements. By observing the discussion among the participants, advocates can learn the answers to questions they would not have thought to ask, and can hear those answers in words the participants, not the advocates, have chosen.

It is one thing to learn that 63 percent of the public favors welfare reform. It is quite another to know why. A focus group might reveal that people vastly overrated the number of individuals receiving welfare, the size of typical benefits, or the ethnic or racial composition of welfare recipients. People may be surprised to learn that children constitute the largest number of welfare recipients or that individuals typically receive welfare for only a brief period.

Words matter. Knowing the words to which people respond, and the language they use to express their concerns, is key to being able to strike chords with which the public responds. Ask the public if they approve of welfare and most often they will say no. Ask the same people what they think of helping those in need and they will probably express support. Speaking in their own words, people might term welfare government "handouts" or waste. They may reveal that their views are shaped by a few highly publicized media stories of "welfare queens," women who fraudulently abuse the welfare system. In contrast, they might express support for welfare when it is described as an effort to feed and clothe needy children or lend a helping hand to those in poverty.

Effective issue advocates must talk the public's language, using the public's words to meet their concerns. But it is only by asking questions and listening to the way the public expresses its concerns that advocates can refine their messages and their campaigns.

Exploring the Territory

Together, polls and focus groups are the primary tools to assess public opinion. The challenge for issue advocates is to use that information to influence public opinion. To do that, advocates use public opinion in several different ways.

Getting the Lay of the Land

At the start of an issue campaign, issue advocates need baseline data about how the public understands a problem or an issue. How important is the issue to the public? Does it affect them personally? How often, if at all, do they think about it? How is the issue connected to other issues in the public's mind?

Advocates concerned with feeding hungry children need to know whether the public believes that widespread hunger in this country is a thing of the past or that existing charities and governmental programs provide adequate food for even the most impoverished family. Advocates who seek more protections for the safety of public drinking water need to know whether the public perceives that the purity of drinking water is at risk.

Baseline public opinion data give advocates a starting point to measure progress as their campaign emerges from Stage 1, as well as insight into how best to influence public opinion. In some situations, initial public opinion data might convince advocates to rethink or postpone their campaign, or even to choose a more favorable forum, such as the courts or the administrative branch, which might be less concerned with public sentiment and more focused on the merits of the argument.

As the issue advances to Stage 2, issue advocates begin to focus on solutions to public problems. At this stage, it is important to know how the public views a problem and its possible solutions. Is the public satisfied with the current health-care delivery system? Would they support a change requiring insurers to cover everyone, no matter what their current health status? How much more would they be willing to pay for such a system? Would people object if they could no longer choose their doctor, as long as they received inexpensive medical care?

Nothing is free. Sad but true. Building more roads to ease congestion costs money and pollutes the air. Ignoring the road system and putting money into improved mass transit may cost more money (and driver aggravation) in the short run while producing savings in air quality for future generations. Does the public understand and accept these tradeoffs? How much will the people pay for clean air or water or a balanced budget? What sacrifices will they make in their own communities? Will they pay higher sales taxes for better schools? More libraries? To keep the neighborhood pool open in the summer?

Public opinion is rarely uniform. Different people feel differently about issues for different reasons. To build a campaign, advocates create "profiles" of likely supporters and opponents. Are married women under thirty with two or more children likely to be opponents? Why? Might they be persuaded with some ingenious argument? Learning as much as possible about how different segments of the population stand on an issue, and why they stand where they do, can enable creative issue advocates to craft targeted strategies to move key constituencies to their side. Knowing who is undecided and why can provide a map for creating an issue campaign to persuade the persuadable.

Testing the Waters

As the issue enters Stage 3, campaigns take form and respond to changing events and shifts in public opinion. From candidates to canned peaches, if you are about to mount an extensive campaign to "sell" the public, you must test the market first. It is no different with issue advocacy. In Stage 3, workable solutions emerge and are tested for public acceptance. "Clever" messages that resonate with those who share an advocate's perspective do not necessarily work with a more important audience: uncommitted or unsupportive members of the public.

Polls and focus groups can "track" public opinion, measuring their response to ongoing campaigns; polls and focus groups reveal the most effective messages and messengers. Mid-course corrections can then take into account feedback from public opinion surveys about the effectiveness of particular advertisements or campaign spokespeople.

Carefully crafted issue campaigns pay as much attention to the messenger as the message. Are lawyers the right group to argue against tort reform? Are doctors good candidates to argue for it? It depends on how the public perceives each group and its stake in the outcome. Who best speaks to the public's concerns? Knowing how the public perceives potential interests enables issue advocates to choose effective spokespeople, both interest groups and individuals, who will appeal to the largest segment of the public. That is why small business owners, not container manufacturers or large cola companies, argue against a deposit on glass containers. That is the reason neighborhood businesses, rather than large oil companies, take the lead in arguing against government environmental and workplace safety requirements.

Assessing the Reliability of Public Opinion

Why It Matters

The Republican's 1994 Contract with America tested well in preelection polls. The public expressed support for its provisions addressing crime, term limits, and regulatory relief. An overwhelming majority of 79 percent of the public supported a constitutional amendment requiring Congress and the president to balance the federal budget. But when the same people were told that balancing the budget would require cuts in social security and Medicare benefits, support dropped to 32 percent.[4]

Is it wrong to say that 79 percent of the public supported the balanced budget? No. But it is misleading. Assuming that cuts in social security and Medicare would have been inevitable (a moot point in this analysis), these poll results illustrate the difference between offhand views and thoughtful judgments. Most public opinion data cited in an effort to influence public policy (or to justify decision makers taking action on public policy) tend to reflect just such offhand and ill-considered opinions.

To be reliable, public opinion must reflect an understanding and acceptance of an issue and its consequences.[5] In a rush to produce instant public opinion, the media (which conduct their own polls and report the results of others') often report "quick and dirty" poll results that fail to probe the public's understanding of an issue. Advocates and decision makers are guilty, too, as their search for the most favorable or supportive public opinion data often leads them to accept incomplete or ill-considered views masquerading as public judgment.

The potential unreliability of public opinion is best illustrated by the drop in public support for a balanced budget amendment from 79 percent to 32 percent, once new facts are introduced and the consequences are explained. Any decision maker (or issue advocate) who took comfort in polls that showed 79 percent of the public supporting the amendment was in for a rude awakening when the public reassessed its views and the poll numbers dropped.

Public opinion is reliable only if it reflects a thorough understanding of the issue and its consequences. The vast majority of issues people care about are difficult problems that defy easy solutions. The solutions often require short-term sacrifices to accomplish long-term goals.

For example, the public may support cutting benefits for welfare recipients. But will it lead in the long run, as some believe, to more crime; a poorer-educated, less competitive workforce; and more children living in poverty and ill health? Is the public aware of, and prepared to accept, the consequences of its choice? Many experts agree that "ending welfare as we know it" may require more money, not less, invested in job training, education, and child-care benefits for welfare recipients. Will the public accept the short-term sacrifice of *higher* welfare costs for the long-term benefits of a healthier, better-prepared workforce?

Too often public opinion is inherently inconsistent because it fails to take into consideration the consequences of public choices. For example, polls may indicate overwhelming support for property tax cuts, while the same polls may show strong opposition to reducing police or fire protection or closing branch libraries. The fact that people have failed to grasp the connection between lowering taxes and closing libraries is a sure sign that their opinion on either subject is unreliable. When the consequences of tax cuts and the connections between lower taxes and less police protection are explained, the public may well change its views.

When President Clinton announced that he was considering sending American soldiers into Haiti to "restore democracy," he knew that he had to build public support for the invasion. Interest groups who shared his position on Haiti were faced with the same problem. A similar situation had faced President Bush when he decided to send U.S. troops into Somalia on a "humanitarian" mission. Both presidents, along with interest groups that supported their positions, attempted to persuade a reluctant public to support the use of troops. President Bush was able to rely on pictures of starving Somali children to win public support. President Clinton relied on our national interest in restoring the legitimate, democratically elected government in nearby Haiti and the need to stop the continuing waves of illegal immigration.

But both situations presented the same problem: would public support for sending American troops pass what Senator John Glenn termed the "Dover test"? Dover Air Force Base in Delaware would be the point of return for the bodies of American troops who died on foreign soil. Would Americans, who initially supported sending troops, maintain their support after American soldiers died? Was the public willing to accept the consequences of its choices? How reliable were polls that showed people supporting these actions? No American politician wanted to rely on poorly formed public opinion that did not recognize and accept that Americans might die in Somalia or Haiti. The quality and reliability of the public's opinion mattered.

Knee-Jerk Opinions and Bumper-Sticker Solutions

Unfortunately, the fact that the public does not fully understand and appreciate the consequences of its choices does not prevent it from expressing an opinion, even a strong one, on an issue. Too often, politicians do not make an effort to determine the reliability of the public's opinion, probably because the public's opinion coincides with their own. They cite the data to support their policy actions, only to discover, as new facts come to light and the consequences of choices become clear, that public opinion has changed. Similarly, issue advocates are too often satisfied with a "quick hit," a persuasive television advertisement or sound bite that, for the moment at least, tips the balance of public opinion.

Talk radio, issue advertisements directed at the public, and the increasing tendency of elected leaders to sample the public opinion waters before and after every speech or vote seemingly push the public to make up its mind without all the facts or an awareness of the consequences of the choices it is asked to make.

The kidnapping and murder of twelve-year-old Polly Klaas in California in 1992 provided the impetus for "three strikes and you're out" laws. The murderer of Polly Klaas had been convicted of numerous previous crimes, but had completed his sentences and was set free. Radio talk-show hosts led the call in California for a law that would put three-time offenders in jail for life. The easy-to-understand principle, as embodied in the catchy slogan "three strikes and you're out," captured the public's attention. The California legislature quickly enacted that principle into law. The clamor for three strikes and you're out did not end at the California border. When Congress considered the 1994 crime bill, popular support convinced it to include a similar provision in federal law.

The federal crime bill would have included another provision, one that the public also thought it understood: "midnight basketball." It seems that cities had formed and funded late-night basketball leagues to give teenagers and other young people a place to go and something to do other than to wander the streets and possibly commit crimes. The public, which had enthusiastically embraced three strikes and you're out as a crime-fighting measure, rebelled at the idea of federal dollars supporting midnight basketball. Labeled as "pork," it received strong criticism, despite the fact that one midnight basketball program had been recognized by President Bush as one of the "thousand points of light."[6]

The public was understandably angry about crime and wanted government to do something about it. Did it further its goals by supporting three strikes and you're out and opposing midnight basketball?

California's experience with its own version of three strikes and you're out is instructive. In Los Angeles, a man was sentenced to life imprisonment after conviction for his third felony, stealing a piece of pizza. Another man went to jail for life after stealing wooden pallets to start a beach bonfire, his third felony. Court costs have skyrocketed in California, as those faced with a third felony conviction demand a jury trial, having lost their incentive to plead guilty. County jails face extreme overcrowding and are no longer accepting prisoners convicted of misdemeanors. Sentences for others are being reduced to make room for more serious felons. Still more prisons need to be built, and paid for, in California.[7]

Former Deputy U.S. Attorney General Philip Heymann described three strikes and you're out as an idea that "sounds terrific" but "doesn't make any sense. It's become too easy to pretend we're going to solve this problem with a set of remedies that look good for the first 15 seconds you look at them and very bad when you get to half a minute." He argued that it placed major new strains on federal resources but did little to reduce violent crime. How and why, he asked, would the federal government pay for the cost of incarcerating inmates over the age of fifty, when they are highly unlikely to commit further crimes?[8]

Does the death penalty deter crime? If not, does it at least reduce costs for taxpayers, since they do not have to pay to incarcerate prisoners for life? Popular support for the death penalty has risen, but studies show that it costs much more in court costs to execute prisoners than to imprison them for life. Even police, judges, and prosecutors believe it is counterproductive.[9]

And what about midnight basketball? Members of Congress and the public argued that what we really needed were "midnight libraries," where young people could be encouraged to read and learn. True, but would that have an effect on crime? Didn't the statistics show that midnight basketball dramatically reduced inner-city crime?[10] But the debate never addressed that question.

Have three strikes and you're out and the death penalty solved the crime problem, or have we just declared victory and moved on to the next issue? Or worse, have we created more problems with ill-considered solutions whose ramifications the public and policymakers have not fully explored? How do we move beyond simplistic solutions that make better bumper stickers than public policy?

Toward Better Public Policy Decisions

Our frenetic democracy has more call-in talk shows and instant public opinion polls than time and opportunity for second thoughts and considered judgments. How do we deal with difficult issues that require short-term sacrifices for long-term solutions? How do issue advocates foster the development of reliable public opinion—public judgment— that takes into account all relevant factors? How can we develop consistent public support that passes the "Dover test"?

It is often difficult for issue advocates to resist the temptation to develop high quantities of low-quality, unreliable public support. But legislators have learned (as we see in chapter 10) to be skeptical of instant polls and to discount postcards and form letters and phone calls generated by radio talk shows as unreliable measures of true public support. And issue advocates have learned to their dismay not to rely on illusory levels of public support that can vanish as soon as opponents raise additional argument or produce new information.

Fortunately, there are ways to foster the development of high-quality, reliable public opinion.[11] Issue advocates must recognize that, as we saw in chapter 2, all issues are not always ripe for action. Many issues move toward action before the public has a full opportunity to discuss and evaluate them. Advocates need to take the time and find the opportunities to educate citizens and help them resolve competing views and apparent inconsistencies, allowing them to understand and accept the consequences of choices, rather than push the public toward formulating an immediate, albeit ill-considered and unreliable, opinion.

That means time must be spent on educating the public when the temptation is to roll out a campaign and mobilize the public. It means finding the time and place for formal and informal public discussions, from conducting town meetings to using mass media outlets to explore the ramifications of an issue. It means speaking the public's language—using its words, but more importantly meeting its concerns, whether real or perceived. Midnight basketball sounds like a waste of federal tax dollars. Advocates never convincingly explained why it worked better than harsh, punitive measures that resonated with the public's anger with crime and criminals.

It means making connections between issues and concerns, instead of attempting to address each issue in a vacuum. The death penalty, gun control, and three strikes and you're out can each be seen as separate initiatives that the public supports or opposes individually. Or advocates can confront the more difficult, underlying issues of reducing crime and violence, thereby addressing the real public concerns that each of those proposals seeks to address. Advocates must be prepared to do what they ask the public to do: resist the easy, short-term solution that does little to address the underlying problem.

Leadership and Public Opinion Polls: Following the Leader?

Global warming. Social security. Health-care reform. Difficult issues require difficult choices and public sacrifices. If we truly believe that profligate consumption of fossil fuels leads to irreversible, disastrous global warming, how do we make the painful, immediate public sacrifices needed to deal with the problem? If the Social Security System is truly on a path to bankruptcy, will we pay more taxes or accept fewer benefits? Health-care costs skyrocket, yet the public insists on being able both to choose its own doctors and to keep costs affordable.

In each instance we have several public policy choices. Our leaders can read the only polls that seem to be available: unreliable ones. They can see for themselves that the public has not thought these issues through and wants to have its cake and eat it too. People want to avoid the consequences of global warming but do not want to turn off their car air conditioners. Powerful senior citizen lobbies refuse to accept any reduction in social security benefits, even for those wealthy enough not to miss the money. And the public wants the best possible health care but does not want to pay the bill. What is a decision maker to do?

The distressing answer is usually the same: nothing. Do not risk alienating the public, as reflected in the unreliable public opinion data, and do not take the time or effort to educate the public on the need for sacrifices and difficult choices.

Perhaps doing nothing is not the worst option. Perhaps it is worse to embrace proposals that do not work (or even exacerbate the problem). Or to do something that is not cost effective and that squanders time, resources, and the rare political moment when an issue captures the public's attention. Or to adopt solutions that appear to work, thus mollifying the public, but only postpone the inevitable day of reckoning.[12]

Solving persistent, difficult, potentially expensive public problems cries out for leaders and leadership. We need leaders who understand the need to help the public accept the costs of finding and implementing hard solutions, rather than pander to the latest fickle poll. Do we elect our leaders merely to translate prevailing public opinion into public policy? Or do we want them to consider our views, but use their own judgment to make the best possible decisions? The question of leadership and judgment, and the underlying dichotomy between representative and direct democracy, surfaces again in later chapters. For now, we recognize that all public opinion data are not equal and that solid solutions must be based on reliable, thoughtful public judgments.

6

Information and Persuasion

Information is the single greatest tool of persuasion in the issue advocate's arsenal. Used creatively, it can shape reliable public opinion and influence decision makers.

Information and Advocacy

Identifying and Bridging the Public Opinion Gap

Issue campaigns are not created in the abstract. Initial polls and focus groups yield valuable clues about how the public views an issue. A careful review of the public opinion data will allow issue advocates to identify the "public opinion gap": the distance between their own understanding of an issue and the public's. What do issue advocates know about an issue that the public does not? And how might that information, if properly packaged and delivered, bridge the gap and change the public's mind?

Campaigns start, of course, with what the public knows—or thinks it knows—about an issue. If 70 percent of the public supports the death penalty, do those supporters believe that the death penalty is an effective crime deterrent? Do they understand the added costs of prosecuting death penalty cases and the lengthy appeals process? Are they aware of the disproportionate number of minorities executed? Do people believe that putting violent criminals to death will at least save society the long-term costs of incarcerating these felons? How will they react if studies show the opposite to be true?

The public opinion gap can be as fundamental as a misunderstanding of the issue itself. Does the public think that requiring employers to provide family and medical leave means *paid* leave? (It does not.) The public may not understand the extent of the problem, such as the magnitude of homelessness or the number of children living in poverty or the cost of cleaning up toxic waste sites. Or it may be confused about the nature of the solution and the likelihood that it will succeed, such as funding midnight basketball programs to prevent crime. Or it may not fully appreciate a problem's costs or a solution's benefits.

Information has the power to persuade. It can bridge the public opinion gap and shift the balance of power in an issue advocacy campaign.

- *Attracting Public Attention.* Childhood hunger in America lacks the gut-wrenching images of starving African children, but malnutrition and its effect on child development and learning are a problem in this country. How could the Food Research and Action Center (FRAC), a Washington, D.C., policy organization concerned with poverty and nutrition, attract America's attention and resources to solve its own hunger problem?

    FRAC began its 1991 Campaign to End Childhood Hunger with an extensive survey of hunger and nutrition among poor children in America.[1] The survey got broad media and public attention and gave the campaign its initial impetus. Without a well-documented study (or pictures of emaciated children), the media and the public would have moved on to the next most pressing issue.

    AIDS is another example of a problem that can be too easily dismissed as happening to somebody else, somewhere else. Like starving children in far-off countries, numbers or statistics can end up in file cabinets or on the evening news' cutting-room floor. But human faces and individual stories are more difficult to ignore. Information—stories—about real people and their problems can make numbers come alive and command attention by the public and decision makers. Pediatric AIDS was a medical problem until the well-publicized cases of Ryan White and Elizabeth Glasser transformed it into a public policy issue.

- *Refocusing the Issue and Attracting New Supporters.* Is health-care reform about access to health insurance? Is it an issue that primarily affects the poor? The elderly? Children? People with mental health problems? Is it about making American industry competitive with its international counterparts by controlling health insurance costs? Is it about the quality of health care? Its affordability? Or is it about caring for the homeless, who may be forced onto the street by their inability to get or pay for necessary health care?

  Information can transform an academic and technical debate about reforming health care into a robust public policy discussion about competitiveness or children or mental health, which might attract new attention and supporters to the underlying issue.

  For example, health-care-reform opponents might gain crucial new supporters with information about the adverse effect reform would have on rural Americans, who already have limited access to health care and few choices. Or they could gain small business support with information about how reform will force marginally profitable businesses to lay off employees or cut wages.

  Advocates for more assistance to the homeless might use information about the large number of homeless veterans[2] to garner the support of veterans organizations and to transform a tired public discussion about homelessness into a rejuvenated campaign to help those who served their country.

- *Giving Credibility to Arguments and Advocates.* Protecting children, small businesses, and veterans benefits are important American values. But invoking abstract values rarely suffices to change public policy. Information can bolster arguments based on values by providing an external and seemingly objective justification for potential supporters, who may be reluctant to rely on values or beliefs alone. For instance, death penalty proponents, who might attract natural allies from those who believe that "an eye for an eye" is an appropriate remedy, could bolster that argument with data, if they existed, on the deterrent effect of the death penalty. Similarly, advocates who support preservation of the rain forest because "it is the right thing to do," could bolster their argument (and, not incidentally, win additional supporters) with information about the potentially life-saving medicines that might be extracted from plants and animals that would otherwise disappear.

Information that buttresses the argument is particularly important when the argument appears counterintuitive. Logic appears to dictate that raising the minimum wage will result in fewer low-wage jobs. But a study of the effect of New Jersey's 19 percent hike in the state's minimum wage concluded that employment in fast-food restaurants (which typically hire many minimum-wage workers) actually increased. The report influenced policymakers in other states and at the federal level, despite the fact that later studies questioned its accuracy.[3]

Information can also earn advocates a seat at the policymaking table. Complex environmental policy decisions concerning clean-air and -water laws and regulations often depend on information provided by the industries to be regulated. After all, isn't the affected industry best able to predict the direct costs to it of cleaning the air or the indirect costs in lost jobs? Environmental and health organizations, in contrast, can develop their own information to counter that produced by industry. Reliable information can effectively neutralize the inherent advantage industry has as the apparent custodian of all the relevant information.

The Center on Budget and Policy Priorities is a liberal interest group concerned with the effect of federal budget decisions on the poor. It bolsters its argument with extensive analyses of legislative budget proposals and is often sought out by members of the media and other interest groups for their expert opinions on the implications of budget decisions.[4] Like FRAC, it uses information to establish its own credibility and make it a more reliable and effective advocate.

- *Explaining Problems and Unlocking Answers.* Problems persist despite our best efforts to apply solutions. Crime increases, the environment deteriorates, good jobs disappear, illegal immigration into the United States grows.

  Information can help predict the consequences of problems and their solutions, demonstrating that problems must be addressed and solutions will work. The time-honored solution to illegal immigration is to hire more border guards and build higher fences. But studies show that most illegal immigration begins when people enter this country on airplanes, with legal visas, then remain illegally when their visas expire. That information suggests the need for new ways to look at the problem and new solutions to address it.

A 1995 study showed that nearly 80 percent of children born to unmarried teenagers without a high school diploma were living in poverty at ages seven to twelve, compared with 8 percent of children born to older, married mothers who finished high school. The study also found that children who grow up without fathers are five times more likely to be poor, twice as likely to drop out of high school, and much more likely to end up in foster care or juvenile justice facilities. Girls raised in single-parent families are three times more likely to become unwed mothers, and boys without fathers at home are much more likely to become incarcerated and unemployed.[5] Armed with this information, advocates can suggest innovative approaches to address the underlying causes of public problems.

Information: All You'd Ever Want to Know

Information is more than facts or data that can be demonstrated as either true or false. For public policymaking purposes, we use "information" broadly to include everything the public and decision makers want and need to know to reach a judgment about an issue.

As a tool to influence or persuade, information can appeal to the head or the heart. It can include careful studies and surveys about the number of jobs potentially lost to environmental regulations that protect trees inhabited by spotted owls. It can also include the personal story, complete with pictures and quotations, of a family forced out of its home and onto welfare because restrictions intended to protect the environment eliminated logging jobs in the Pacific Northwest. And it can also include appeals to conscience and religious faith that question the wisdom of humans allowing one of God's creatures to become extinct.

Which form of information is most persuasive and for what audiences? Are hard facts and cold statistics ever enough to persuade? What about revealing anecdotes about people and their experiences?

Individuals and policymakers want and need more than numbers and probabilities to justify changing public policy. They are reluctant to make (or accept) public policy decisions based on the statistical chance that implementing a new program or terminating an existing one will produce the claimed benefits. They want and need to know how it will affect "real people," and the normative or value component inherent in the choices they are asked to make, whether as citizens or legislators.[6] It is rarely enough to say that a certain number of casualties are expected to occur if we send troops into battle, such as in the Gulf War. The public wants to understand the moral and ethical component of a decision to send troops to a foreign country. People want to know what will happen to individuals: American soldiers, Kuwaitis, even Iraqi citizens.

They also want to know what others think about the issue. Public opinion data can be important information in an issue advocacy campaign, just as in an electoral campaign. Rising public support, as reported in the polls, can persuade the undecided: there is "safety in numbers." And falling public opinion numbers can have the opposite effect. This phenomenon is often magnified by media reporting that focuses more on poll numbers (as in health care reform) than on the merits of the issue.

Doing Studies and Telling Stories

Information is not always factual, and facts are not always true. In this section we examine the different kinds of factual information usually adduced in public policy debates, and how each might best be used. In a later section we look behind the numbers and examine their reliability.

During the Reagan administration the nation seemed to focus for the first time on the problem of homelessness. A deep recession had left large numbers of individuals and children without homes and living on the streets. Society tried to adapt to these individuals in a compassionate way, even changing how we described them. No longer were they bums or panhandlers or even street people. They were homeless, and many were mentally ill. Homelessness was a problem that needed to be addressed, but how serious a problem was it? What was the extent of homelessness? The debate soon became about numbers, rather than compassion.[7]

The Reagan administration sought to minimize the extent of the problem, arguing that private charities, rather than government programs, were in the best position to solve the problem. Church groups and others, who were trying to meet the needs of the homeless, produced their own, larger numbers, to demonstrate that homelessness was much more prevalent than the administration claimed. Who was right, and more important, is it possible for anyone to produce a definitive number of the homeless people in America?

If you pass the same person sitting on the same street corner every day, you can determine whether that particular individual is homeless. The "fact" of that person's homelessness can be established. It is the kind of fact that courts or agencies or Congress can resolve.

But facts about individuals or particular events or situations are not generally the foundation for making public policy (although, as we see, telling stories about real people can be very persuasive). Most often, public policymaking depends on less easily determined facts. While we are capable of deciding, on a case-by-case basis, whether any individual is homeless, facts about the precise extent of homeless—in a city, state, or the nation as a whole—are at best estimates or educated guesses. Estimates differ and are subject to interpretation, depending on how the information is collected and analyzed. We often term these facts "legislative facts" because legislative bodies must use their expertise and judgment to evaluate conflicting information, since a precise number is impossible.

Legislative facts are inherently imprecise and subject to challenge. And stories about individuals and their experiences provide an unsteady cornerstone for public policymaking. Yet both types of information are important advocacy tools.

Studies and Statistics

Despite the difficulty in establishing beyond doubt the validity of legislative facts, studies and statistics dominate efforts to persuade decision makers and the public. Reliable studies are usually a necessary predicate to establish the prevalence of problems, the workability of solutions, and the costs and benefits of each. No matter how speculative or open to interpretation, studies can at least provide "expert" reassurance that solutions will accomplish their goals.

As the 104th Congress considered reforming the nation's tort laws, lawmakers were flooded with studies and surveys attempting to demonstrate the harm caused by rampant product-liability lawsuits. Doctors and manufacturers lined up to support tort reform, while trial lawyers and consumer interest groups lined up against it. Since the costs of liability suits are more easily quantifiable than the speculative benefits of safer products or medical care, reform proponents (who were in the best position to know the costs) produced a volume of statistics to demonstrate that tort suits raised the price of consumer products and health care. Their studies showed, for example, that one-half of the price of a child's $200 football helmet went to pay liability insurance, as did $20 of the price of a $100 stepladder. Studies revealed that $8 of an $11.50 dose of the common childhood DPT vaccine paid the cost of liability insurance.

Liability insurance premiums in America were twenty to fifty times higher, studies showed, than for foreign competitors. Only 200 product-liability suits are filed each year in Great Britain, versus 70,000 in this country. And to top off the argument, studies demonstrated that only one-third of any damages awarded went to injured parties; two-thirds went to their lawyers.[8]

When Vice-President Quayle announced his support for litigation reform in 1991, he chose one study's $80 billion cost figure. Others quickly criticized that number, contending that the real cost was $29 billion. Still others claimed it was as high as $300 billion.[9] Yet it is relatively easy to quantify costs. Companies know the liability insurance premiums they pay for specific products or transactions. It is much more difficult to determine the total economic costs of product-liability suits, so costs can be weighed against benefits in the balance of public policymaking.

Trial lawyers and consumer groups questioned the reliability of these studies, as we see later in this chapter, but had little statistical evidence of their own to produce. Both sides did, however, supplement the dry and lifeless numbers with real stories about real people and their problems.

Anecdotal Information

Personal stories about individual experiences—anecdotes—are powerful advocacy tools. Just recall Myra Rosenbloom's tale, and try to imagine a similar campaign succeeding using only studies and statistics. If the public's eyes glaze over when presented with statistics, people are often drawn to personal stories with which they can identify. Issue advocates tell "stories that stay" to breathe life into numbers and facts.

Despite all the numbers, tort reform failed to interest the American public. Until Stella Liebeck purchased a cup of coffee at a McDonald's in Albuquerque, New Mexico. Driving away from the restaurant, she placed the cup of coffee between her legs, where it spilled, burning her. She sued McDonald's, claiming the coffee was too hot. A jury agreed with her and awarded her actual and punitive damages totaling $2.7 million.[10]

Tort reform advocates had a field day with Mrs. Liebeck's story. Suddenly tort reform was transformed from an obscure issue argued with lifeless statistics into a story about a real person's real experience. This was a symptom of the harmful effects of product-liability litigation that all Americans could understand. They knew, or thought they did, that reasonable people do not put hot coffee between their legs, and if anyone was to blame it was Mrs. Liebeck. One story was worth a thousand statistics.

Of course there was another side to this story, including the more than 700 people who were also burned by coffee McDonald's knew to be excessively hot.[11] And there was another side to the tort reform debate: pictures of people burned by exploding gas tanks or women maimed by faulty breast implants.[12]

We analyze in greater detail how different types of information can be used to persuade lawmakers and regulators in chapter 9.

Painting Pictures and Putting Numbers into Perspective: Using Creativity and Imagination to Communicate Information

President Reagan liked to bring the national debt down to human scale by describing a trillion dollars as a pile of $1,000 bills reaching sixty-seven miles high. He knew that people learn something only if they can relate it to something they understand. And understanding is a necessary precursor to persuasion.[13] The public is so inundated with numbers and statistics that, no matter how reliable and accurate, they often fail to communicate and therefore to persuade. Issue advocates can package and present their information using creative comparisons and dramatic presentations to penetrate the information fog.

Antismoking organizations can cite facts and figures about the harm caused by tobacco or the difficulty people have quitting once they begin smoking. Or they can relate the dangers and costs of smoking to things that people understand. For example, that deaths from smoking in this country are equivalent to one fully loaded jumbo jet crashing every day. Or that, in the words of the surgeon general, "smoking is more addictive than heroin."[14]

Figure 1.

A schoolroom of California kids shot dead every two weeks.

Isn't that enough?

Handguns have become the leading killer of California's children...the murder weapon of choice and the #1 teen suicide method. California is selling a thousand more each day and more kids are getting their hands on them with tragic results. Many responsible Californians agree on four steps that must be taken:

 Ban Saturday Night Specials. These cheaply-made, cheap-to-buy handguns are disproportionately represented in homicides and other crimes. Imports were banned 25 years ago. Domestic Saturday Night Specials, 80% now made in Southern California, weren't.

 Let communities decide what rules to live by. Most states preempt local gun controls with looser state laws, California among them. But where sensible laws rule, handgun violence declines. Twelve California counties account for most youth killings in the state. Wouldn't home rule make our streets and our children safer?

 Increase the potential penalty for carrying a concealed handgun. Right now, it's a misdemeanor to carry a non-permitted, loaded pistol in your jacket pocket or tucked in your waistband— like jaywalking, or dropping a gum wrapper— while brass knuckles can be prosecuted as a felony.

 Treat handguns like other consumer products. There are now more safety rules on teddy bears than on handguns, and basic devices that could prevent most accidental shootings are not required. Why not bring safety standards for handguns under the jurisdiction of the Bureau of Alcohol, Tobacco and Firearms?

These proposals were presented as part of a recent videoconference among 1,500 Californians and others who want to prevent handgun violence against kids.

It looked at handgun violence as a public health menace, and how to reduce it.

As Donna Shalala, U.S. Secretary of Health and Human Services, noted "...gun violence against children is not an inner city problem. It's not a problem of poor people. It's not a problem confined to certain genders or ethnic groups.

"And, most important, it is not— nor will it ever be—somebody else's problem.

"It is our problem."

In response to the tragic consequences of violence in our society, The California Wellness Foundation is dedicating more than $35 million over five years to support a comprehensive Violence Prevention Initiative. To learn more about the Campaign to Prevent Handgun Violence Against Kids and other projects of the Initiative, please write us.

The California Wellness Foundation
6320 Canoga Avenue, Suite 1700
Woodland Hills, California 91367

Reprinted with permission

Handgun control advocates effectively dramatized the scope of gun violence by comparing its victims to "a school room of California kids shot dead every two weeks." The comparison places gun violence in a larger context, and not incidentally relates it to children who may be its innocent victims (see Figure 1).

When President Clinton contemplated invading Haiti to restore democracy, he knew he had to convince a skeptical American public that it was the right thing to do and that Haiti's size made it a manageable military operation. He could have described Haiti as a country of approximately 11,000 square miles, which would have been perfectly accurate but totally useless. People no more think in units of thousands of square miles than they do in trillions of dollars. To give a more useful picture of Haiti's size, one can compare it to something people know: Haiti is approximately the size of the state of Maryland. Advocates must know their audience, of course, and if that audience is European, the appropriate comparison would be with Belgium, not Maryland.

In 1995 the Pentagon sought more than $30 billion to buy twenty additional Stealth bombers. Opponents translated the $30 billion figure into numbers the public could understand. Thirty billion public dollars, used in other ways, could immunize all the children living in poverty; fully fund the National Endowment for the Arts for ten years, provide job training to 400,000 people trying to get off welfare, and do much more. In addition, they described the B-2 Stealth bomber as costing "more than its weight in gold"[15] (see Figure 2). Not incidentally, funding opponents suggested appealing alternatives for spending the requested money.

Sometimes the challenge is to make seemingly small numbers appear large. When Energy Secretary Hazel O'Leary was criticized for spending $46,500 of federal money to monitor media coverage of her agency, her opponents tried to make that number seem large, even in the context of a $1.5 trillion federal budget. They described it as representing "the entire tax obligations of 21 average American households," a figure to which the average American taxpayer could clearly relate.[16]

Is a picture really worth a thousand words? (Actually, that may not be a very effective way to communicate a picture's worth: who knows how many words are a thousand? Do people really relate to that number?) Pictures, graphics, charts, displays, and telling objects are im-

Figure 2.

IT'S BACK...

THE BOMBER THAT COSTS MORE THAN ITS WEIGHT IN GOLD

For the **$31.5 Billion** to build 20 additional B-2 Stealth Bombers, we could:

• Immunize all the children living in poverty in the United States	($541 million)
• Fully fund the National Endowment for the Arts for 10 years	($1,700 million)
• Restore federal public library construction funds cut in 1995	($18 million)
• Fully fund the program to eliminate tuberculosis in the U.S.	($484 million)
• Fund the Safe & Drug-Free Schools program for 5 years	($3,300 million)
• Fully fund the National Endowment for the Humanities for 10 years	($1,800 million)
• Electrify and upgrade 5,000 miles of rail	($15,000 million)
• Restore all education funds and student aid cut in the 1995 budget	($622 million)
• Fully fund the Corporation for Public Broadcasting for 10 years	($3,000 million)
• Purchase & operate mobile health clinic vans in 100 cities	($30 million)
• Fully fund summer youth programs in 100 cities	($1,000 million)
• Provide job training to 400,000 people trying to get off welfare	($2,000 million)
• Contribute $2 billion to deficit reduction	($2,000 million)
TOTAL:	**$31,495,000,000**

......and still have $5 million in change.

Cost of 20 B2 planes is estimate from Air Combat Commander John Loh, testtimony before the House National Security Committee, 4/6/95.
Sources: Children's Defense Fund; L.A. Times 9/9/93; National Commission for Economic Conversion & Disarmament; Wall Street Journal 8/5/94; Washington Post 7/1/93.

Council for a Livable World Education Fund ● 110 Maryland Ave. N.E. ● Washington, D.C. 20002 ● (202) 543-4100

Reprinted with permission

portant tools to communicate information and persuade. Numbers can certainly impress, particularly when compared to everyday notions people understand, but graphical or visual representations of numbers can do even better.

That is why 100,000 signatures on a petition is much less effective than 100,000 people demonstrating for the same purpose. It is also why the huge, unfolded AIDS quilt, with personal representations of the lives and deaths of so many AIDS victims, can communicate more about the extent of AIDS than numbers or statistics.

And that is why, when gun-control advocates marched on Washington to support increased restrictions on handgun sales, they reinforced their message with a dramatic display of 40,000 pairs of shoes. Each pair was brought or sent to Washington by a friend or parent of a youthful victim of gun violence.[17]

A display in the U.S. Holocaust Museum includes shoes taken from Holocaust victims. Accompanying home photographs of people killed in a village destroyed by the Nazis, the shoes reveal the human-scale tragedy behind 6 million deaths. And the Vietnam Veterans Memorial conveys the enormity of the loss of American life during the war with each dead soldier's name etched in black stone.

The burden that government reporting requirements impose on small businesses can be expressed in numbers of forms to be filed, hours required to complete the task, and money spent to comply with the requirements. Or all the required forms can be piled on the desk of a typical small businessperson, in front of a camera that records the scene and displays it on the front page of the *Washington Post*.[18] The effect is magnified if an enterprising reporter decides to follow the trail of paper inside the government, only to discover that the information is rarely used.

Ross Perot used charts and graphs to explain the need to eliminate budget deficits. The raw numbers may have meant little to viewers, but the diverging lines representing revenues and expenditures presented a telling message. And Senator Robert Dole attempted to portray the bureaucratic complexity of President Clinton's health-care-reform proposal with an intentionally complicated chart demonstrating, in Dole's view, the byzantine structure of health-care delivery under the Clinton proposal. No amount of words could trigger the impression conveyed by a chart full of lines and arrows and boxes. Long after the words fade, the visual memory invoked by the charts, graphs, or shoes remains.

In chapter 7, we focus on how information can capture and hold the media's attention.

Dueling Data: Sources and Reliability of Information

Suppose you want to learn about the extent of hunger in America. The U.S. Department of Agriculture, which administers the school lunch and food stamp programs, no doubt has some data, as do local governments. Interest groups such as FRAC and the Children's Defense Fund have additional information to contribute, as do think tanks concerned with government agricultural price supports or international agricultural trade. Church groups that feed the poor have relevant data, as do social workers and foundations that support their work. The private sector, including agricultural interests and food manufacturers and distributors, could provide useful information. Academics have no doubt published studies and surveys of the problem. Even the media may have produced reports about hunger in America. Not surprisingly, once you assembled all the relevant information on hunger (and tossed out the obviously unreliable) you would discover that all the expensive studies and surveys did not reach the same conclusion.

People instinctively believe that while opinions and arguments are subjective, facts—data, studies, or surveys—are either true or false. But we have seen that legislative facts, on which most public policy decisions are based, cannot be definitively labeled true or false. Worse, making public policy requires speculative judgments to predict the probable consequences of events. Is caffeine harmful, and if so, at what levels? Does alar sprayed on apples as an insecticide cause cancer in humans? How well should hamburger meat be cooked to avoid illness? Do cellular phones cause brain cancer? Does drinking two glasses a day of red wine lower one's risk of heart disease? Are nuclear power plants safe? In each instance, we need to rely on facts or information developed from sources we believe are reliable.

Yet none of the "facts," on which public policy must be based, is capable of being resolved. Advocates, the public, or decision makers will search in vain for the one perfect study or survey to resolve all doubts. Academic analyses are routinely challenged by other academics and contradicted by other studies. Respectable experts differ on the health effects of moderate wine drinking or the economic benefit of cutting the capital gains tax.

Information is a tactical advocacy tool. Advocates determine what information is required to close the public opinion gap, and then find or create it. Dueling data and competing studies require advocates to produce the most reliable studies and to cast doubt on the reliability of the opposition's information. With plenty of experts and studies to choose from, advocates understandably select the most credible and convincing.

Issue advocates are not scientists, they are advocates. They are not in pursuit of "truth" but of supportive information. Interest groups develop and use information that supports their positions, often ignoring or dismissing contradictory studies. They are free to pick and choose from thousands of published and unpublished scientific and technical studies. Policymakers—legislators, regulators, and the courts—must resolve factual disputes in the adversarial crucible of public policymaking.

Individuals and policymakers determine the reliability of factual information by carefully scrutinizing the information itself, its source, and the interest that supports it. Is government information inherently more reliable than interest-group information? Is a government study concluding that "second-hand" cigarette smoke causes cancer less reliable because the government official who produced the report is a known opponent of the tobacco industry?

Is academic information, by its very nature, more reliable than interest-group information? Does an academic study lose some of its credibility if it is funded by an interest group and used to support an issue campaign? Is a tobacco company study that concludes the contrary, produced by a respected epidemiologist complete with appropriate scientific protocols, suspect because the tobacco company that paid for the study will benefit financially from its conclusions? Would the same study, reaching the same conclusions, be more believable if it were produced under the auspices of a major university? In that instance, would it matter if the study were funded by a grant from the same tobacco company? And what if the tobacco company does not fund the study directly but provides major support for the university?

Unfortunately, there are no easy answers to these difficult questions. Even federal government census data, perhaps the most exhaustive and painstakingly collected government data, are routinely challenged by states, cities, and issue advocates for undercounting certain populations: the homeless, children, minorities.

The only inescapable conclusion is that when advocates use information to influence public policy, the information's reliability will always be challenged. Advocates cannot rely solely on the presumed independence of government or academia or think tanks to authenticate the integrity of their information. They must present their information as credibly as possible and be prepared to defend it from inevitable attack.

(A final note about reliability: It can be dangerous and even fatal to use information that is inaccurate or has not been verified. Tort reform advocates depicted the Girl Scouts as victims of frivolous lawsuits, even going so far as to air advertisements calculating the number of boxes of cookies the scouts must sell to pay for their liability insurance premiums, an otherwise effective way to present that information. Unfortunately, as the Girl Scouts were quick to point out, and the media quick to publicize, it was not true.)[19]

"Laundering" Information: Buying Science

An oil company that opposes legislation requiring it to use double-hulled oil tankers to minimize the risks of spills faces a choice. It can produce its own analysis demonstrating that double-hulled tankers are actually more likely to be involved in accidents than single-hulled tankers because they are heavier, slower, and less maneuverable. Or it can fund an "academic" or "independent" expert to produce the same study. The choice is easy.

The public and decision makers respect "academic" and "independent" experts, presuming they are engaged in the scientist's search for truth rather than the advocate's search for supportive information. That is why issue advocates often attempt to "launder" information, washing it clean of the taint it might otherwise have if it were known to have come directly from the affected interest. By separating those who produce the information from those who pay for it and use it to advance their policy interests, advocates hope to invest their information with increased credibility.

The simplest illustration is the "professional expert" who has the necessary academic or other credentials, but whose work is clandestinely supported by the affected industry and whose conclusions appear to favor it. For example, many states that are chronically short of revenue are seriously considering legalizing casino gambling. But how much will casinos contribute to the state's economy and its treasury, and will those benefits be outweighed by increased crime? Not surprisingly, casino gambling advocates produced "expert" studies and opinions. Unfortunately for the advocates, the media were quick to realize that the studies were paid for by the industry and the experts were mere spokespeople for the industry's interests.[20]

Some interests even create self-styled "independent" research councils or committees to produce "expert" information. These research organizations attempt to benefit from the credibility and independence the public associates with truly independent academic, scientific, or technical institutions. But information produced by research organizations created or supported by interest groups may lack credibility and independence precisely because they are funded by specific business or economic interests. Nevertheless, the media often report these expert studies and surveys without acknowledging that the organization's expertise was purchased by the affected interest, such as an expert witness or professional advocate.

By usurping the independent science community's mantle of authority, these "expert" groups have the potential to exert a lasting influence on media, public, and decision-maker opinion. They can commission a variety of studies and can manipulate the data to reflect the views of those who purchase it. Even if their experts or research papers are not unassailable, advocates can use them to create doubt around already settled issues, such as the connection between smoking and health, or to call into question the results of other, more reliable analyses.

For example, the American Council on Science and Health (ACSH) issues a flow of purportedly independent "scientific" reports on such subjects as pesticides, nutrition, and food additives, which seek to discredit independent scientific findings and regulatory initiatives critical of the food, drug, and chemical industry, which are ACSH's principal funders.[21]

Other examples abound: Representative Henry Waxman (D-Calif.) described a tobacco industry-funded research organization, the Council for Tobacco Research International, as "public relations masquerading as science. . . . From the very beginning, the council was a public relations ploy—a seemingly independent research body whose real purpose was to promote the idea that smoking is safe."[22]

Healthy Buildings International (HBI), an "independent" indoor air consultant, published a study placing tobacco smoke as the least likely complaint about indoor air quality. HBI is funded almost entirely by the tobacco industry. In congressional hearings, three employees of the company revealed that the study data were intentionally manipulated to produce results more favorable to the industry. The Department of Justice investigated HBI for perjury.[23]

Procter & Gamble, a leading manufacturer of disposable diapers, commissioned and paid for a study by the prestigious Arthur D. Little consulting firm to refute growing public concerns about the environmental consequences of disposable diapers. The consultant's study concluded that cloth and disposable diapers had the same effect on the environment. Procter & Gamble effectively used the study to defuse public concerns about its disposable diapers. The Arthur D. Little study certainly was not the only or last word on the issue, but it was sufficiently credible (although other studies differed) to create confusion and influence public and private behavior.[24]

As one observer noted: "When studies differ, there are many legitimate-sounding—and possibly legitimate—reasons. But the flood of deliberately contradictory studies ensures there will be no definitive proof of anything. If a study contradicts another study's position, buyers of research can simply commission more studies."[25]

How can issue advocates help the public and decision makers cut through this information fog? First, by exposing the sources of funding and presumed bias of the challenged information. Second, by producing genuinely independent experts to analyze and refute dubious information. Third, by urging the media to explain the sources and potential biases of information they cite and on which they and the public rely.

Information will always remain open to dispute, particularly when it is used to predict the consequences of public policy choices. In the next section we explore how the public and decision makers make those choices, relying on necessarily imperfect data and uncertain assumptions.

Making Policy Choices with Imperfect Information: Striking a Balance Between Costs and Benefits

Even the best scientists and the most reliable analyses cannot provide all the answers policymakers need. They cannot determine with certainty the precise tolerance level for lead in drinking water or pollutants in the atmosphere. Sociologists and psychologists cannot tell with certainty that the death penalty will deter youthful criminals or that denying public support to welfare mothers who have additional children while on welfare will reduce the cycle of dependency. Nor can studies or surveys definitively establish that requiring a three-day wait before purchasing a handgun will reduce crime and violence.

On every issue, policymakers engage in social and scientific experiments as they attempt to solve public problems. For each proposed solution, they need the best possible information to determine the likelihood that the solution will work and that its benefits will outweigh its costs. Weighing the benefits of solutions against their costs is not new, but it is even more important as we recognize that we have only limited public resources, which must be allocated among competing demands; and that some solutions that have been tried cause more harm than good: their costs outweigh their benefits.

The 1973 Endangered Species Act sought to halt the rapid and irreversible destruction of species that have existed from time immemorial. It reflected a public consensus that protecting endangered or threatened species was a desirable goal. Over time, however, we have become increasingly aware of the costs of the act. First it was the Tellico Dam project that was halted because it threatened the endangered, inch-long snail darter. Then it was the infamous spotted owl, protection of whose northwestern habitat would cost logging and timber-related jobs and "endanger" the communities dependent on those jobs. As Congress debated renewing the Endangered Species Act in the 1995 climate of limited government and scarce resources, a key question—one not asked in 1973—was whether the price we pay for protecting each and every endangered species is worth the benefits we receive.

The cost side of the equation—how many jobs will be lost—is eagerly addressed by businesses that create (and profit from) those jobs, and the workers and communities that depend on them. They readily produce studies and analyses "quantifying" the act's high costs. But how do we measure the benefits? Religious groups that support the act rely on the admittedly unquantifiable benefit of protecting all of God's creations. Environmental groups argue that maintaining the existing biodiversity is essential to the balance of life on earth and that by wantonly destroying species we risk great, albeit unknowable, harm. Pharmaceutical companies can produce speculative information about the benefits of yet-undiscovered lifesaving medicines that can be derived from endangered plant species.

How do policymakers make judgments when costs and benefits are so difficult to measure, and no two measurements of the same phenomena will likely produce the same result? Technical and scientific experts can and do produce "best guess" estimates that form the basis for policy decisions. How much long-term harm is caused by human consumption of certain food additives? Estimates can be made based on animal studies and chemical analyses. But they are only estimates, and other studies can reach different conclusions.

Let us examine how this works in practice. Assume that a manufacturing process emits a gaseous by-product, zenon. Tests on laboratory animals indicate that at certain levels zenon can cause respiratory problems, including lung cancer. Regulators must decide what limits to impose on zenon emissions. First, they must assemble the facts. On the cost side of the equation, it turns out that while zenon is naturally produced in the manufacturing process, expensive measures can be taken to limit its release into the atmosphere. Costs rise as the amount of zenon released diminishes. As costs rise, profitability declines; the manufacturer can raise prices for finished goods just so much. At higher costs, production would have to be cut back, along with wages and possibly jobs. And consumers would have to pay higher prices.

On the benefit side, reduced emissions would lead to fewer health problems. But experts can only make educated guesses about how to translate animal testing studies (which are themselves open to interpretation) into data about humans. After many assumptions and imprecise calculations, they can produce an estimate of the total number of human deaths different levels of zenon emissions produce. More experts can assign a dollar figure to each life, as courts and judges routinely do in wrongful-death cases.

Regulators can match the costs against the benefits and arrive at an emissions level where the costs of further reductions would outweigh the benefits. In theory, that is the precise amount of emissions regulators should permit. In practice, politically responsive regulators, unlike scientists and economists, are unwilling to rely solely on dispassionate calculations that assign monetary figures to human lives.

Individuals and society constantly assess the risks inherent in certain activities and choose a course of conduct that minimizes those risks at a reasonable cost. Individuals decide whether or not to pay extra for the added safety of automobile airbags or antilock brakes. They implicitly assess the risk of not wearing a seat belt versus the benefit of increased comfort and avoiding creased clothing. They decide whether to smoke and how much to drink and which kinds of foods to eat, aware that there are potentially harmful effects implicit in each choice. They do not make precise numerical calculations, and often they do not even make conscious risk assessment decisions. They do not have to; they are making individual decisions, not public policy.

Public policymaking demands a more rigorous approach, however. But if the information on which they base those decisions is inherently speculative and predictive, how do policymakers decide? The answer is to have the best possible information about the problem, the need for government action, and the consequences of that action.

For example, when the Federal Aviation Administration (FAA) considered requiring infants to be strapped into specially designed infant airplane seats, it faced a classic dilemma. Yes, studies showed that infant seats could potentially save lives. But parents who currently do not pay to take their infants aboard airplanes would be forced to buy a seat for them. Polls indicated that about one-fifth of parents would choose not to pay for the infant passenger and to drive to their destination instead. And studies showed that driving is much more dangerous for infants (as well as their parents) than flying, even without infant safety seats.[26] The FAA weighed the costs and benefits and decided not to require infant safety seats on airplanes.

In the end, scientists and experts do not regulate; they only provide the factual underpinning for elected and appointed political leaders—members of Congress, the Food and Drug Administration, the Occupational Safety and Health Administration, or the Federal Aviation Administration—who must make the ultimate public policy decisions.[27] The result: regulatory decisions that affect public health, safety, and welfare are often based as much on political and popular pressure as on "expert" scientific and technical assessments of risk and rewards.[28] The problem for government policymakers, which in turn can be the opportunity for issue advocates, is that experts and the public often disagree in their risk assessments. The public, for example, hears and worries about toxic waste dumps and nuclear power plant accidents, while the experts worry about indoor air quality and cigarette smoking as more critical public health hazards.[29]

For example, in 1989, the Natural Resources Defense Council released a lengthy study claiming that the pesticide alar, commonly used on apples, caused cancer.[30] With Meryl Streep testifying before Congress against the use of alar, and *60 Minutes* drawing public attention to the problem, public pressure mounted for government action. The media eagerly embraced the story about apples, children (major consumers of apple juice), and cancer, and the public voted at the grocery store by refusing to buy apples grown using alar. The public pressed Congress and the EPA to act, even though scientists minimized alar's danger and the EPA had already decided to phase out its use.[31]

Issue advocates must find ways to supplement credible and persuasive information with public demand for action if they seek to convince policymakers to act in the face of uncertainty. And the main tool for educating and mobilizing the public is the media, to which we now turn our attention.

7

Media Advocacy

If information is the primary tool to influence public opinion, the media are the mechanism to transmit that information.

$$\text{Information} \rightarrow \text{Media} \rightarrow \text{Public Opinion}$$

The media present opportunities and obstacles for issue advocates, who must capture and hold the media's notoriously short attention span to communicate a message in a way that resonates with prevailing public values, and ultimately to change public opinion.

Issues and the Media

The dictionary defines a medium as a substance through which something is transmitted. In a busy and complex society, individuals lack the time and resources to identify and explore most issues for themselves. Nor can interest groups and issue advocates communicate personally and directly with every citizen, particularly on state or national issues. While people still meet and talk about issues in small and large communities, and neighborhood activists still go door to door seeking support for their issues, issue advocacy is wholesale, not retail, politics. Advocates must rely on the media to disseminate their message.

For better or for worse, the media, particularly the mass media—newspapers, newsmagazines, television, and radio—provide most of the people most of the information they will ever get on most issues.[1] But the media are more than passive message disseminators. The media decide what the public learns about issues, and when and how they learn it. The media do not just reflect public concerns, they help shape them.

Media coverage, including news coverage, does not just happen; and even when it does, coverage does not automatically convey the issue from the advocate's perspective. Media advocacy promotes broad-based media coverage of an issue that frames and captures the symbols of public debate, thereby building public support for policy initiatives.[2] It begins with the principle that advocates must apply as much effort to media advocacy as they do to developing information, building coalitions, mobilizing the grassroots, and lobbying decision makers. Media advocacy is part strategic communications, part public relations, and part image building.

Covering the News

With even the best of intentions, the media cannot cover all the news impartially and thoroughly. And many media outlets make no pretense of doing so. Newspapers, magazines, and television networks are generally commercial enterprises with audiences and shareholders to satisfy. Individual reporters and editors have their own prejudices and predispositions, especially on major issues. You do not have to be cynical about the media to recognize that newspapers are concerned with whether a story sells papers and television news outlets battle for rating shares. Issue advocates must adapt to this environment if they want to use the media to bring favorable public attention to their issues.

The media play many roles in informing the public about issues. Among them:

- *Select* what issues and events to cover. Media outlets have limited resources and ever-present deadlines. Despite the *New York Times'* masthead commitment to "All the News That's Fit to Print," there is always more news—more stories, more people, and more events—than any media outlet has time, resources, or room to cover. Every newsroom must evaluate the newsworthiness of people and events, taking into consideration their audience's interest and a story's intrinsic importance. Scientists may sound alarm bells about global warming, or economists may release reports about impending savings and loan failures, but the media must decide whether and how to report on their concerns.

Many interest groups and issue advocates hold press conferences and issue press releases or press advisories, but relatively few press conferences result in news stories, and even fewer press releases lead to media coverage. Issue advocates and interest groups ask themselves a variation on the age-old question: "if you give a press conference (or give a speech or issue a report), that is not covered in the media, did it really happen?"

- *Edit* issue coverage. Even when they decide to cover an issue, media outlets do not reprint press releases verbatim or show unedited videotapes of press conferences. They decide how to cover an issue: what reporters to assign, whether to tell the story through pictures or words, how much digging to do into government reports or interest-group pronouncements; what aspects of an issue are important, whose voices to seek out and whose views to report. The media choose who to interview and which comments from an hour-long interview to transmit to the public. They choose the adjectives to apply and the camera angles to show for every story they cover. When Newt Gingrich was named *Time Magazine*'s Person of the Year for 1995, the picture that graced its cover showed a brooding figure with a five o'clock shadow. No doubt many other photographs were available.
- *Highlight* the importance of issues. The media decide how often to cover an issue and where to report it. A story might appear at the top of the nightly television newscast or "above the fold" in the morning newspaper. There may be stories explaining the issue's impact on people and other issues. The media may follow up with additional stories about the same issue, thereby signaling the issue's importance. Front-page coverage may be supplemented with related stories in the local, lifestyle, sports, business, and health sections. AIDS coverage can be limited to raw numbers buried deep inside the daily papers, or it can appear in stories about sports figures, entertainers, and children who suffer from AIDS.
- *Analyze and interpret* issues. The media place issues in context, relating them to other events and issues. They explain how issues affect people and society. Congressional debate about tort litiga-

tion reform can be depicted by the media as an effort to limit "lawsuit abuse" as typified by "horror stories," such as Stella Liebeck's suit against McDonald's for serving the scalding coffee she spilled on herself. Or it can focus on disfiguring injuries suffered by people whose Ford Pinto gas tanks exploded. The choice is the media's.

- *Opine* on issues. News stories are intended to be impartial renditions of events. But the media routinely supplement news coverage with editorials that express the views of (primarily) newspaper editors and owners on issues of concern to them. Merely selecting an issue on which to opine reflects an editorial judgment that the issue is an important one to which readers should pay attention. Readers who are uncertain how to respond to issue developments may take their cue from editorial opinions.
- Provide a *forum* for public discussions of issues. Newspapers devote a portion of their editorial page to letters and articles from citizens who want to make their voices heard. Talk radio allows many individuals to be heard with a minimum of editing. Sunday morning television public affairs programs, and continuous radio and television news coverage, such as CNN, afford time and opportunity for many voices to be heard on issues.

In these and other ways the media function as issue gatekeepers, interpreters, analyzers, and shapers of public opinion.

Influencing Events

The public gets its information from the media, but so do decision makers. Media stories about government action or inaction can directly affect public policymaking. The media can make news as well as report it. And issue advocates can use the media to influence policymakers directly.

$$\text{Information} \rightarrow \text{Media} \rightarrow \text{Policymakers}$$

"There's only one way to make an agency respond, and that's to get them on the evening news." You might be tempted to feel sorry for the lonely, ineffectual issue advocate who uttered that statement. After all, the advocate obviously has no other tools available to advance his or her interest. Except that the author was former Congressman Mike Synar, who once chaired a powerful subcommittee of the House Energy and Commerce Committee.[3] And the power to which he referred is not confined to administrative or executive branch agencies. The media wield the same power over elected officials and even nongovernmental institutions, such as corporations, universities, or hospitals.

Why do the media have this awesome power to influence policymakers, and how can issue advocates use it? The power derives from the media's ability to shine light on activities that policymakers prefer to keep hidden away in a dark cabinet. When the Department of Agriculture in the Reagan administration sought to revise the nutritional requirements of the school lunch program, it did so in an obscure government regulation, buried in the *Federal Register*. If not for stories about it in the media, the department might have been successful in its effort to classify ketchup as a vegetable.[4]

When the police beat Rodney King after his arrest, the only factor that distinguished that event from other allegations of police brutality was that a bystander with a video camera provided a tape of the beating to a television station which broadcast it to the world. The resulting public outcry forced the resignation of the Los Angeles police chief and the police department to reexamine its practices.[5]

Many fast-food restaurants stopped using highly saturated and unhealthful tropical oils and animal fat when the media carried stories detailing restaurants' hitherto unknown cooking practices.[6] Publicity forced tuna fish processors to stop using fishing techniques that ensnared and killed dolphins along with tuna.[7] And grisly television news pictures of baby seals being clubbed to death forced the Canadian and Norwegian governments to find other ways to deal with seal overpopulation.[8]

Why did government and corporations respond in each instance? Because the public scrutiny brought to bear on decisions otherwise made in secret embarrassed and shamed those organizations. Once public attention was focused on the decisions, those who made them were, for the first time, required to justify them. In many cases, rather than explain their actions, those responsible changed their policies and practices.

Shining media light on questionable activities is a particularly effective issue advocacy strategy. It works best as a tool to influence undemocratic institutions, such as corporations, but it is also useful to influence bureaucratic actions that are otherwise not directly account-able to the public.

Shaping the News Coverage

It's Important to You, But Is It News?

Every press conference advocates call, every study they release, and every public comment they make is "news"—to them. But very little, if any, of it is reported by the media. Of course advocates can pay to advertise in the media (as we discuss later in this chapter), but getting an issue covered as news, rather than through an advocate's paid ad-vertisement is important. News coverage carries with it (whether de-served or not) a presumption of credibility and impartiality. Others are speaking the advocate's words; even if they are merely quoting them. The fact that they do so gives the words added significance.

Where Is It News?

The average daily newspaper provides a myriad of opportunities to discuss a problem or an issue. The most obvious place to expect issue coverage might be the "hard news" section. But newspapers and the people who read them have many different interests and dimensions. Advocates can leave no media stone unturned to communicate infor-mation about their issue so that it resonates with how people think about their lives and the problems that affect them.

For example, welfare reform is an ongoing issue that is ripe for action at the federal, state, and local levels. The average daily newspa-per presents advocates on either side numerous opportunities for cov-erage. They include the following:

- *National* news of studies and statistics describing who receives welfare, how much they receive, and the level of waste, fraud, and abuse.
- *Local* stories about how welfare affects communities, with perti-nent facts and figures about the local area.
- *Lifestyle* stories where real people relate their own experiences struggling to get off welfare or even living well on welfare benefits.

- *Business* stories about the dearth (or glut) of jobs for welfare recipients; or success stories about businesses that have provided training to welfare recipients enabling them to obtain jobs and leave the welfare rolls.
- *Sports* stories about successful professional athletes who grew up in poor homes, and how welfare enabled their families to survive.
- *Arts and culture* stories about the artistic accomplishments of people who once received welfare.
- *Comic strips* that portray sympathetic (or greedy) faces of homelessness or hunger.
- *Editorials, op-eds, columnists, editorial cartoonists and letters to the editor* that express opinions about the need for or problems with welfare.

While we chose a daily newspaper for our example, the same basic principles apply to news weeklies, monthly magazines, radio, and television.

How Is It News?

Media outlets receive a deluge of story proposals and press releases from interest groups seeking coverage of a wide range of issues. How do advocates attract the attention of an assignment editor or an enterprising reporter? By putting themselves in the reporter's or editor's shoes. Instead of insisting that the media have an "obligation" to cover an issue, advocates tell their story so that readers and viewers will want to read and watch it.

Advocates recognize that news stories must meet the commercial media's need to attract and hold viewers. Stories must be interesting and important so readers and viewers will want to read and watch them; they must be "newsworthy."

Advocates can increase the chances of news coverage if they tell good stories that have the elements of good drama:

- *Controversy or conflict* is a necessary element of any good story, whether it is one aggrieved and determined individual seeking justice from the legal system or a small property owner refusing to sell out to a big developer. Stories about good versus evil or a seemingly powerless victim fighting back against a villain attract media attention. A lone worker risking life and career to expose her employer's corporate misdeeds makes a more interesting story than a union's report about the same business practices.

When health-care-reform advocates sought to air a prore-form television advertisement making the point that Pizza Hut paid for health care for its workers in Europe, but not America, television stations in Washington, D.C., refused to run the ad lest they anger Pizza Hut, a major sponsor. The stations' re-fusal (prompted by Pizza Hut), and the controversy it created, became the story. The ad was shown repeatedly on news re-ports that centered on Pizza Hut's efforts to suppress it, even more than on the facts revealed in the ad.[9]

- *Injustice* done to undeserving individuals can make a story news-worthy by provoking powerful emotions: anger, fear, envy, hatred, sympathy, outrage. Does the story tug on viewers' heartstrings? Does it make them want to pick up the phone and express their outrage? Stories about unfair treatment, particularly of children, have an enormous impact. When young Ryan White was ostra-cized by his neighbors and refused admittance to public school, the story was about the injustice of mistreating those with AIDS, no matter how they acquired the disease.[10]

- *Irony* attracts attention. The Center for Science and the Public Inter-est (CSPI) is concerned with beer advertising and children. It sur-veyed fourth graders, asking them to name as many American presidents and brands of beer as they could. Students were able to name more beer brands than presidents, and were more likely to spell the beer names correctly than the names of the presidents. News coverage focused on education, youth, and alcohol—precisely the connections CSPI wanted to make.[11] Similarly, a study pub-lished in the *Journal of the American Medical Association* drew widespread media attention to tobacco marketing targeted to youth when it concluded that young children were as likely to identify "Joe Camel," cartoon animal spokesperson for Camel cigarettes, as they were Mickey Mouse[12] (see Figure 3).

The problems of pesticide misuse got media attention when an interest group released a study "flunking" the U.S. Capitol building itself for its use of pesticides that cause cancer and reproductive and other health problems to deal with mice and cockroaches.[13]

Figure 3.

Eighty-five percent of children who smoke prefer the three most advertised brands (Marlboro, Camel and Newport). That's no coincidence.

Tobacco companies spend billions on cartoon ads, billboards near schools and mountains of free merchandise that kids love (T-shirts, caps, backpacks, jackets). The results:

- *Three thousand kids start smoking every day.*
- *Nearly all adult smokers begin as children.*
- *One-third will die from their addiction.*
- *Tobacco companies are making $200 million a year from sales to children and addicting a new generation of customers.*

The nation's top health experts have proposed new limits to keep tobacco marketing from seducing children and to make cigarettes less accessible to kids. But industry lobbyists are scheming to snuff these rules out.

It's time we stopped trusting tobacco companies with our children's lives.

- *Tell the FDA you support the proposed limits* (Food & Drug Administration, Docket 95N-0253, Room 1-23, 12420 Parklawn Drive, Rockville, MD 20857).
- *Tell your Members of Congress not to endanger America's children for tobacco company profits.*
- *Learn more by calling 1-800-284-KIDS.*

This ad sponsored by the National PTA, American Nurses Association, National Association of Secondary School Principals, National Coalition of Hispanic Health and Human Services Organizations (COSSMHO) and over 100 other organizations throughout the country.

Reprinted with permission

- *Celebrities* attract the media's and the public's attention, even when they are not acting or singing or throwing a baseball. As we saw in the last chapter, the use of the pesticide alar on apples was not new, but Meryl Streep's willingness to be the public spokesperson for the anti-alar campaign attracted the media's attention.

  Organizations drew media attention to the unseemly connection between sports and alcohol at a press conference featuring a well-known race-car driver who refused to take money from a beer company to advertise on his car because he disliked the connection between drinking and driving. And when a prominent baseball player objected to television announcers' linking his name to a beer company's advertisement, he drew media attention to the issue of promoting beer in connection with sporting events.

  A celebrity's presence can turn a mundane occurrence into a media event. A boring congressional hearing on energy policy made news when Ted Danson testified. The media turned out to see Christopher Reeve when he lent his star power to still another dull press conference, urging federal funding for the National Endowment for the Arts.[14]

- *Milestone events* are opportunities to draw the media's attention to an individual event or occurrence that is not otherwise newsworthy. In a large city, a teenager's murder by a drug dealer might be newsworthy if it were the 100th murder committed in a city in a year, prompting a story that examines the causes of violence. Stories such as this help advocates make "news" out of events that are not new.

- *Large numbers*, particularly large round numbers, attract attention, whether it is thousands of people demonstrating to support · or oppose affirmative action or temperatures reaching 100 degrees for an extended period of time as a possible indicator of global warming and the greenhouse effect.

- Events or occurrences that might otherwise escape coverage can be newsworthy if they fit the *est* phenomenon—the big*gest*, small*est*, new*est*, or old*est*. A fire at a toxic waste site might be just another fire if it were not portrayed as the biggest fire in the county, requiring the largest number of firefighters. One more drunk-driving arrest might not catch the media's attention if it were not the highest speed ever clocked by an arresting officer.

- *People* are at the center of every good story. Stories about how real people cope with poverty or health problems or educational deficiencies are more likely to be newsworthy than dry statistics or studies. Reports of child labor in Central America may attract little media attention, but no media outlet can resist the real story of one teenage girl's experience working in an El Salvador factory that makes clothing sold in America.[15]

  A single story about a child (and a child's innocence makes its suffering more poignant) made ill by an undercooked hamburger will get more coverage than a dozen scientific studies linking raw meat to disease.[16]

  Poverty and hunger are real, but statistics often fail to communicate the individual hardship and suffering behind the numbers. Real stories about real people's experiences can provide the necessary emotional drama to capture the media's attention. One woman's—Rosa Cunningham's—story about her family's struggle to overcome poverty and the drug culture made front-page news and communicated more about poverty and its problems than raw numbers ever could.[17]

- *Local* aspects of national stories can attract the attention of local media that fill a different niche from the national media. An interest group that releases a report about the extent of childhood hunger in the United States can multiply the report's coverage by including statistics and examples from each state and locality. Local leaders and experts can be recruited to comment on national stories; their commentary can be newsworthy even if the issue itself would not have been.

Taking the Media Initiative

Media coverage, like change, does not just happen. Every day's newspaper starts out as blank paper. News outlets are constantly looking for good stories to fill their pages or air time. If an advocate's story, told from the advocate's perspective, does not fill some of that space, another story will—and if it is a contested issue of public concern, it very likely may be a story initiated by the opposition. If advocates initiate a story, they are more likely to be able to exercise some control over it, such as by suggesting people to interview or information to include.

"Hooking" a Reporter

The more advocates know about the demographics and interests of the audience, the more effective they will be in pitching a story. Just because a story interests or outrages advocates does not mean that every media outlet will feel the same way. Different media have different needs. A "great story," one that has all the elements described in the last section, will get nowhere if advocates do not tailor it for the type of news medium and the specific media outlet. Radio stations need sound bites and articulate interviewees; television needs pictures and action. News must be timely, but weekly newsmagazines depend less on breaking news and more on synthesis and analysis.

The first step in getting media coverage is identifying media outlets and learning how they differ from each other. Community newspapers are not the same as the nightly network news. And the network news is not the same as *60 Minutes* or talk radio. Advocates match their stories to the audience and goals of the media outlet.

Reader's Digest, Newsweek, TV Guide, People Magazine, and the *National Enquirer* are all available at the grocery store checkout stand, and some people buy all five. But each attempts to appeal to different demographic audiences and selects and presents information in different ways. Advocates who understand media outlets will best be able to identify those most likely to cover their story. Just as some people will buy all five publications, each of them may choose to cover the same story, but in a different way and with a different spin. Creative media advocacy might lead to a story in each of those publications, but not if advocates pitch the story in the same way to each of them.

The second step requires delving into the operational structure of each media outlet to learn as much as possible about its audience, deadlines, people, and procedures. It requires reading, watching, and listening to potential media outlets so that stories can be matched to an individual outlet's interests and capabilities. Knowing the style and interest of individual journalists and assignment editors can be important, since they often pursue their own leads in deciding which stories to cover and how to cover them. A reporter who has written one story on the environment or food safety is a likely target to write another.

The third step is preparing background materials to help the media understand the advocate's story, their organization, and its perspective. Reporters and editors are notoriously harried; they have little time or resources to do background or other research on an issue, at least not before deciding a story is worth pursuing. That is why advocates prepare a "media kit" to supply background information, position papers, fact sheets, biographies of issue spokespeople (even including sample quotes), and organizational contacts—anything and everything to stimulate the reporter's or the editor's interest in the story and the issue, and to make their job easier.

The backbone of the media kit is the "news release." News releases are short, clearly written accounts of an event, accomplishment, or report. They include journalism's five "Ws" and an "H"—who, what, when, where, why, and how. Some small media outlets with limited staff will even print a thorough, well-written news release verbatim, passing off the advocate's story as their own.

Finally, people and relationships matter. Just as media outlets have interests and "personalities," so do particular reporters and editors. Issue advocates can cultivate mutually beneficial professional relationships with reporters or editors. Running a story by a reporter in an informal telephone call—where the reporter already knows the advocate and the organization—can often be as effective as holding a press conference or preparing a media kit.

When all else fails, advocates can make their own news, with demonstrations, protests, sit-ins, and creative "issue theater." For example, in 1990 Philip Morris sponsored a national tour of the Bill of Rights. In cooperation with the Virginia State Library, Philip Morris announced that it would transport Virginia's copy of the Bill of Rights to each of the fifty states. Antitobacco advocates sought to call attention to what they believed was a subtle tobacco marketing tactic, particularly one aimed at children, such as the school groups and Boy and Girl Scouts who were invited to participate in the tour. The advocates built a satirical statue, named "Nicotina," based on the Statue of Liberty, which included a pack of Marlboros in its hand and an electronic board displaying messages criticizing the promotion. An adjoining "death clock" showed the estimated number of tobacco-related deaths since the tour began. The board displayed such messages as "Philip Morris tobacco will help kill 400,000 Americans this year." "Eighty percent of smokers get hooked by the time they are 18." "Teenagers will spend $1.26 billion on tobacco this year." "Enjoy their Bill of Rights tour—don't get addicted to their tobacco." A bronze plaque on the statue's base read, "Give me your tired, your poor, your women, children, and minorities yearning to breathe free."[18] The visual image of the statue, coupled with its antitobacco message, generated substantial media coverage and contributed to forcing Philip Morris to cancel the tour soon after it began.[19]

Beyond Reporters

Just as news stories do not just happen, editorials do not just appear. Most newspapers have editorial boards or editorial page editors who scan the news to determine which issues are important enough to their readers to take an editorial position, and which position to take. Issue advocates can submit written "editorial memoranda" (draft editorials, with appropriate background data) to editorial boards. They can also meet with editorial boards, although this will be less likely in large markets; to meet with the *New York Times* editorial board, advocates will have to wait for an invitation.

All editorials are not equal. Influential newspapers, such as the *Wall Street Journal*, *New York Times*, *Los Angeles Times*, and *Washington Post*, carry the most weight on national policy matters, for example. Favorable editorials in generally unsympathetic papers can carry the most weight, such as a *Wall Street Journal* editorial supporting union organizing practices or a *Washington Post* editorial opposing President Clinton's budget.[20]

Many newspapers devote space opposite the editorial page to "op-eds": serious, thoughtful opinion pieces, usually written by credentialed experts, which express alternative views (to those of the paper) or which opine on other issues. A well-written, authoritative piece can be submitted for publication either blindly, by dropping it in the mail, or after a conversation with a member of the newspaper's editorial staff. The bad news is that most papers draw on a stable of syndicated columnists to fill most of their op-ed space, although there is often more room for other views in weekend editions. The good news is that advocates can target potentially sympathetic columnists and send them materials about an issue, including news releases.

When all else fails, advocates can write a letter to the editor. The "Letters to the Editor" section of a newspaper is among its most highly read parts; it appears every day and is intended to, and often does, reflect the mood of the people or a current debate within the community. Most important for issue advocates is that decision makers, particularly elected officials, read the letters to the editor to get a sense of the community's views.

Advocates can raise issues or respond to a previous letter or article with another perspective. Even a letter applauding another letter writer, a journalist, or an editorial position may get published. Generally, a letter to the editor responds to an article or editorial that omits important facts, gives false or misleading information, or makes key points that need clarification. Exposing the private or special interests of the author of a published letter or of a source in an article (if his or her true affiliation, funding, or allegiance was not identified) is also a good reason to communicate with the paper and the public.

Newspaper editorial policies for deciding which letters to publish vary widely. Major dailies place a greater emphasis on publishing letters from credentialed authorities, while smaller papers are generally more inclined toward publishing letters from local citizens, businesses, or institutions. A barrage of letters can help set a community agenda, stimulate editorial and news coverage, and help educate community leaders and politicians on an issue. If nothing else, many letters on the same subject can pique an editor's interest in a problem or an issue, perhaps stimulating a subsequent news story.

Sometimes the news is funny, and sometimes the comics get serious. The prime example, of course, is Garry Trudeau's *Doonesbury*, which takes on politicians as well as issues such as gun violence and tobacco. Organized cartoon campaigns have drawn attention to issues such as hunger, homelessness, and illiteracy. Individual cartoon strips have addressed war toys, teen pregnancy, eating disorders, abortion, smoking, drug addiction, AIDS, child abuse, dyslexia, recycling, animal rights, and many other social and public health concerns.[21]

Readership demographics and cartoon topics indicate that adults read the comics more than children and that comics are among the most widely read sections of the newspaper. While no scientific research has measured the influence of cartoons on society, individual readers, politicians, or government officials, there is little doubt that cartoons help put a "spin" on an issue and may provide advocates with another avenue to get their message across.

Just when advocates think an issue is not "ready for prime time," they discover that it is. Prime time—network television's serious and comedic efforts at entertainment—often addresses serious issues of public concern. If anyone doubts that people take prime-time discussions of issues seriously, they need only recall how Vice-President Dan Quayle criticized the "lifestyle choice" of the fictional character "Murphy Brown." Of course, Murphy Brown's producers and writers struck back, pillorying the former vice president. But they also took on hard issues themselves, such as when Murphy's car was stolen and she discovered that her neighbors had guns and alarms. She began to explore the problem of crime, ending with a plea (on her fictional newscast) for better education and job opportunities and more money to prevent drug abuse and child neglect.

Murphy is not alone in her prime-time crusading. In 1992 *L.A. Law* portrayed the experiences of a Central American farmworker made sterile by unregulated and indiscriminate use of pesticides on food intended for export to the United States, depicting the "circle of poison."[22]

In 1993, two prime-time entertainment programs whose main characters portray doctors, *Picket Fences* and *Northern Exposure*, wove the then-current health-care-reform debate into their story lines. On *Picket Fences*, the television doctor lamented the likelihood that her earnings would decrease if the Clinton health-care plan passed. And on *Love and War*, the fictional owner of a restaurant makes a plea for tort reform after she is sued for donating spoiled food to the homeless.[23]

By identifying and working with receptive producers and writers, issue advocates can influence prime-time coverage of their issue.[24]

Doing the Media's Heavy Lifting

Sometimes advocates discover it is more difficult to get and hold a reporter's attention than to write and edit the news themselves. News releases can be sent to potentially receptive media outlets, some of which, hungry for news, might even use the release verbatim. More often, media outlets look for something more. Fortunately, the technology exists for issue advocates to produce and transmit live or recorded "news" stories, prepackaged for broadcast.

Radio "actualities" (and their video cousins, video news releases) are "interviews" prepared by issue advocates for radio or television broadcast. A well-produced audio or video can contain a mock interviewer asking questions of issue experts. Media outlets do not have to worry about assigning a reporter and crew or even coming up with appropriate questions. They can air the tape as part of their own news broadcasts.

"Satellite feeds" enable an issue advocate to sit comfortably in a studio and electronically appear live on a series of radio or television interview programs or news broadcasts. Taking the initiative one step further, advocates can produce and syndicate prepackaged programs, such as *It's Your Business*, produced by the Chamber of Commerce. Sponsored by business interests, these programs have the look and feel of weekly news interview shows, except that the host and guests are recruited (and often paid) by issue advocates.[25]

Buying the Media's Attention

When the media speak, people listen. Even when news reports merely echo advocates' press releases, the mere fact that the information appears in the media gives advocates' views credibility. It is always preferable to have the media speak those views, but, as we have seen, media coverage is unpredictable. Sometimes advocates have no choice but to pay to have their message disseminated through the mass media. They advertise.

Advertising Your Issue: The Hard Sell

"Harry and Louise" are the most famous issue salespeople. Advocates used extensive commercial advertisements to sell health-care reform, the North American Free Trade Agreement, and tort litigation reform. They bought radio, television, and newspaper advertisements to convince the public to support their position and communicate that support to members of Congress. As we have seen, "Harry and Louise" and their progeny were natural outgrowths of the political campaign ads that had just finished running in 1992, both in form and tone.

Unfiltered by news judgments or the media's effort to cover the news objectively, advertisements can play on emotions, exaggerate, and ignore the issue's other side. Issue advertisements have the advantage of allowing advocates complete control over the content, tone, and placement of the ads (as long as they can afford them).

For example, Omaha businessman Phil Sokolof suffered a heart attack after his cholesterol level exceeded 300. He changed his diet and regained his health, but when studies revealed that many fast-food restaurants used highly saturated, unhealthful tropical oils, he decided to do more. Mr. Sokolof paid for full-page newspaper advertisements educating the public about the dangers of tropical oils and challenging fast-food companies to use other, more healthful products. Sales plummeted as public attention focused on the problem, and most companies stopped using tropical oils.[26]

Sellers of automobiles or beer can buy advertising time when and where it is most likely to reach target audiences. Issue advocates can do the same, choosing media outlets in key states or congressional districts or those that are more likely to reach individuals who (revealed by polls and focus groups) are capable of being persuaded on an issue. Advertisements that seek to influence the public or decision makers often contain an explicit "call to action," with a phone number to call or an address to write. (We discuss in detail how advocates use advertisements to mobilize the public in chapter 10.)

One disadvantage of issue advertisements, of course, is that the media are filled with dubious product claims that a skeptical public discounts. Even children have learned that the animated figures they see in commercials are smaller and less attractive than they appear on television. Certainly their parents have learned that health care or tort reform will not live up to the promises their advocates make for them in slickly produced, thirty-second commercials.

Another problem, which was illustrated by the health-care reform/Pizza Hut advertisements that stations refused to air, is that media outlets are under no obligation to sell advertising time or space to issue advocates. While most are willing to accept those ads, the rules that require broadcasters to air candidate ads do not apply to issue advertisements.

With limited resources, issue advocates can use paid advertisements to shape the news coverage. In 1989, antitobacco advocates bought a full-page newspaper advertisement asking President Bush's drug czar, William Bennett, to take a "drug-free challenge" and quit his two-pack-a-day cigarette smoking habit. They sought to focus public attention on tobacco as a dangerous, addictive drug. Many newspapers subsequently ran stories prompted by the advertisement, including the *New York Times*, which editorialized about the irony of an addicted smoker as drug czar.[27] In 1994 the same advocates targeted the heads of tobacco companies and media outlets that carried cigarette advertisements with their own ad asking, "How do they live with themselves?" (see Figure 4).

Figure 4.

Tobacco is an addictive drug — as addictive as heroin.*
Tobacco addiction is America's leading cause of preventable death.*

How do they live with themselves?

Si Newhouse

He could voluntarily refuse to push tobacco in his magazines, as many major magazines do. But he hasn't. His magazines probably do more to make smoking seem attractive and sophisticated — what every young person wants to be — than any others. *Fortune* puts his net worth at $5 billion.

Rupert Murdoch

Tobacco advertising is banned on TV, so tobacco companies go after kids in Murdoch's *TV Guide*. He could say no. He's worth $3 billion.

Larry Tisch

As the man who controls Lorillard Tobacco, he could ask Congress to halt all tobacco advertising and promotion. The tobacco companies would save $4 billion a year. That's $4 billion more annual profit for their shareholders — in the short run. In the long run, fewer kids would be enticed to replace smokers who die or quit. But is that bad? *Fortune* says Tisch is a billionaire.

Henry Kravis

Since his company, RJR, began using a cartoon character to push Camels, Camel's share of the teen and pre-teen market has jumped from 1% to 32%. He could become a health hero by joining with Tisch in asking Congress to ban all tobacco promotion — and boost the industry bottom line by $4 billion. Judging from the *Forbes* 400 list, he can afford this risk. He's worth half a billion.

Michael Miles

Miles runs Philip Morris. Who'd have more reason to want a total ad ban than the shareholders of Philip Morris? Marlboro smokers wouldn't quit buying Marlboros just because the advertising stopped; yet Philip Morris could quit spending all those billions trying to defend its market share. Miles — who himself quit smoking long ago — made $5 million last year.

> Like most people who profit from the sale of addictive, unhealthy substances, these men have the good sense not to use those substances themselves. Not one of them smokes cigarettes.

Si, Rupert, Larry, Henry, Mike: If you'll agree it's crazy for a society to *promote* its leading cause of preventable death, and stop doing it, we'll take out an ad **twice as big** honoring you and saying thanks. There's no greater contribution you could make to America's health.

*U.S. Surgeon General

STAT *Stop Teenage Addiction to Tobacco*
NATIONAL OFFICE 511 East Columbus Avenue, Springfield, MA 01105 (413) 732-STAT

For a free book, KIDS SAY DON'T SMOKE, send four 29-cent stamps. If you can help us pay for more ads like this, we'd appreciate it!

Reprinted with permission

Not every interest group has the resources to purchase issue advertisements. On some policy issues, advocates can use "public service announcements" to convey their message. The genesis of public service announcements, or PSAs, is in the electronic media's obligation, as a condition of its license, to serve the public interest. They are therefore willing to air limited advertisements (produced at the advocate's expense, but without charge for the air time) on issues of public concern. These ads are generally limited to noncontroversial issues, particularly efforts to change individual behavior (to stop littering or smoking or drinking and driving). PSAs are less useful (and much less likely to be aired) when they concern public policy issues; it is one thing for a PSA to urge teenagers not to smoke; it is quite another to urge citizens to support legislation to outlaw cigarette vending machines because they are often used by teenagers to circumvent restrictions on youth smoking.

Advertising Yourself: The Soft Sell

Business interests understand that public policy affects their bottom line, whether the issue is tort reform, mandatory recycling, or health care. As we see in chapter 9 businesses have developed sophisticated programs to influence public policies. They have also applied their effective advertising resources toward "strategic communications": developing and transmitting messages that go beyond asking the public to buy their products. Strategic communications improve corporate or industry images, make their voices heard on public policy issues, provide alternative sources of information, and mold public and decision-maker opinions.[28]

Pharmaceutical manufacturers advertise their dedication to finding lifesaving products. Lumber companies tout their efforts to grow trees and protect the environment. Defense contractors proudly display their latest fighter bombers. Labor unions portray the jobs lost when consumers and public policy fail to support American-made products. Beer manufacturers promote responsible drinking, and tobacco companies urge young people not to smoke. Dow Chemical tried to remake its image twenty years after napalm and the Vietnam War with commercial advertisements directed at young people looking for jobs, contending: "Dow lets you do great things." And Mobil Oil touts its innovative energy research and exploration (see Figure 5).

These advertisements are all intended, at least in part, to influence

Figure 5.

Getting ready for a changing world

Nobody can expect the world to stand still, and nowhere is there more proof that we must remain geared to change than in today's—and tomorrow's—international oil industry.

For one thing, those companies that expect to thrive in global competition will be going places we could not go in recent history, as new frontiers have opened up in Eastern Europe, Central Asia, the former Soviet Union and Latin America. Companies and countries that have been unfamiliar to each other will seek common ground to form new relationships to develop natural resources, build economies and share revenues. New alliances will be forged between companies developing economies of scale or dovetailing operations. And new technology will add reserves heretofore deemed unrecoverable.

New-frontier nations will open their borders to companies with a demonstrated capacity for leadership, project experience, financial strength and a history of technology transfer. On the other side of the equation, the countries that will appear more attractive to private investment will be those that are willing to provide reasonable contract terms and the promise of long-term stability—politically, economically and legislatively.

The process will necessarily be one of give-and-take and, with worldwide competition for capital funds, money, like water, will flow where fewer obstacles will obstruct its path. In this world of constant change, it will be as important for governments as it is for companies to recognize the need to reexamine economic philosophies and tax policies.

New alliances—both domestic and international, and in all segments of the business—will become increasingly important for companies striving to build a stronger asset base and develop economies for future growth. Because of the diversity of companies involved, such alliances will also provide greater opportunity for developing new technology—a must in this business where it is critical to be a low-cost supplier. Many capital programs the industry has on the drawing boards would not have produced the necessary payout to be considered just a few years ago if it were not for recent advances in technology.

The many advances in subsea production and well-completion technologies, for example, have eliminated the need for much more costly systems and greatly improved the economics of a number of high-cost projects.

Breakthroughs of recent years have enabled us all to find and develop oil and gas at much lower costs and to recover more from existing reservoirs. Moreover, we've accomplished those tasks while at the same time improving the industry's environmental record. Again, technological advances enabled us to perform that mission effectively.

And, as we find and develop the world's energy more economically through technology, we also get more out of the crude oil and natural gas as we process it in our refineries and chemical plants. Technology has given us higher yields and improved product quality in our downstream operations.

Within the petroleum industry technology has many faces, and all of them are turned to the future. The companies that are prepared to embrace technology and can apply new developments quickly and effectively throughout their operations will be the industry leaders of tomorrow.

We're planning on being one of them.

Mobil®

public policy. But instead of a "hard sell"—asking the public or decision makers to take action—they focus on improving the advertiser's
image. Why, if the goal is to influence public policy, do they take a
softer approach? Because a skeptical public discounts commercial appeals. Instead, the ads attempt to build corporate credibility and favorably dispose the public to drug manufacturers or tobacco companies.
The commercials portray the companies as concerned for the broader
public interest, rather than their corporate bottom line. They minimize
or eliminate the direct connection between the interest and the issue, so
when the time comes for the interest to ask the public to make its voice
known, or decision makers to act, it may find a more receptive audience, one more inclined to believe its message.

Sometimes, commercial advertisements in any form are too much of
a "hard sell." Even subtler strategies can improve an advocate's public
image. Perhaps the best example is corporate support for the arts, culture, libraries, universities, hospitals, and other charities. When Exxon,
a major oil company, attempted to remake its image after the *Exxon
Valdez* disaster, it joined with the National Fish and Wildlife Foundation to establish a highly publicized Save the Tiger Foundation. Not
coincidentally, the tiger is Exxon's symbol for its corporate identity.[29]

When corporations support Public Broadcasting, they gain access to
large markets without appearing to sell products. Corporations with no
products to sell to the target audience vie to get credit for their support
for *Sesame Street*. Allied Chemical and Union Carbide, for example,
funded the *MacNeil Lehrer Newshour* in the wake of corporate public
relations disasters.[30] Presumably, viewers would be subtly persuaded
to think more favorably about the sponsors' activities as a result.

The Chairman of Arco, a major oil company, said that as a direct
result of his company's contributions to public broadcasting, "we gain
an image of quality. Our sponsorship of the Wolf Trap concerts resulted in a tremendous response from people in government. And, my
God, you walk into the departments [of government], or the Congress,
and you're identified as Arco, and there's a feeling of warmth. There's
no question but that it's helpful to our lobbying effort."[31]

Developing a Media Message

Message development requires understanding how an issue relates to prevailing public opinions and values. Only then can media messages be

designed that will broaden advocates' base of public support. How advocates talk about an issue can be as important as what they say about it.

Words Matter

"We ought to forget the word 'homeless.' If we talked about the mentally ill, it would be a much different discussion."

—Andrew Cuomo, assistant secretary of housing and urban development.[32]

When the 1995 budget standoff between President Clinton and the Republican Congress forced the federal government to shut down, only "essential" workers stayed on the job. The public fumed at the notion that their taxes funded "nonessential" government workers. If they were "nonessential," then by definition, they were *never* needed. The Clinton White House quickly changed its language. Now "emergency" government workers had to report, while "nonemergency" workers stayed home. The public furor died down, although nothing had changed but the words the White House used to describe the event.[33]

When the Washington, D.C., subway system installed machines to enable passengers to purchase the additional fare needed to exit from a station if their fare card lacked an adequate amount, they called those machines "Addfare" machines. But riders with sufficient fare to exit the station continually tried to use those machines to add still more money to their fare cards, as they normally did at designated fare card machines. Unfortunately, Addfare machines were limited in number and purpose. They would not accept fare cards with sufficient remaining fare to exit the station, and their use by those patrons clogged the system, trapping those without adequate fare. The solution: change the name of the machines to "Exitfare" machines. Patrons got it immediately.

Words help determine how we understand an issue. Frank Luntz, often called the chief pollster for the 1994 House Republicans, advised them on how to talk to America: "Say you are cutting 'bureaucrats,' who have no friends, not 'eliminating programs,' which have lots. 'Putting the government on a diet' tends to resonate extremely well with the average American likely to have gained four pounds between Thanksgiving and New Year's Day."[34]

Polls reveal that a majority of Americans oppose "welfare." But they express support for government help for the poor and the needy.

A 1994 poll revealed that a majority of the public opposed the "Clinton health plan." But when the poll takers described the substance of the plan—and omitted the label "Clinton health plan"—a majority of the public supported it.[35]

Well-chosen words can communicate a lasting, memorable message. When American automakers argued against legislation that would require them to make more fuel-efficient cars, they contended that the government should instead focus on developing a "super-efficient car within 10 years." Daniel Becker, a Sierra Club lobbyist, said that automakers are using the "super car," which they may never build, as an excuse to avoid meaningful action now. "It's the Wimpy defense," said Mr. Becker, referring to the character from the *Popeye* cartoons. "I will gladly pay you Tuesday for a hamburger today."[36]

In each instance, well-chosen words conveyed a message that registered on the public psyche more deeply than the issues they described. Words can demystify confusing and complicated public policy issues. And symbols can often be more powerful than words. The American flag stirs powerful feelings of patriotism; the swastika communicates hatred and evil as no words can.

Finding Words That Work

Words and symbols can shape public attitudes about issues. The right ones can position an issue so that it favorably resonates with prevailing public concerns and attracts a broad and deep base of diverse supporters. Many labels and symbols capture and reflect widely shared public values. Though we are a notoriously heterogeneous nation, Americans respond with surprising unanimity to a set of core public values: freedom, justice, security, family, health, fairness, opportunity, choice, community, caring. The more an issue campaign positively evokes these core values, the more likely it is that public attitudes toward that campaign will be favorable.

Mirroring these affirmative public values are a set of negative values that evoke disapproving responses: unfairness, oppression, harm, deceit, greed, favoritism, dependency. When an issue campaign succeeds in associating one or more affirmative values with its position—and associating the opposition with one or more negative values—it greatly improves its chances of generating broad public support.

The media are the battleground in which each side seeks to secure to its cause the most powerfully affirmative symbols and to attribute to its adversaries the most negative symbols. How issues are framed in the media, and how they can be strategically reframed, can determine the outcome of an issue campaign. "Framing the issue" is the process by which advocates develop and convey their message to maximize the affirmative and minimize the negative values associated with it. The critical message development task for any issue campaign is to broaden the core base of supporters—individuals and interest groups—by finding and using themes that engage the intellect and emotions of those who are not ready supporters.

"Protecting the environment" and "preserving the earth for future generations" had been successful messages or frameworks to build support for many environmental proposals over nearly a twenty-year period, from the creation of the Environmental Protection Agency until the early 1990s, when an antienvironmental backlash occurred. Landowners and businesspeople who opposed many environmental initiatives began to talk about the "wise use" of our limited environmental resources, stressing "free enterprise," "property rights," "economic growth," and "job creation." Property owners stressed their "rights" as landowners to use their property as they wished, contending that the government should not interfere with those rights by "taking" their property without compensation and "due process of law."[37] The environmental debate continues, but its terms have changed. It is no longer just about preserving the environment; it is now a question of balancing the "rights" of landowners and businesspersons against the benefits of protecting the environment.

Other examples of competing frames and efforts at reframing abound: "abortion rights" advocates learned that they can gain more supporters if they framed their position as "pro-choice," implicitly painting their opponents as "anti-choice." Not to be outdone, opponents of abortion realized that their position would have more broad-based appeal if they adopted a positive symbol. Instead of being "anti-abortion," they became "pro-life," tacitly labeling their opponents as "anti-life."

When President Reagan sought to deploy a missile defense system that would enable U.S. missiles to shoot down incoming hostile missiles, scientists differed sharply on whether such a system would be feasible, and peace activists argued that it would be destabilizing and in violation of the Anti-Ballistic Missile Treaty. The president labeled the system the "Strategic Defense Initiative" and later attempted to describe it as a "Peace Shield." Opponents, attempting to stress the unworkability of such a system, referred to it as "Star Wars." The public may not have understood astrophysics or international law, but it grasped the implausibility of "Star Wars."

The Public Matters: Testing the Message

Where do effective, powerful themes and frames come from? As we see in chapter 10, they should ideally emerge as the end result of a lengthy public opinion assessment process. Too often, however, they arise, full-blown, from the fertile imagination of an issue advocate, and proceed directly from there into the public arena.

The preferred process involves several important steps. First comes recognizing that the purpose of the message or frame is not to resonate with the well-informed, already convinced, issue advocate, but to appeal to (and persuade) a carefully targeted public audience. Before developing a message, issue advocates test public opinion and identify likely supporters and opponents, and the reasons behind their opinions. They then use polls and focus groups, targeted to key, persuadable constituencies, to find a message to which the public responds. Finally, there is the art of the catchy, well-turned phrase that attracts and keeps the media's and the public's attention.

That is what Frank Luntz did in rendering his advice to the victorious Republicans in January 1995, even going so far as to chide incoming Speaker Newt Gingrich. Luntz's focus groups found public support for moving children of teenage welfare mothers, who have been victims of abuse, to new homes. But when the new home was described as an "orphanage" (Gingrich's frame), the support was significantly less than when the new home—the same new home—was described as a "foster home."[38]

And that is what opponents of the Supreme Court nomination of Robert Bork did. Working with pollsters, advocates designed and conducted focus-group sessions. Recognizing that the message should not be developed in Washington, the campaign held focus groups in Philadelphia and Birmingham, Alabama. Those sites were chosen carefully: they were the constituencies of key members of the Senate Judiciary Committee, and they were swing areas populated with undecided voters.

The campaign soon learned that most people gave little thought to the Supreme Court. Yet working-class people in Alabama did not want to refight old civil rights battles. They were reluctant to become involved in a campaign to stop Bork's nomination, but at the same time they did not want to disturb fifty years of Supreme Court civil rights decisions. The focus-group results convinced the coalition that the themes that worked for the campaign were "not going backward" and "not tipping a balance [on the Supreme Court] that had been achieved," as well as "choice." Equally important, the focus groups told the advocates that some of their favorite themes, conceived in Washington, did not work. The public no longer responded to or cared about Robert Bork's role in Watergate's "Saturday Night Massacre."[39]

Finally, there is a danger in letting public opinion dictate issue frames or messages verbatim. Perhaps the public, even after focus-group testing, has not thought the issue through thoroughly or misunderstands key points. When those points are clarified in the crucible of public debate, or when second thoughts occur to the public, the initial theme might be less effective. Issue advocates bring to message development a healthy understanding of political, social, and cultural forces, including prevailing public concerns. That, combined with a thorough understanding of the issue's dynamics, and input and testing from the public, can lead to the most convincing campaign messages and themes.

Ethics and Messages

Messages and themes are developed in an adversarial setting; one "side" seeks to "defeat" the other. Does that inevitably lead to deception and confusion? Probably no more so than any other component of issue advocacy, where opponents argue about the consequences of change: litigation reform can lead to lower prices and innovative goods and services, or it can result in more dangerous products and unchecked medical malpractice. The answer depends on one's point of view.

Gun owners seeking to protect their rights can frame the issue as one of "safety," stressing how much safer law-abiding citizens would feel if they knew they could protect their families with a gun. The hypothetical "Safe Society Act" could protect the rights of citizens to own and carry handguns, which might make some people feel safer, but still others feel less safe. Indeed, the "Safe Society Act" could describe a law supported by gun-control advocates designed to prohibit most gun ownership.

Under either formulation of the hypothetical law, supporters and opponents will likely argue that they are trying to make people "safer." The debate over the role of gun-control legislation in making society safer is a lengthy one, relying on studies, surveys, and educated guesses and predictions. Who is to say whether people will genuinely be "safer" if they have more, not less, access to guns? The theme or message might suggest a different way of looking at the same issue; but by itself it is no more persuasive or probative than any other information adduced in the debate. Nor is a theme or frame any more confusing or misleading than any other information. Who wins the battle for control of the themes and symbols of the debate, and what information and argument they use to do it, is at the essence of issue advocacy.

8

Finding Strength in Numbers: Building and Managing Coalitions

Coalitions are an important part of all politics: electoral, legislative, and issue. But they are the lifeblood of issue advocacy.

Candidates construct electoral coalitions of voters to win an election day majority. They craft their positions on issues such as the environment, education, civil rights, and crime in an effort to win support from sufficient numbers of voters who share their views. But people vote, not interest groups. Voters and interest groups who form a candidate's electoral coalition do not act in concert and are unconcerned with the candidate's coalition-building strategy. Interest-group endorsements can be helpful in persuading voters, but groups do not coordinate their endorsements across issue lines: education, environmental, and civil rights groups do not unite to back candidates. It is the voters' job to assess competing candidates' positions and cast their votes one at a time.

Legislators assemble legislative coalitions of other legislators to pass bills. Farm-state representatives join their inner-city colleagues to increase the food stamp program. Senators from tobacco-growing states such as Kentucky and North Carolina form a coalition with those from sugarcane-growing states such as Hawaii and Louisiana to protect crop subsidies. The legislators then go their separate ways on other issues, taking positions and casting votes to further their constituents' interests.

Issue coalitions are the building blocks of issue advocacy campaigns. Interest groups enlist other interest groups to build the necessary support for an issue campaign. The coalition's members are interest groups, not individuals whose votes are accountable only to their consciences, or legislators who represent a diverse constituency of citizens with many different views on every issue. Interest groups bring their own issue agenda to a coalition. Every action they take—every coalition they join—must advance their issue agendas. In this chapter we examine the special problems and opportunities of issue coalitions.

Issue Coalitions

Issue coalitions enable minority interests to build majority support. Just as individuals increase their influence by joining together with like-minded individuals in interest groups, organizations and interest groups establish or join coalitions that multiply their power. Coalitions allow different interests to work together and at the same time to maintain their separate policy agendas.

A coalition is an alliance, usually limited in time and purpose, between organizations with differing agendas, working together for a common policy advocacy goal. The term *coalition* encompasses a great diversity of alliances formed to advance a shared public policy goal. Coalitions can be formal or informal, permanent or temporary.

Coalitions can unite diverse civil rights or environmental organizations as they formulate and advance complex, long-term agendas. Or they can provide a mechanism to coordinate short-term activities, such as opposing the Supreme Court nomination of Robert Bork or supporting the balanced budget amendment to the Constitution. Organizations committed to preserving the oceans unite with those concerned with rivers to oppose water pollution. Interest groups representing cigarette manufacturers work in coalition with those representing convenience stores to oppose increased cigarette taxes. The recent explosion in interest groups has led to a corresponding increase in the number of coalitions.

Businesses form trade associations that can act as issue coalitions, such as the National Association of Manufacturers, the Chemical Manufacturers' Association, and national and local chambers of commerce. Or they create temporary alliances to defeat health-care reform or support regulatory relief.

As issues enter Stage 1, coalitions begin as issue networks. An "issue network" is less formal and less action oriented than a coalition. At its simplest, an issue network is nothing more than a mechanism to facilitate communication and cooperation between individuals and organizations who share common concerns about public policy issues. Networks afford issue advocates an opportunity to share information and keep abreast of relevant technical, scientific, policy, public opinion, and other news and developments.

Networks often precede coalitions, just as individuals or organizations sharing information and common concerns may gradually coalesce into an association or organization—an interest group— designed to influence policy. Since networks rarely adopt public policy positions, they can reach broadly for members while avoiding the difficult process of reconciling members' differing policy agendas. Once some or all network members identify a shared public policy goal, and the issue enters Stage 2, the network begins the transformation into a coalition.

A coalition is an alliance between *organizations*, each of which brings its own *agenda* and decision-making process to the coalition table. Since coalition members are organizations, not individuals, they do not have the same freedom of movement that individuals have. Interest groups that join coalitions must be sure that the coalition shares the fundamental goals of the organization and its members. An organization may not be permitted to join a coalition without approval from an internal committee, its board of directors, or even its members. Organizations may be reluctant to join coalitions out of fear that the coalition will take positions or make public statements that are at odds with the organization's goals.

Individual organizations each have their own priorities, which may or may not coincide squarely with the coalition's. Issue advocacy inevitably requires compromise, and individual organizations may find themselves uncomfortable with the compromises required for a coalition to accommodate the differing agendas of all its members. Some members will inevitably be more deeply committed to a common goal than others; one member's minor issue might represent another's bottom line.

Coalitions can be slow and cumbersome; achieving agreement on even minor objectives can be time-consuming and energy-consuming. And that can hamper the coalition's ability to respond to crises and opportunities. Group rivalries can erupt, along with the understandable reluctance of organizations and individuals to subordinate their own identities to the coalition. Hard feelings can fester and grow, especially when some groups or individuals work harder than others, and still others only show up in time for the victory celebration, claiming an unfair share of the credit.

Coalitions are at the mercy of their members and can achieve only what the members permit them to achieve. Their only resources—people and money—are those that members provide.

Large, permanent coalitions, such as trade associations, have permanent staff, office space, and resources, all dedicated to achieving the coalition's goals. Member organizations pay substantial dues to support the coalition and its infrastructure.

But most coalitions are ad hoc, voluntary assemblages of organizations, with little power to compel the member organizations to commit time and resources to the coalition or to fulfill their coalition commitments. They are usually staffed by "volunteers" from the member organizations, some of whom may even be detailed to work exclusively on coalition projects.

Coalition memberships are frequently shifting, with new members appearing at some meetings and others disappearing entirely, as each weighs the benefits of coalition membership against its costs. The individuals who represent their organizations around the coalition table are busy staff members within their own organizations, with tasks to perform and bosses to whom they must report. Coalition work often takes a back seat to the press of day-to-day responsibilities. And even when individuals agree at a coalition meeting to take a position or perform a task, they often lack the authority or power to fulfill their coalition promises.

While all coalitions are composed of different organizations with different agendas working together, there are numerous ways to organize and manage coalitions. The best coalitions are flexible enough to adapt to their members' needs and the common goal that has brought them together. The basic variations fall into two broad areas: identity and operating structure.

Identity

A coalition can choose to have a high or low profile. It can select a catchy name that encapsulates its mission, send letters on stationery emblazoned with its own logo, communicate its message to the public and decision makers in the name of the coalition, and rent office space with its name stenciled on the front door in gold letters.

Or a coalition can be nearly invisible to the public, operating behind the scenes, with each coalition member carefully coordinating advocacy tasks with each other, but performing those tasks in the name of their own organization, rather than the nameless coalition. The coalition could meet behind the closed doors of some hospitable law firm or one of the anonymous coalition's members.[1]

A distinct coalition identity can serve many purposes. The term coalition implies unity of purpose and strength, and many coalitions proudly adopt a public identity as a way to proclaim a broad base of support.[2] Three small organizations that comprise a coalition may not appear very strong or powerful, but when they unite under a coalition banner, they give the appearance of greater strength and power. By using a separate coalition identity they may make it easier for other organizations to join their efforts. An organization that might not want to forge an alliance, however public, with organizations with which it might not agree on every issue (or with which it might compete for business or members or just publicity) might willingly be part of a coalition whose name provides a broad umbrella for the identity of its members.

Naming a coalition can give its members an opportunity to remake their image, broaden their appeal (to the public or decision makers), and even hide their members' identities. The now-famous "Harry and Louise" advertisements that raised questions about the Clinton administration's health-care-reform plan were produced by and credited to the Coalition for Health Insurance Choices. As we discuss in chapter 10, by choosing and publicizing that name, the coalition's members, predominantly insurance companies who were seeking to advance their financial interests, were able to portray themselves and their positions as being in the broader public interest. Citizen organizations and other interest groups that may have been reluctant to join an insurance company-led coalition could find a comfortable place under a coalition's broad umbrella.

By contrast, nameless, faceless coalitions can be most effective when their very existence is unknown to the broader public. It may not help the cause of tort reform opponents to be led publicly by trial lawyers, whose livelihoods depend on continuing the existing system and who are blamed by reform advocates for creating more problems than they solve. Even a cleverly named coalition might not shield the lawyers' membership from persistent reporters. Yet it might be vitally important for consumer organizations who are fighting tort reform to coordinate their legislative strategies with the trial lawyers. The resulting coalition might well remain publicly nameless, meeting in another organization's offices, and taking no public positions in its own name.

Operating Structure

Coalitions can pool their resources to hire staff or assign tasks among the member organizations. Coalitions with broad policy agendas that are unlikely to be accomplished in a short period of time often raise the necessary funds to establish a formal legal entity for the coalition, complete with bylaws, a board of directors, and permanent staff.

In contrast, the vast majority of coalitions are focused on a narrow issue, or set of issues, and are short-lived. Coalitions typically begin with little or no concern for operating structure or even membership. If they evolve out of issue networks, they may be unaccustomed to raising money, assigning and accomplishing tasks, and resolving conflict.

They rarely have detailed operating procedures and usually avoid, as long as possible, addressing procedural issues such as decision making and voting. Not until differences of opinion on tactics and goals arise do these coalitions take the time to address how to resolve those differences. But when coalition members appear divided over which strategy to pursue, it is probably too late to debate whether coalition decisions should be reached by consensus, rather than by majority vote.

Coalition leadership can be fixed, with members voting to elect a single leader, or it can be informal and rotating, with members taking turns chairing meetings. The leader can be one of the members of the coalition, each of which represents his or her own organizations, or it can be an individual selected and hired by the coalition and directly accountable to the coalition, rather than to individual members.

Why Organizations Join Coalitions

Coalitions afford interest groups an opportunity to achieve public policy goals they could not reach working alone. Coalitions allow narrow interests, which are deeply committed to affecting policy, to reach out and build the broad base of support necessary to make change. By forming coalitions, interest groups mimic their members, who have decided to band together to increase their power and effectiveness.

By choosing their identity carefully, coalitions can reframe the issue and change the terms of the public debate. Major automobile manufacturers, who opposed raising the federal fuel-efficiency standards for new cars, formed the Coalition for Vehicle Choice to advance their interest. They recruited coalition partners who shared their concern that higher fuel-efficiency standards might lead to fewer large cars and vans. By reframing the issue, they also sought to recruit new interest groups, such as disabled veterans and seniors' organizations that rely on large cars or vans.

Coalitions multiply the amount and kind of resources and expertise available to interest groups. Coalition partners can contribute different resources: research and policy expertise, money, grassroots power, different values, media expertise, and lobbying skills, among others. Tasks—from advertising to polling—can be parceled out among coalition members, to take advantage of members' expertise and avoid duplication.

Coalitions allow individual organizations, each of which would otherwise be acting independently in pursuit of the same goal, to coordinate effective action. Unifying themes and messages can be developed; advertising and grassroots mobilization can be coordinated with "inside" lobbying.

Individual organizations potentially have much to gain from joining a coalition. Smaller, less powerful organizations can have the opportunity to perform on a larger stage, increasing their visibility both within the community of issue advocates and with the general public and decision makers. They can "become a player," building an ongoing power base to increase the organization's impact on a broad range of issues. Organizations can expand the scope of their activities: community-based organizations can join a national coalition to address larger issues. Just by participating in coalitions, organizations that have not previously worked together can develop mutual trust and respect.

For the longer term, coalitions can shift power. Coalitions have the potential to transcend narrow policy issues to create lasting changes in local, state, and national power structures. Civil rights organizations that worked together to fight segregated schools, poll taxes, and employment discrimination became a powerful political voice for their members' interests through their coalition efforts. Community-based organizations unite in coalitions to give voice and power to individuals and organizations that had been previously disenfranchised or had not shared proportionally in community resources. Small, cooperative steps taken in issue coalitions can subsequently lead to involvement in electoral politics and fundamental change.[3]

Lasting, long-term power shifts can also be achieved when business interests come together in coalitions, such as concerted business efforts that began in the 1970s and 1980s to oppose government regulation and pursue regulatory relief. Business cooperation in opposing President Clinton's health-care-reform plan helped empower business groups, leading to progress on litigation reform, regulatory relief, and the Contract with America.[4]

Building a Coalition: Membership

Coalition building is akin to grassroots organizing. Grassroots organizers may go door to door, address civic groups, or meet in church basements to talk about neighborhood or national issues. Their challenge is to help busy people make the connection between their individual and personal concerns—family, home, health, and money, among others—and public policy issues. They seek to enlist people, who are worried about paying for a new car or the next vacation, in a campaign to reduce the level of contaminants in the municipal water supply.

Similarly, coalitions must recruit organizations with full and busy agendas. Businesses are concerned with rising interest rates or falling market shares, as they focus on keeping employees and shareholders happy; unions are concerned with layoffs, wage hikes, and corporate restructuring. Then along comes a cross-cutting issue such as health-care reform. Unless organizations see a clear connection between their interests and the new issue, they may be reluctant to make room for still more work on an already full plate.

Most coalitions are built by word of mouth. Coalition members are recruited one at a time, usually by personal contacts between a key individual in one organization and his or her counterpart in another organization. The initial core members recruit colleagues in organizations they know and trust, with which they have worked in the past, who share their organization's agenda, and who are likely coalition partners.

The coalition's initial core membership is comparatively easy to recruit. Core members are organizations whose policy agendas substantially overlap. They are accustomed to working together on common issues. They have a history of trust and a shared policy agenda. Most environmental groups, for example, are eager to join a coalition to strengthen the Clean Water or Clean Air Acts; many business groups are willing partners in a coalition to oppose those efforts.

Recruiting the coalition's core membership amounts to "rounding up the usual suspects." But while it is necessary to identify and recruit "natural allies," it is only a first step. The more that coalition members reflect the same or very similar interests, the less effective the coalition will be. Each member may bring additional resources to the coalition, but the supporter base will remain narrow.

The most powerful coalitions, by contrast, represent a broad range of interests that the public and decision makers cannot ignore. That is why environmental groups supporting the continuation of the Endangered Species Act joined in a coalition with religious groups concerned with preserving all of God's creations. They also brought together poor communities fighting pollution, and excessive commercialism and consumption.[5]

To identify coalition partners beyond the core membership, issue advocates begin with a thorough analysis of the issue's dynamics, employing the power-mapping and issue-mapping techniques described in chapter 2. With a map to guide them, advocates can identify other interest groups and organizations that care (or potentially care) about the issue, and why they care. They can then refine that list to include those that support (or potentially support) the coalition's position. In the process, of course, issue advocates map their expected opposition.

Mapping the power—identifying the key power sources on an issue—can lead to identifying potential coalition partners. A legislative committee chair may have considerable power over an issue. That could lead the coalition to recruit partners from the chair's state or legislative district, or who have a good relationship with the chair, or even those whose support can frame the issue in a way that is known to appeal to the chair. Coalitions can also map their own power and recruit new members to fill gaps in their advocacy skills, such as lobbying or grassroots mobilization.

Issue advocates increasingly spend time and resources persuading interest groups (and their members) to take positions and join coalitions. This "cross-lobbying" is a valuable technique to build coalition and public issue support.[6]

Strange Bedfellows: The Power of Unlikely Alliances

Coalitions begin with organizations whose issue agendas largely overlap. The initial recruitment process locates those whose agendas, while different, still show substantial areas of agreement. Finally, coalitions attempt to recruit organizations whose agendas rarely overlap with those of core coalition members. In some cases, core coalition members may even try to persuade other organizations to stretch their issue agendas to include the coalition's issue.

Why would coalitions recruit so widely for allies, even going so far as to include organizations with whom they have never worked on any issue? Just imagine the reaction of a legislator who opens his office door only to find lobbyists on both sides of the abortion issue working together on another issue. "Unlikely alliances" make decision makers and the public sit up and take notice: If people who disagree on so many things agree on this issue, then maybe there's some merit in their position.

The coalition opposing casino gambling in Maryland joined religious organizations, who traditionally opposed gambling on moral grounds, with restaurants, bar owners, and race tracks, who opposed casinos because they feared increased competition. The coalition partners had no doubt opposed each other on issues such as Sunday hours and the standards for granting liquor licenses, yet they identified a common enemy—casino gambling—and saw the advantages in joining forces. The restaurant and bar owners had considerable experience lobbying the state legislature, including making campaign contributions, while the religious groups had a set of values and a large grassroots presence to bring to the coalition.

Immigration reform is a complex issue. One legislative proposal would require national identity cards; another would eliminate immigration preferences for relatives of American citizens. The liberal American Civil Liberties Union joined with the conservative Americans for Tax Reform to oppose national identity cards. Religious organizations and high-technology companies (eager for well-educated immigrant workers) joined to oppose provisions to limit family reunification.[7]

Taxpayer organizations and environmental groups combined forces in 1995 to form a "Green Scissors" coalition to propose environmentally responsible ways to balance the budget. One coalition member described it as "an odd couple coalition. It unites the anger we see in America, the anger about government waste and the concern about the environment."[8] By joining together, they had drawn new attention to their individual concerns and found a unifying theme.

An unlikely coalition can attract media attention. The American Civil Liberties Union (ACLU) and the National Rifle Association (NRA) each took predictable positions opposing increased authority for federal law enforcement agencies to fight terrorism. But when they united in a coalition, the media sat up and took notice, reporting that "an unlikely coalition of gun rights advocates . . . and the American Civil Liberties Union called on Congress yesterday to reject legislation that would give more power to federal law enforcement agencies and concentrate instead on curbing their abuses."[9] The fact that the ACLU and the NRA were acting together was news in itself.

Coalitions can build issue bridges between traditional adversaries. Conservationists and lumber companies can work together to protect bears that move beyond national forests to adjacent logging lands.[10] Oil companies can work with senior citizen groups to help seniors weatherize their homes and lower their heating bills.[11] Even when the alliance does not focus on changing public policy, it can set the stage for possible future cooperation and build trust and understanding between disparate interests.

In New York, pro-choice women's groups joined religious and other pro-life organizations in the Common Ground Network for Life and Choice to press for government policies that facilitate adoption. Together they were able to attract more public attention and support for adoption than either of them could have done acting in coalition with more "traditional allies." The coalition partners were able to open legislative doors for each other that neither could have opened alone. Finally, they were able to build bridges to each other, recognizing that there was much on which they could agree, and much that they could accomplish by working together despite their fundamental differences.[12]

These examples all illustrate the value of unlikely alliances and a basic principle of issue advocacy: there are no permanent friends and no permanent enemies, just permanent interests.

Bringing all potentially interested organizations to the coalition table as early as possible may seem a desirable goal, but how far should a coalition reach for new members, and at what cost? The most obvious cost is that new members may be less committed to the coalition's goals than the original core members. They may be "weak" members, who cannot or will not deliver on their commitments. A weak member might be prevailed upon to take a public role in the coalition, only to leave the coalition in an equally public defection when a compromise is reached that is unacceptable to the weak member.

Organizations considering joining a coalition have many questions to answer. How comfortable will they be aligning themselves with others with whom they may disagree on a broad range of issues? Are the existing coalition members organizations or individuals with whom they want to work? Will they lose flexibility and influence over how the issue campaign is planned and executed? How will joining the coalition affect their organization—its credibility and power—long after the coalition disbands?

Managing a Coalition: Governance

Coalitions are fragile organizations. With fluid membership and varying levels of individual and organizational commitment to the coalition's goals, it is sometimes surprising that coalitions accomplish anything at all.

The worst coalitions are peppered with distrust; adversaries or business competitors can make recalcitrant coalition partners. Coalition meetings can disintegrate into feckless discussions reflecting fundamental issue differences. The coalition is at the mercy of its members and their varying levels of commitment to the coalition and its goals. A single, deeply committed organization can discover that its hard work is frustrated by the inability or unwillingness of its coalition partners to perform their assigned tasks.

Yet coalition governance and management usually receive little attention until problems arise and the coalition's integrity and effectiveness are threatened. Unlike managing projects within organizations, coalitions require a lighter touch to accommodate the differing needs, resources, commitments, and abilities of diverse coalition partners. And unlike maintaining a membership organization of individuals, losing a coalition partner can mean losing an entire interest, including its members, resources, and values. When one environmentalist drops out of the Sierra Club, it is an insignificant problem. When the Sierra Club leaves a coalition, it takes all of its members—and possibly even the environmental movement—with it.

Problems and Pitfalls

The path to coalition success is fraught with obstacles and dangerous detours. Even the most committed coalition member is likely to sigh heavily when trying to fit still another lengthy meeting into an already crowded schedule. And meetings can often bog down as reluctant members express reservations about coalition policies and tactics, or as new members are brought on board and take valuable time to get accustomed to the coalition and its members.

Process can stall progress as coalition members from different kinds of organizations with different organizational styles want to debate and discuss, while others from different organizational cultures want to act. Taking a vote or reaching a consensus on seemingly minor points can require lengthy discussion and debate. Individuals accustomed to acting on behalf of themselves and their organizations can be frustrated by the slow pace of coalitions. Even the simplest coalition letter and statement may have to be drafted by committee, with each phrase approved by every member. Many coalition decisions must be deferred until individuals can clear them with their respective organizations.

All member organizations are not equal, although they may appear to be. Theoretically, every organization that sits around the coalition table is entitled to (or thinks it is) an equal say in coalition matters. But some organizations are always more equal than others, whether they be the core advocates who convened the coalition or the larger, better funded, more established, more powerful organizations.

Some individuals are also more equal than others. Coalition representatives are chosen by their organization, not the coalition, so it is possible for the head of one organization to sit at the coalition table next to a much-lower-level official representing another organization. The first member may expect greater deference from the coalition because of his or her organizational position, rather than the importance of that organization to the entire coalition. The member may be unaccustomed to taking direction or deferring to others. To complicate matters, the second member may not be able to speak for his or her organization without checking with organizational superiors, which is obviously not the case with the first member. Even choosing the coalition's chair can raise issues of clashing egos.

Coalition members, who are not fully committed to the coalition's goal or are unable to pull their weight in the coalition, can be a source of problems. They may raise questions and doubts about issues on which there is general agreement. Some may agree to perform tasks for the coalition, only to find they are unable to accomplish them or find support within their organizations for allocating the necessary resources. The voluntary nature of a coalition makes it nearly impossible to compel individual members to perform their tasks, or to perform them up to the coalition's standards.

Compromises or concessions are necessary in any coalition, but often they can be achieved only by lengthy, volatile, and sometimes painful debate, which can undercut feelings of solidarity. Some members may be eager to embrace a proposed compromise, while others may be reluctant to accept anything but total victory. Compromises may make some coalition members question the value of continuing to participate in the coalition.

Compromises on strategies and tactics can also raise problems. One member may urge the coalition to denounce a political leader, while others, who may have worked with that leader in the past (and hope to do so in the future), may oppose that strategy.

A few members may end up doing most of the work. They may do it willingly, perhaps antagonizing other members, who feel shut out by the dominance of powerful members or organizations. Or they may end up doing it reluctantly, when others cannot or will not do their share. A few members may claim most of the credit, which might be appropriate if they are the same members who do most of the work; too often they are not. Some members may get public credit in the media, when others believe they are more deserving.

Factions and group rivalries can arise and lead to internal coalition politicking distracting members from the coalition's goals. Valuable time can be spent healing rifts and maintaining the integrity of the coalition, while more nimble advocates on the other side can concentrate on advancing their interests.

Organizational members' credibility can suffer when the coalition takes controversial public positions or produces work of questionable quality. Internal and external perceptions of the organization can be affected by what others do or say under the aegis of a coalition. Organizations that compete for members or funding may also compete for media attention; each wants a high public profile for itself and may resent seeing a competitor quoted in the media as the coalition's spokesperson.

Solving the Problems and Avoiding the Pitfalls

Several basic rules can make coalitions more effective and avoid the more serious pitfalls.

- The goals and objectives of the coalition should be clearly stated so that organizations who join will fully comprehend the nature of their commitment. At the same time, coalition members should openly acknowledge their potentially differing self-interests. By recognizing these differences, coalition leaders can promote trust and respect among the members, while stressing common values and vision.
- Coalitions should reach out for broad membership but should not include those who are uncertain or uncommitted to the coalition's goals or strategies. The most effective coalitions have a solid core of fully committed organizations, which can draw together shifting groups of allies for discrete projects or campaigns. Overreaching for members can result in paralysis and suspicion. There is nothing worse than a strategy-planning session where coalition members are eying each other suspiciously instead of openly sharing ideas and plans. It is always possible that reaching broadly for supporters can yield coalition members who have close ties to the opposition and, intentionally or not, may provide coalition strategies and tactics to that opposition.

- A coalition should be able to work with a great diversity of organizations, but all groups need not belong as formal members. Different categories or levels of membership can accommodate organizations that are reluctant to become full partners in the coalition. Organizations whose goals are more radical, or whose tactics—such as boycotts or picketing—would not meet with full coalition approval are often more comfortable and effective working outside the formal coalition structure and informally coordinating their activities with the coalition.
- At the heart of every successful coalition, there should be a small directorate of leaders who are deeply committed to the issue and to the coalition. They should be able, when necessary, to subordinate the narrow interests of their individual organizations to the overall goals of the coalition. Coalitions, by their nature, are grateful for any contribution their members make (and rarely have the luxury of turning any contribution down), but the best coalition leaders need to be carefully selected and recruited. Good leaders are probably too busy to volunteer for the position. Rotating the coalition leadership among the members may be an appropriate way to share coalition responsibilities and authority.

  The coalition's leaders should have strong ties to the major organizations within the coalition. And the commitment of those organizations and their leaders should itself be strong. This commitment should be communicated within the organizations so that staff members clearly understand that coalition work is a high priority.
- Coalitions can be formal or informal, tightly organized or loose and decentralized. The kind of coalition chosen will depend on the kind of issue as well as the styles of the people and organizations involved. Coalitions evolve naturally and should not be forced to fit into any one style. But the best coalitions establish principles of governance before they are needed. Must all decisions be reached by unanimous vote? By majority vote? By consensus? Who can speak to the media on behalf of the coalition? Who has the power to commit the coalition in meetings with outsiders? Who can invite new members to join the coalition and who must approve their membership?
- By starting out with a manageable first task, a coalition can discover its strengths and weaknesses with minimal risk. Interim

policy objectives—and the necessary advocacy strategies and tac-tics—should be carefully chosen to build good working relation-ships. They should be significant enough to involve organi-zational members, but sufficiently modest so that there is a rea-sonable expectation of success. They should have the potential to involve a broad membership base and be of sufficient importance to gain public and media attention.

- Coalition tasks and responsibilities should be clearly defined and assignments equitably apportioned. Leaders should overcome their reluctance to hold fellow coalition members to high perfor-mance standards. Assigned tasks must be done—and done well—or the entire coalition suffers. At the same time, the coalition should find ways to take advantage of each member's resources and abilities. This will likely mean that some organizations as-sume a disproportionate share of the coalition's workload. Those members who are asked to do less should still be made to feel they are valued coalition members.

- Coalition meetings should be viewed by members as a necessary responsibility, not an opportunity for an occasional visit with old friends. As much as possible, members should be encouraged to designate a single individual to represent the organization at co-alition meetings; "fill-ins" should be discouraged.

- Once the coalition is organized, member organizations should consider hiring at least one staff person who would be responsible to the coalition, not the member organizations. At the least, one member organization should temporarily assign or "detail" an employee to work for the coalition full-time, for the duration of the coalition's effort. Scheduling meetings, taking and circulating minutes, reminding members of their commitments, coordinating communications, and preparing and copying materials all require considerable time and energy.

- Coalitions are made, not born. The best coalitions unite organi-zations that are not accustomed to working with each other. Skepticism and even active distrust may pervade early coali-tion meetings, requiring time to air and acknowledge differ-ences. Patient coalition leaders should allow time and oppor-tunity for discussion and debate, while keeping the coalition goal-oriented.

- Credit for success should be distributed fairly, but coalition leaders should remember that much can be accomplished if no one cares who gets the credit.

* * *

The difficult task of building and sustaining a coalition is more than rewarded by the power and energy of a well-constructed and well-maintained coalition, which can quickly become more potent than the sum of its individual members.

9

Persuading Decision Makers

Until now, we have examined how individuals and interest groups assemble the power and resources to make change. When an issue becomes ripe for action, it is time—for them and for us—to focus on persuading the people and organizations who can make change happen.

This chapter analyzes how issue advocates persuade decision makers from the "inside." The next chapter explores how they mobilize popular support to put "outside" pressure on those same decision makers. Taken together, chapters 9 and 10 describe the strategies and tactics advocates use to influence how laws and policies are made, interpreted, and administered.

Lobbying and Lobbyists

Even before Ross Perot made the word "lobbyist" R-rated, lobbying had an image problem. To many, lobbying has unsavory connotations of arm twisting, backroom bargaining, and trading money for influence. Yet citizens and interest groups who lobby are participating directly in the making of laws and the governing of the nation; they are exercising their constitutional right to petition the government.

Legislators hold hearings to solicit the views of the public; they invite their constituents into their offices; they attend town meetings in their districts so that they can stay in touch with the people they represent. They conduct their legislative business in public (for the most part), even broadcast it on television, so that citizens can know what their government is doing and have an opportunity to influence it. And the more the public participates, the more government truly reflects the will of the people.

At least in theory.

Individual citizen-lobbyists—the Myra Rosenblooms—are the exception, not the rule. Walk the halls of Congress, or any City Council chamber, and you will encounter a dozen highly paid, professional lobbyists for every citizen-lobbyist. That imbalance of resources and power is at the root of lobbying's unsavory reputation. It is not just the money used to hire a bevy of lobbyists, armed with computerized profiles of each member of Congress, but also the money to contribute to the member's reelection campaign, through individual contributions and the growing number of political action committees (PACs).

But lobbying is not just for smoke-filled rooms anymore (if it ever was), and it is not just for well-heeled economic interests. Lobbying is a profession, one that is analyzed and studied in law schools and political science programs. And the representatives of business and industry are no longer its only practitioners. Increasingly, consumers, public interest groups, and individuals concerned with homelessness or civil rights or public health are learning and using lobby skills alongside lawyers and former members of Congress.

Bill Gradison, meet Myra Rosenbloom.

There are no qualifications for being a lobbyist, but there are professional lobbyists who combine their experience, knowledge, and personal contacts to lobby on behalf of paying clients. Law firms are home to many who lobby; even more inhabit lobbying or public affairs or public relations firms and offer their services to any individual or interest willing to pay. Still others are employed by businesses or trade associations in offices in Washington or state capitals. Lobbyists have their own trade association, which even has its own lobbyist.

While lobbying focuses on, and has its origins in, influencing lawmaking, its common meaning is broader. We speak of "lobbying" someone who has to make a decision, no matter what the forum, no matter who the decision maker. Lobbying as a word and an activity has become generic.

Lobbying includes influencing the many actions that Congress (or state and local legislative bodies) and individual legislators take that go beyond enacting legislation. For example, the U.S. Senate confirms agency heads and cabinet members nominated by the president. Both Houses of Congress oversee government agencies to ensure that they carry out their responsibilities in accordance with the will of Congress. Individual members of Congress help constituents solve problems with their social security benefits or the bureaucracy's reluctance to approve a new drug or an export license.

Lobbying also includes influencing the executive or administrative branch of government, because sooner or later every government official is lobbied. As we saw in chapter 4, important policy decisions are made throughout the executive branch. And agencies that make rules are merely exercising power delegated to them by Congress to make laws.

A Day in the Life of a Lobbyist

Contrary to popular belief, lobbyists do not spend their days prowling the halls of Congress or the state legislature, buttonholing legislators and changing their votes. Most of their best work is "behind the scenes": it is much less glamorous and much more important. In this section we get a better understanding of what lobbyists do and the skills they need to be successful.

The lobbyist, whether he or she represents a large corporation, a small business, a broad-based coalition, or a citizen interest group, wears many hats and has many titles. Lobbyists, who sometimes term their task "government relations" or "issue management," have broad responsibility for understanding and influencing government policymaking so that it reflects their clients' interests.

In the course of a busy day, lobbyists' tasks include the following:

Monitoring

First and foremost, lobbyists monitor government activities and policymakers. Effective lobbyists create formal and informal issue networks to share and analyze two basic kinds of information about government policymaking: (1) publicly available information that everyone knows but few understand, such as what bills are introduced, which administrative rules are proposed, and when hearings are held; and (2) information that few people know, such as the preliminary views of government policymakers or the initial reactions of legislators to informal proposals and contacts.

By carefully monitoring government activities, lobbyists can establish an "early warning system" to identify potential policy actions before they are set in stone, and while the lobbyist's influence can still shape the decision. It is much easier to change an agency's proposed rule before the agency head "signs off" on it and proposes it for comment in the *Federal Register*. Similarly, it requires much less effort to insert language in legislation before it is introduced than to make the same change on the floor of the Senate.

There is no shortage of people and institutions to monitor.

The Formal Government

Monitoring federal government and legislative policymaking begins with reading and understanding formal, public sources of information, such as the *Congressional Record* and the *Federal Register* (which report on the public activities of Congress and the executive branch) and court decisions. Because important decisions are often made elsewhere, lobbyists in Washington also monitor activities in the states, including the state court systems.

There will literally be dozens of federal agencies and congressional committees (not to mention fifty times that number of state agencies and legislative committees) to track. For each agency, lobbyists monitor proposed and final rules, administrative interpretations of the law, changes in agency policies and procedures, speeches and testimony by key officials, and even personnel changes. For each committee member, lobbyists monitor public statements and press conferences, and even the legislator's daily schedule. Is the member scheduled to address your issue in a major speech or meet with your opponents at a fund-raising dinner?

What may seem like an impossible task is made easier by commercial services, such as the Commerce Clearing House and the Bureau of National Affairs, which publish looseleaf "reporters," containing compilations and analyses of government actions on issues such as taxation, the environment, labor relations, telecommunications, among others. Because issues are so interconnected, few lobbyists have the luxury of focusing on only one narrow issue; major corporate lobbyists must be aware of developments in all those areas, and probably many more.

Less widely known, but equally useful, are commercial publications devoted to particular issues and government agencies. *Inside EPA*, *Communications Daily*, and *FTC Watch* are examples of targeted newsletters that follow specific agencies, developing sources from within the agencies as well as those subject to their jurisdiction. Disgruntled employees frequently "leak" documents or give "off the record" interviews that yield valuable insight into internal agency decision making. Lobbyists can identify hitherto unknown champions of their positions within agencies or obstacles to progress.

The People Behind the Government

Understanding government policymaking requires identifying and learning about the people who constitute the government, their motivations, and likely positions on issues. Congressional staff members have access to their bosses' offices and their mental processes. Legislative staff act as their member's eyes and ears, both inside the legislative process and with interest groups and constituents. Busy legislators rely on personal and committee staff to make initial decisions and convey public concerns to them.

Much of the lobbyist's work focuses on the bureaucracy, but only a few hundred federal bureaucrats are appointed by the president and confirmed by the Senate. Thousands of individuals toil behind the scenes, devising and implementing programs and policies that affect the lobbyist. They constitute the "real" or permanent government, and though they are relatively anonymous, their actions can have an important impact on their bosses' and their agencies' actions.

Probably the most valuable agency document is its phone book. In it lobbyists can find organizational charts and up-to-the-minute information about who occupies which key internal positions. A lobbyist seeking to influence a decision to be made by the head of the Environmental Protection Administration, for example, can trace that decision back through the agency bureaucracy to the desk of the (probably) career government official preparing the first draft of the decision. The lobbyist can meet with that employee (and his or her supervisors) in an attempt to probe their initial concerns, provide information to bolster or rebut those concerns, and track the decision through the bureaucracy, meeting with appropriate officials along the way.

Personal relationships are important. Behind every legislator or bureaucrat there is an individual. It is important for a lobbyist to get his or her calls returned, but it is more important to know enough about key individuals to understand what motivates them, what positions they are likely to take, and what information and which individuals, organizations, and interests can persuade them. Profiles of key executive branch appointments are available, providing lobbyists with insight into the background, interests, and political motivations of those officials.

The Issue

Anyone can see change happen in the rear-view mirror. The challenge is to identify it early in its life cycle, when it can be most easily influenced and when one's own options are broadest. The final resolution of an issue usually comes only at the end of a lengthy process. Even before the first government official contemplates drafting a solution to address a problem, social and political forces are already at work shaping the issue and bringing it to public attention.

Lobbyists monitor issues by identifying broad social and political trends that may influence their issues, garnering information from newspapers and general-interest periodicals, as well as academic and technical analyses of issues. Networks and coalitions help lobbyists monitor issues by convening symposiums, conferences, and meetings, and by publishing newsletters and reports that keep abreast of recent issue developments.

Monitoring the media enables lobbyists to understand how the public learns about an issue. Commercial services can alert the lobbyist to every mention of an issue in the general media, both print and electronic. What messages are the media conveying about an issue and how are those messages being received? Are the media increasingly inclined to discuss environmental issues in terms of the rights of property owners? Do the media describe telecommunications reform as a way for consumers to have more choices? To whom are the media turning for expert analysis and commentary? Whose opinion pieces or letters to the editor are being published?

When the Environmental Protection Administration announces a proposal to classify "second-hand smoke" as a carcinogen, lobbyists should not be taken by surprise. They should have been reading the scientific and technical literature on smoking and cancer and monitoring society's growing intolerance with smoking in public places. They should have seen the issue coming and have been actively working to influence it long before it became a gleam in a bureaucrat's eye.

At an early stage, advocates can define the terms of the public debate, such as by framing litigation reform as an effort to promote job creation and product innovation, rather than to deny consumers protection from hazardous products or medical malpractice. At an early stage, relatively small exertions of power and resources can mute one's opposition before it has an opportunity to gain public support and accumulate the resources needed to wage an effective issue campaign.

The Public and Everybody Else

The lobbyist eats, drinks, and sleeps an issue. But who else cares about it, and what are they doing or saying about it? The lobbyist can learn much by identifying and monitoring his or her opposition (not to mention coalition partners). What position are they taking on legislation? How are they articulating their position to decision makers and their members? When and how are they mobilizing their grassroots supporters? On what studies, surveys, and other information are they relying? How are they replying to opposition arguments? A major oil company lobbyist can monitor the newsletters and action alerts issued by environmental organizations, either by joining the organizations or by following their actions on the Internet or their worldwide web pages or gopher sites.

In addition to monitoring the media and public debates, lobbyists monitor public opinion directly by conducting surveys and focus groups and analyzing published public opinion data. They try to understand what the public thinks about an issue and how its views are reflected in letters to the editor, calls to talk radio, and national and community discussion forums.

Representing

Lobbyists are often the chief public representatives of their organization, interest group, or issue. They represent—and speak for—the organization when meeting with legislators and policymakers, when attending network or coalition meetings, and in a host of formal and informal social and political contacts, including receptions and political fund raisers. Any chance meeting or communication can lead to finding and supporting potential allies and coalition partners, as well as developing relationships with potential opponents.

Lobbyists stand for the issue in the eyes of decision makers and the media. Simply by "showing the flag," such as by attending an important meeting or hearing, lobbyists demonstrate their organizational interest in, and commitment to, an issue. Lobbyists establish themselves as the organization's representative on an issue, and merely by being present when and where issues are discussed and decisions made, the lobbyist can be in a position to be consulted by, or have access to, decision makers.

Educating

At its core, lobbying is educating. It is making decision makers and the public aware of the ramifications of issues and their effect on the lobbyist's organization and the larger public interest. The lobbyist fosters understanding and builds bridges between different worlds: between businesses and government administrators; between lawmakers and people with AIDS.

Lobbyists bridge cultures and translate organizational positions and expertise into language and concerns policymakers understand. Lobbyists accompany scientists, experts, ordinary citizens, and organizational officials on visits to decision makers, briefing them on how to make effective presentations and guiding them through the maze of governmental decision making. They convene policy briefings for lawmakers and their staffs to explain the "real world" consequences of government decisions. An automobile company lobbyist faced with the prospect of a law requiring more fuel-efficient automobiles can bring scientists working on electric cars to explain their limitations to lawmakers enamored with the idea of nonpolluting vehicles.

Lobbyists explain government actions and policies within their own organizations as they formulate issue positions and make internal decisions on governmental policies. Just as lobbyists interpret science and business for the government, they interpret government for scientists and businesspersons. Should corporate resources be invested in a new product, or will government approval be delayed for still more studies and analyses? Must automobile manufacturers develop electric cars, or will government fuel-efficiency standards be relaxed?

Lobbyists identify the public opinion gap and help develop and deliver information to close it. They are a source of information and expertise for the media, which are always eager to solicit or accept the views of interested parties on matters of public concern. Being a public spokesperson requires a lobbyist to understand the media culture, even to "speak in sound bites" when necessary.

In working with the media, lobbyists often enlist the help of public affairs or public relations firms, whose specific task is to shape media coverage of controversial issues. They prepare and disseminate press releases, "opinion" pieces for publication, and make issue spokespeople available to the media through satellite feeds.

Coordinating

Effective lobbyists coordinate their organizations' efforts to influence public policy by cultivating relationships within their own organizations and having sufficient internal authority and respect to mobilize diverse organizational resources to support their public policy advocacy efforts.

Lobbyists prod their organization into taking the most appropriate positions on public policy issues and then develop and manage a comprehensive issue advocacy plan, including the "outside" or grassroots mobilization strategy. They commission polls and focus groups to assess public opinion, develop campaign themes and messages, identify key decision makers who need to be persuaded by paid advertisements run in their districts, direct campaigns to stimulate letters or calls from the legislator's constituents, and even coordinate their organizations' political action committee campaign contributions.

Because issues are rarely resolved in one forum or arena, lobbyists coordinate litigation and legislative strategy, helping to formulate the organization's response to (or commencement of) lawsuits. An effective lobbyist also knows when administrative action will likely be more favorable than legislative action, and an issue should best be left to the bureaucracy. Since federal, state, and local bodies frequently share jurisdiction over an issue, lobbyists coordinate strategies used in each forum, identifying, for example, situations where federal preemption of state laws might be appropriate, or where state or local action may be preferable to federal action.

Persuading

Ultimately, lobbyists identify who to persuade and how to persuade them. Their persuasive power depends on the power of the interest they represent and the way that power resonates with a decision maker's concerns. Knowing what motivates a decision maker enables lobbyists to articulate or frame their argument so that it will receive a favorable reception. A legislator who represents a district with many labor union members will likely be more concerned with the effect of an issue on workers. Lobbyists may represent large corporate interests usually at odds with their labor unions; but in the best tradition of finding "unlikely allies" and working in coalitions with them, lobbyists can enlist the support of unions to defeat a proposal that would lower their client's profits by focusing instead on the wage cuts and layoffs that would result.

If the target is a congressional committee chair, lobbyists map the sources of influence over that member. A lobbyist who represents the YMCAs of America or the association of universities or even the Girl Scouts will cultivate relationships with local affiliates of the national organization. Then, when it comes time to lobby the member, the lobbyist accompanies the local representative to a meeting with the member, giving a national problem a local face and voice the member knows and respects.

Information and Lobbying

> Information is the currency of Capitol Hill, not dollars. And not friends."
> —Lobbyist Jan Schoonmaker

Like any professional, a lobbyist has a large and varied bag of tools at his or her disposal, and one of the most important is information. Information may rank second only to demonstrated grassroots support in its power to influence elected officials; for bureaucrats, information is without peer.

This section discusses the ways information has increasingly become a tool of persuasion, outdistancing backroom politicking, pledges of campaign support, and even campaign contributions. In the next sections we analyze how lobbyists use information to persuade elected legislators and in the following section we discuss how administrative decision makers can be influenced.

As we discussed in chapter 6, there are many different kinds of information and many different uses to which it can be put. The same tightly reasoned, factual argument that builds a formal record before an administrative agency may have to be supplemented by an emotional and popular appeal before a legislative committee.

There is a continuum of persuasion that reflects the continuum of process, from formal, evidentiary cases presented before courts and some administrative agencies to political arguments made before legislatures. The more formal the process, the more lobbyists must rely on accurate and persuasive information and argument that can withstand cross-examination and rebuttal.

Persuading courts depends on one party to a lawsuit producing more reliable, probative information than the opposition. Persuading government administrators requires a mix of fact-filled information and political influence, depending on the type of agency decision. And persuading Congress traditionally depends much more on the politics of the issue than the technical arguments behind it. Congress, after all, is accountable to the people; bureaucrats are accountable to the law and process. While Congress holds public hearings and writes reports explaining and justifying its legislative enactments, it does not weigh the evidence presented to it, nor is it bound to justify its decisions based on that evidence, as are judicial and administrative bodies.

That historic paradigm is changing, primarily because Congress and the people are demanding that it change. First, increased public scrutiny of congressional actions, through C-SPAN telecasts of floor debates and committee hearings, and heightened public awareness of policy differences between President Clinton and the Republican-controlled Congress beginning in 1995, have led to more public argument and discussion about the merits of issues. When Congress is divided and issues become more partisan, particularly when the president's party does not control Congress, there are inevitably more public issue disagreements. The media have joined the fray, attempting to understand and explain the ramifications of issues, all in an effort to satisfy people's desire to know how issues will affect them. What will be the consequences of health-care reform for the elderly or the poor? Will revising clean-air and clean-water laws help or hurt business or the environment? How?

Second, the trend toward requiring "cost/benefit analyses" and "risk assessments" for regulatory decision making (discussed in chapter 6) has had a predictable effect on legislative decision making. The principle that regulatory policies should pass a cost/benefit test—a determination that the benefits of government actions outweigh their costs—applies equally to congressional lawmaking and administrative rulemaking.

It is no longer enough to support protecting the environment in general, or endangered species in particular, by arguing that it is "the right thing to do." Now issue advocates need to find and present reliable information to justify their legislative proposals. Since the emphasis is on being able to understand and predict the consequences of laws, the lobbyist's task is to provide information about how many jobs will be gained or lost if a bill is passed. The lobbyist must explain the long-term benefits and short-term costs of further deregulating telecommunications, both for the economy and the consumer. The final decision on reforming medical malpractice laws may not be based solely on a cost/benefit analysis, but both sides still must adduce persuasive information to address the question of whether it will lead to better-quality medical care at a lower cost.

Information has not completely supplanted all other forces in legislative decision making—laws are not yet required to pass a cost/benefit test—but it has become increasingly important. Sound public policymaking now requires that lawmakers have at least a plausible basis for concluding that the benefits of their actions will exceed their costs. Lobbyists must provide that basis as the cornerstone of their issue advocacy campaign.

Lobbying the Legislature

A Look Behind the Scenes

Do lobbyists actually change votes? Sometimes, but much less often than the public believes (or lobbyists boast). Lobbyists are more effective at providing support for legislators who agree with their position than at persuading undecided or opposing legislators. They can reassure friendly legislators, provide supporting information, share intelligence, and help identify allies.

Lobbyists learn about legislators. They study their biographies, their voting records, and the predilections of their constituents. They examine members' policy agendas and how they may be changing, their political situation, their constituents' views on issues, and the strength (and identity) of their likely opposition in the next election. They scour such vital information as the legislator's religious affiliation, previous employment, and spouse's name and occupation, all in an effort to understand how best to persuade the legislator. Federal Elections Commission records and financial disclosure forms provide names of contributors and personal information (such as stocks owned and clubs joined) that can aid the lobbyist in finding ways to influence the member.

Lobbyists target members for lobbying by identifying key "swing" votes: legislators who are capable of being persuaded. They then use voting records, election statistics, public statements, and information about the member and the district to find the right "hook" to persuade the right member, including grassroots mobilization that reinforces their inside lobbying efforts.

Lobbyists create a favorable environment for their issue by drawing friendly legislators' attention to the problem. They work with legislators to craft a solution, suggest potential legislative allies, and identify other interest groups that might be supporters (and how to appeal to them) or opponents (and how to neutralize them).

Lobbyists seek strong congressional champions and support them, making sure they get—when desired—proper credit, both at home and in Washington. Lobbyists motivate and gently prod reluctant congressional leaders. The lobbyist waiting off the House floor or in the Senate cloakroom when the hour is late and the day has been long is an important signal of support and appreciation to members overwhelmed with requests for help. A lobbyist's effectiveness can often be measured by the nature of the relationship he or she maintains with members and their staffs.

Lobbyists help legislators with the nuts and bolts of legislating. They aid receptive legislators in turning an unformed idea into a carefully drafted law, avoiding (or creating) loopholes and unintended consequences. They help lawmakers anticipate and refute opposing arguments.

Lobbyists are their interest's eyes and ears in legislative hearing rooms, members' offices, and the corridors and cafeterias of Congress, the state capitol, or the City Council. Their presence is evidence of their interest's concern for an issue, and intention to hold legislators accountable for their votes.

"Building the case" for legislative action requires appealing to the legislator's head and heart. Hard facts, studies, cost/benefit analyses are the essential foundation on which to build the case for legislative action. But they rarely suffice. Elected politicians respond (as do the media) to authentic and dramatic personal stories that show the human consequences of a policy issue. That is why Myra Rosenbloom's depiction of her husband dying at a hospital without doctors was so effective in lobbying the Indiana legislature. That is why the Clinton administration, in an attempt to defend its actions against the Branch Davidians in Waco, Texas, in 1993, made sure that the first witness at widely covered congressional hearings was a young girl who was sexually assaulted by David Koresh. And that is why supporters of American involvement in the Gulf War arranged for a young Kuwaiti woman to testify before Congress on her personal observations of the atrocities visited on Kuwait by the invading Iraqis.

Donna Rosenbaum, a California housewife whose child died from ingesting *E. coli* bacteria in undercooked meat, testified before Congress and the Department of Agriculture in favor of stricter meat labeling and inspection. She concluded that "one victim's family [appearing at a congressional hearing] is worth 20 lobbying visits. When you hear the extent of tragedy that food-borne illness brings to their lives, it's impossible not to react."[1]

Lobbyists cannot do it all alone. That is why they often work in coalitions with other interests. Sometimes they even spend time lobbying other interest groups, "cross-lobbying," to persuade them to take supportive positions or mount their own lobbying campaigns. Small business interests successfully persuaded the American Medical Association to abandon its support of the "employer mandates" provisions in President Clinton's health-care-reform plan. The AMA's opposition proved more effective than any direct lobbying efforts by small businesses.[2]

A good lobbyist will establish a mutually beneficial relationship with legislators. The lobbyist should be of value to legislators, and not just by buying tickets to the legislator's favorite political fund raiser or charity dinner. The lobbyist can provide important facts, arguments, intelligence, and even political muscle to support the legislator's position. An effective lobbyist will establish himself or herself as an authoritative information resource, thereby gaining access, credibility, and standing.

Trust and relationships matter. Just as interests and interest groups have credibility, so do individual lobbyists. A member or a staffer who knows, respects, and trusts a lobbyist because they have been through many campaigns together will likely give the lobbyist's ideas a fair hearing.

Knowing process and procedure counts. The lobbyist with a command of the intricacies of Capitol Hill procedure, for example, can successfully negotiate the labyrinthine corridors of Congress, while always anticipating his or her opponent's next move. How can a bill be drafted so that it gets referred to the most favorable committee? How can differences in competing versions of legislation be resolved without a floor fight? Successful lobbyists anticipate the problems and know the answers.

Legislators are busy people; much of the initial work of lawmaking inevitably falls to their staffs. Staffs have a mixture of technical expertise and political savvy. Most important, they have the ear and trust of the member. They will know the prospects for legislation, its likely opposition, and when hearings are scheduled, often before their bosses. Staffs can function as an early warning system for a lobbyist, alerting him or her to developments, exchanging information, serving as gatekeeper and sounding board, rejecting and refining a lobbyist's ideas, even championing an idea to members or others on the staff. In many instances lobbyists will never get past the staff and will be no worse for it.

All the skills and expertise in the world will do a lobbyist little good without "access" to legislators. Access is a result of many things, primarily of the interest or cause the lobbyist represents and the issue's significance to the legislator and his or her constituents, close allies, campaign supporters, and contributors. Access is also a product of a lobbyist's value to the legislator and of his or her credibility and reliability. Did the lobbyist support the member's last campaign? Will the lobbyist support the next one? Has the lobbyist always been candid and forthright, even when disagreeing with the member? And finally access is a product of the lobbyist's political and personal connections. That is why so many lobbyists worked for—or even served in—Congress.

Lobbyists link the political process of making laws with the people and the world those laws affect. Legislators are political animals, who are continually trying to gauge public sentiment. But assessing how an issue can potentially affect a myriad of different interests requires perspective and knowledge that a legislator may not have at his or her fingertips. Lobbyists provide political intelligence as well as expertise and perspective. Members who support legislation need to know the political consequences of their actions, both positive and negative.

Lobbyists can be reliable guides to the strength and depth of both opposition and support. Some issues are always more important than others, but legislators may not be able to evaluate an issue's importance to an interest group without the help of lobbyists. "Our organization's members will oppose that provision" is a crucial piece of intelligence for a legislator to have *before* he or she takes a position on a bill. A good lobbyist can help a legislator decide how much a vote is worth—or will cost—politically. Political intelligence also includes insight into the deliberations of the other house; a lobbyist often knows more about the outlook for legislation in the House than a Senator.

Lobbyists understand the larger picture. They know how their issue fits into a member's agenda and the broader legislative, political, and public policy picture. Lobbyists make connections between issues, such as crime, education, welfare reform, and children's health. They explain why an issue is best resolved in Congress (or a state legislature) rather than through the courts or the bureaucracy. They know how courts address the issue, and whether a pending Supreme Court case might make Congressional action moot.

There is no substitute for lobbying experience and issue continuity. Issues that rise to the top of our national agenda are rarely finally and definitively resolved. Environmental problems did not end with the establishment of the EPA. Lobbyists who were present for the creation of the Clean Air Act have an obvious advantage when the time comes for reauthorization. And those who would join in the confirmation battle over a Supreme Court nominee would have an advantage if they honed their skills and their grasp of the issues on the Bork nomination.

Holding Elected Officials Accountable: Issues and Elections

The 1960 presidential campaign is best remembered today for the televised debates between the articulate, smiling, telegenic John Kennedy and the nervous, uncomfortable, seemingly unshaven Richard Nixon. The debates were held at the height of the Cold War, and one of the hotly contested issues concerned two islands off the coast of mainland China, Quemoy and Matsu, claimed by Taiwan and occasionally bombarded by China. Needless to say, history has long forgotten which candidate took which position on that issue, and voters probably based their choice more on Kennedy's smile and Nixon's five o'clock shadow than on the likelihood of war in Asia.

But election campaigns do provide issue advocates with opportunities to force candidates to take positions on issues and to hold them accountable for the votes they cast while in office. Legislators can equivocate, but candidates on the campaign trail have little choice but to confront issues. They are more accessible than at any other time, and more willing to discuss issues openly. Interest groups routinely ask candidates to declare their positions on issues through written questionnaires, to which candidates, eager for votes, usually respond. The media question candidates on the issues and publish the results. Candidates appear at public forums in their state or district, where issue advocates can ask public questions and record the answers.

The presidential campaign had not quite started in the summer of 1995, when President Clinton and House Speaker Gingrich journeyed to New Hampshire to meet a senior citizen's group. They discussed health care and Medicaid and responded to questions. When one audience member, Frank MacConnell, suggested that the president and the Speaker reform campaign finance by appointing a bipartisan commission, the two agreed and shook hands. Skeptics will add that bipartisan cooperation on campaign finance reform disappeared after that handshake. But for one brief moment before a gathering of seniors and a national television audience, two powerful politicians were forced—by one citizen's question—to take a stand on an issue that often divided them.[3]

Election day presents issue advocates with the opportunity to demonstrate their support when and where it counts most: at the ballot box.[4] Between elections, issues advocates take advantage of elected officials' need to be in touch with the electorate, appearing on talk radio, speaking to local community gatherings, and responding to citizen questions. Each presents an opportunity for lobbying far from the distractions of the capital, when lobbyists and ordinary citizens can have their leaders' undivided attention.

"Just Say No"

Policy inertia works against making change. Legislators and policymakers are cautious by nature. Change may be good, but the "devil you know" may be better than the one you do not know. Individuals and organizations, including government policymakers, become comfortable with existing laws, even those they may not like. They learn how to ignore or avoid them when necessary; they understand the procedures they require and their implications. Laws become settled through administrative interpretations and court decisions. People know the consequences of current law; but what will change bring? Will it cause more harm than good? Will it have unintended consequences?

Opponents of legislative or policy change therefore have a different—and easier—task than proponents. Drafting a law or regulation requires precision and certainty; opposing the change requires only finding flaws, inconsistencies (both internally and with other laws or policies), or unintended or speculative consequences. Just as it is easier to ask questions and poke holes than to find answers and implement solutions, opponents of change need only raise doubts.

President Clinton's abortive 1993 effort to reform health care illustrates the different tasks of proponents and opponents. Reforming health care required the president to draft comprehensive legislation to restructure nearly the entire health-care delivery system to accomplish the goal of controlling costs and provide health insurance for all.

President Clinton discovered to his dismay that opponents could create substantial public opposition merely by planting seeds of doubt about how the intricate plan would work in practice. Might it lower the quality of health care? Would people have fewer choices of doctors? While the public initially supported the concept of health-care reform, the devil was truly in the details. And when details of the Clinton reform plan surfaced, the existing system did not look quite so bad.

The public, it seemed, was prepared to accept the current system, with all its flaws, rather than venture into the unknown, even with the promise of universal insurance, portability of coverage, and no exclusions for preexisting conditions.[5] There were, of course, no guarantees that the plan would work precisely as the president claimed, but its complicated nature afforded doctors, insurers, and small businesses an opportunity to raise sufficient public doubts to sink the proposal.

Taking Many Bites from the Same Legislative Apple

Increasingly complex legislative and budgetary agendas have created more opportunities for accomplishing the lobbyist's goals, and for his or her opponent to do mischief. In addition to the normal committees and subcommittees that have jurisdiction over an issue or an agency, congressional oversight committees have proliferated. Each committee can be a source of legislative and policy initiative; each has to be monitored and lobbied. The lobbyist who cares about the environment must now master the legislative authorization, oversight, and appropriations process.

Congress's inability to solve our national budgetary and deficit problems has led to an increasing round of emergency, last-minute budget requests and spending bills. The bills, even in the sanest of times, have often resembled Christmas trees, festooned with ornaments placed on them by every interested member. Nor have the ornaments been the simple kind, mandating spending on a member's favorite project. Instead, they have become opportunities for interim, substantive legislation. Appropriations committees are accustomed to working far from the spotlight. Their deliberations are poorly understood and infrequently reported by the media. The resulting bills are lengthy and complex, and because passage is required to fund important government activities, Congress often approves them without focusing on their details.

In the late 1970s, when administrative agencies such as the Federal Trade Commission were flexing their regulatory muscles, they encountered growing industry opposition. Each time the agency's budget came before Congress the battle between rival lobbyists was joined. It was not uncommon for the agency's budget to emerge from Congress with provisions that "no money appropriated shall be used to investigate ————"—and here a member, with the help of a lobbyist, would fill in the name of a least favorite FTC investigation or rulemaking proceeding. The situation got so bad, with only President Carter standing up against interest-laden appropriations bills, that the agency shut down on more than one occasion for lack of an appropriations bill.[6]

More recently, when members of the House Appropriations Subcommittee with jurisdiction over the National Labor Relations Board were dissatisfied with the board's handling of an unfair labor practice complaint, they cut 30 percent from the agency's annual budget. This strong signal of congressional disapproval was prompted by lobbying by the company that was the subject of the unfair labor practice complaint.[7]

The same strategy was pursued by opponents of the Department of Housing and Urban Development's antidiscrimination regulations for property insurers[8] and EPA's enforcement of clean-air and clean-water laws.[9] It is often easier to cut an agency's budget to the bone through the appropriations process than to revise or repeal the laws it administers.

Even when laws are passed and advocates share a celebratory glass of champagne (or gather over beers to lick their losing wounds), the issue is rarely settled. A corollary to the coalition-building principle that there are no permanent friends and no permanent enemies is that there are no permanent victories and no permanent losses. One Congress can undo or revise the work of a previous Congress or reverse an administrative agency's decisions. And the bureaucracy can interpret or enforce the law in ways that frustrate (or hearten) issue advocates.

Lobbying Government Policymakers: Yes, Even the President

The explosion in public concern for the environment is reflected in the many different federal government policymakers whose actions affect the environment. For example, the Environmental Protection Agency ensures clean air and water; the Department of Interior protects national parks and endangered species; the Pentagon disposes of huge quantities of hazardous materials; the Department of Energy operates nuclear reactors and disposes of radioactive waste.

Still other centers of power and influence affect federal environmental policies. The president signs or vetoes legislation, proposes agency budgets, and issues Executive Orders to control government procurement; The Office of Management and Budget prepares the president's budget and coordinates all agency rulemaking; even Vice-President Gore has responsibility for "reinventing government," which includes how regulations are made and public health and environmental risks are assessed.

Congress recognized the importance of administrative decision making on issues such as the environment and wisely afforded the public explicit opportunities to shape most agency actions. As we discussed in chapter 4, the most far-reaching agency actions are rules that have the force and effect of laws. The process of administrative rulemaking shares many characteristics with lawmaking, so it is not surprising that lobbyists employ all their advocacy skills to influence rulemaking. While agency rulemaking provides specific opportunities to submit information and make presentations before an agency, most administrative decision making is more informal, with irregular and unscheduled opportunities for lobbyists to make their voices heard. That is where the lobbyist's creativity and persistence pay off.

While lobbyists use many of the same tools of persuasion they employ in lobbying Congress to influence administrative agencies, they adapt their efforts to the peculiar nature of administrative decision making. Lobbyists begin the process of influencing administrative policymaking by recognizing that administrative agencies are composed of people who respond to information, politics, and public opinion.

People

In chapter 4 we saw how President Clinton's secretary of health and human services reversed a decision by her predecessor, who was appointed by President Bush. With a sweep of her pen, Secretary Shalala repealed the "gag rule" that had prohibited federally funded clinics from even discussing the possibility of abortion. A different secretary viewed the same issue differently from her predecessor and exercised her discretion to change the law.

The surgeon general of the United States has few responsibilities but immense power. He or she commands no army of bureaucrats; instead, the surgeon general is the nation's chief doctor and the most important medicine in his or her black bag is the power of persuasion. In 1964, Surgeon General Luther Terry announced that cigarette smoking caused cancer, and health advocacy has never been the same. Surgeon General C. Everett Koop became an outspoken AIDS-prevention advocate. More recently, Surgeon General Joycelyn Elders campaigned against teenage pregnancies. In each instance, the people in the position made a difference. Another surgeon general might have hesitated to attack the tobacco industry or shied away from public discussions of sexually transmitted diseases or teenage sexuality.

Federal environmental policies are administered primarily by the EPA and the Department of the Interior. Even without changes in the law, the Clinton administration's EPA head, Carol Browner, and Interior Secretary Bruce Babbitt produced very different policies from the Reagan administration's appointees, Ann Gorsuch Burford and James Watt.

Lobbyists know that the right people in the right positions in the administrative branch can dramatically affect issues. That is why advocates pay so much attention to lobbying the president to appoint government policymakers who are sympathetic to their viewpoints.

Information

Administrative policymakers have wide latitude in deciding how to exercise their discretion, but as we discussed in chapter 4, that discretion is much more restricted than Congress's powers (which are limited only by the Constitution). Courts generally have the power to require that administrative decisions be based on sound information. Making a persuasive and well-documented case before an administrative agency is thus a crucial first step in influencing the agency's decision making.

Information provides the bedrock foundation on which agencies must build when they formulate and implement policy initiatives. Agency heads may be personally moved by poignant stories of real people's problems, but they know they will ultimately need a sound evidentiary record to justify their decisions. Lobbyists provide that record.

Advocates "make their case" before an agency by producing statistically valid studies and surveys to demonstrate the prevalence of a problem and the effectiveness of a solution. Advocates need the kind of reliable, accurate, and convincing evidence generally required to persuade judges and juries. They must anticipate that evidence they present before agencies will be scrutinized by the agency staff and tested by their opponents in the crucible of administrative policymaking by rebuttal evidence, possibly even cross-examination.[10]

Politics

Administrative agencies face a dilemma. On one side, they are often required to follow procedures that afford the public an opportunity to make its voice heard. They are required to give serious consideration to those voices, and their decisions must be based on solid information.

On the other side, administrative agencies (even the so-called independent agencies designed to be somewhat insulated from political pressure) are political creatures. They depend for their budgets on the initial support of the president and his Office of Management and Budget, and ultimately on the legislative appropriations process. Their actions, their budgets, and even their very existence is subject to review and oversight by Congress (or state legislatures for state agencies).

Sometimes the most effective way to influence an agency's decision is to identify and persuade those with political power over the agency. Administrative agencies are always conscious of and responsive to the political landscape: the views of the president who appointed the agency head, the position of important agency constituencies (whether farmers or environmentalists), the wishes of key congressional committees and subcommittees, and the public's position on important issues.

It is not unusual for an administrative agency to announce a decision only to find itself explaining that decision to Congress at hearings to cut the agency's budget or enact legislation to reverse the agency's action. Even the best evidentiary record, demonstrating beyond doubt that a product causes cancer, may not be enough to withstand congressional oversight that focuses not on the record but on political realities, such as lost jobs.

Since administrative decision making has political roots and involves exercising considerable latitude or discretion, lobbyists use all the sources of political power over agencies, and all the tools available to influence them. Unable to influence the Federal Trade Commission directly, lobbyists for food and toy manufacturers, and national advertisers and broadcasters, turned their attention to Congress, which reined in the powers of the Federal Trade Commission when it proposed rules restricting advertising to children.[11]

Public Opinion

As we saw in chapter 6, public shaming or embarrassment is a powerful tool to influence bureaucracies that prefer to remain faceless and operate out of the limelight. Administrative agencies, unlike elected representatives, usually eschew publicity. Except for a few highly publicized actions—the secretary of the interior visiting a storm-ravaged national park and pledging to rebuild it or the EPA head announcing new clean-air regulations—agency actions usually come to public attention when the media uncover scandal or malfeasance.

School boards do not make news when they successfully educate thousands of children; instead, the media are drawn to fire-code violations or crime on school property. The Department of Agriculture, which administers the school lunch program, does not get media attention for the numerous hungry children it feeds, but rather for its attempt to reduce the number of vegetables served at school lunches by classifying ketchup as a vegetable.

Negative publicity—shining public light on administrative action (or inaction)—can force decision makers accustomed to operating in relative obscurity to justify their decisions to the public. Even decisions made with the best of intentions and the soundest evidence can be overturned in the court of public opinion.

* * *

The Food and Drug Administration's recent efforts to regulate cigarettes illustrates the interplay of these four forces. Historically, cigarettes and other tobacco products have not been regulated by the FDA, under the theory that they are neither foods nor drugs. That position remained unchallenged for many years, until an accumulation of public opinion, information about tobacco company practices, political power, and an activist FDA commissioner reexamined the issue beginning in 1993. In that year, tobacco company officials were summoned before the Health and Environment Subcommittee of the House Energy and Commerce Committee to explain their use of nicotine in cigarette manufacturing. Questions arose about whether tobacco companies manipulated the levels of nicotine in cigarettes, in an apparent effort to maintain smokers' addiction.

Food and Drug Administration Commissioner David Kessler also appeared before the subcommittee. He indicated his belief that the FDA did have the power to regulate cigarettes, but he expressed reservations about exercising that power.

While the regulatory decision was Commissioner Kessler's to make (under authority delegated to the FDA by Congress, but also subject to public comment and court and congressional review), the clear implication of his statements was that he would not act until a political consensus for regulation developed. Tobacco regulation, which was within his discretion, would be done not as a matter of law but as a matter of policy, and only when the agency knew there was public and political support for that policy.

That support finally came in 1995, when President Clinton announced his backing for Food and Drug Administration regulation of tobacco sales and promotion to youth. On August 11, 1995, the Food and Drug Administration, at the urging of President Clinton, proposed rules to regulate the sale, advertisement, and distribution of tobacco to young people.[12]

The FDA's decision whether or not to propose the rules was an unreviewable decision entrusted to the FDA commissioner. Yet the decision was clearly influenced by the changing political and public opinion climate surrounding the issue of tobacco and health. Anti-smoking, health-care, and children's advocates all lobbied the FDA and, more importantly, the president (including the First Lady) to propose the restrictions. In fact the restrictions were announced by the president and explained in a White House news conference by the FDA commissioner accompanied by the secretary of health and human services. Political forces, including the weakened power of the tobacco lobby and the president's desire to find a popular issue, combined to influence the FDA's decision.

The scene shifted from Congress to the FDA after the rules were proposed and the public comment period began. The FDA's final rules would be subject to judicial review and so would have to be supported by substantial evidence. Lobbyists seeking to influence the outcome of the rulemaking therefore focused their comments on the legal and factual questions surrounding the issue, as well as the policy reasons why regulation was or was not appropriate. Comments centered on the legal authority of the FDA to classify cigarettes as a drug or a medical device, and the effect of cigarette advertising, promotion, and distribution on adolescent smoking. Studies and surveys were submitted by proponents and opponents, each attempting to demonstrate in a statistically valid and scientifically reliable way that the rules should or should not be issued. Tobacco industry studies attempted to demonstrate that teenagers start smoking because of peer pressure, not advertising or promotion, while antismoking advocates tried equally hard to demonstrate that tobacco advertising targets underage smokers. In all, the FDA received more than 500,000 comments from the public on its proposal.[13]

The first decision the FDA must make is whether it has the legal power to issue the rules it proposed. If it concludes that it does (and that decision will doubtless be revisited by the courts and Congress), it must then determine what specific action to take and whether that action is in the broad public interest. And unlike Congress, the FDA must justify its decision, basing it on the weight of the evidence. Without evidence that its proposed restrictions will accomplish their goal, the FDA's rules cannot withstand court review.

It is interesting to note that FDA Commissioner Kessler was appointed by President George Bush. Presumably, Kessler's views on tobacco had not changed with the incoming Clinton administration. But it took a combination of Clinton's political backing, growing negative public opinion about cigarettes and tobacco companies, and new information revealed in congressional hearings and company documents to provide the impetus for action.

Influencing Corporate and Institutional Behavior

In chapter 4 we analyzed how corporate and institutional behavior can affect public policy. In this section we explore how individuals and interest groups can influence nongovernmental institutions.

Corporations are different from legislatures, bureaucrats, and courts. Corporate officials are not public servants, sworn to uphold a higher public good. Corporations are not public democracies, and their leaders are not popularly elected. Their concern is for the corporation's "bottom line" and the price of its stock. Corporations are accountable to their shareholders and their boards of directors, not to the public.

But corporations are not entirely insulated from public pressure, especially if that pressure comes from individuals or organizations with economic (or, less likely, political) power over them. Corporations are concerned with their public image, primarily as it affects their financial position. Corporations are quick to respond to allegations that their products are hazardous or defective. They recognize, either in acknowledging the possibility that the allegations are correct or in forcefully denying them, that corporate credibility—their public image—is important.

Influencing corporations requires identifying constituencies who are potential sources of influence over the corporation. Just as advocates would be unlikely to persuade a senator from New Jersey with calls and letters from citizens in New Mexico, corporations pay attention to relevant audiences. Issue advocates seeking to influence corporate or institutional policy begin by creating a power map of the corporation or institution and its key individual decision makers. For a business, those with power over the corporation include members of its board of directors, shareholders, customers, suppliers, the corporation's own employees and their labor unions, and community leaders in cities and towns where the corporation has offices or plants. For a nonprofit hospital, sources of power include doctors, nurses, board members, large donors and benefactors, insurers, and patients. For a university, those sources include students (and their parents), faculty, alumni, and contributors whose names adorn campus classrooms.

Corporations are people too. Because corporations and institutions are run by individuals, issue advocates can identify the sources of power over those individuals, including social and professional colleagues and community leaders. Like politicians, as individuals businesspersons might be swayed by their doctors or religious leaders.

While members of Congress might be influenced by the editorial pages of their hometown newspaper, the *New York Times*, *Washington Post*, *USA Today*, *Washington Times*, or *Wall Street Journal*, corporate decision makers might pay attention to other opinions. They might start with the same *Wall Street Journal*, but also heed specialized newspapers and magazines, including *Forbes*, *Fortune*, *Business Week*, even the *Harvard Business Review*. Those publications might be more appropriate targets for media advocacy, including opinion pieces and letters to the editor.

Doctors, hospital administrators, and nurses all have publications to which they look for guidance on policy issues. They may pay more attention to the *Journal of the American Medical Association* or the *New England Journal of Medicine* for news on health-care reform than the *Washington Post*. University officials deciding whether to divest tobacco company stocks from their portfolios might pay particular attention to the *Chronicle of Higher Education*. Issue advocates focus their efforts on arenas where decision makers are paying attention, not the newspapers and magazines advocates read or with which they are most familiar.

Boycotts and Bad Publicity

Interest groups recognize that the public has no vote on the business practices of corporations. At the same time, the public has the power of the purse: the ability to boycott the corporation's products. Boycotts hurt the bottom line, of course, and as such they can directly influence corporate policies.

There is a long and partially successful history of interest groups boycotting consumer product companies in an effort to change their policies on issues such as civil and human rights, labor practices, doing business with South Africa, the sale of infant formula in developing countries, and environmental policies.[14] Cesar Chavez catapulted the plight of migrant farmworkers into the limelight in the 1960s with a call for a national boycott of grapes. Recently, consumer boycotts have been successful at influencing McDonald's to stop using environmentally harmful styrofoam packaging, Burger King not to buy cattle from ranches created by destroying rainforests, and Starkist to stop killing dolphins in the process of catching tuna.[15] When Shell Oil Company announced that it planned to dispose of an obsolete offshore oil rig by sinking it in the North Sea, the environmental group Greenpeace led a consumer boycott of Shell gasoline by European drivers, which forced the company to change its plans.[16]

Boycotts also attract media attention, tarnishing images that corporations spend considerable time and resources to burnish. No corporation wants negative publicity, particularly about its products. That accounts for efforts by corporations, in response to consumer and interest-group demands, to stop purchasing goods from suppliers who use child labor and to conduct their businesses in environmentally responsible ways.[17]

Successful boycotts are often conducted as one part of a more comprehensive issue advocacy campaign. Advocates who opposed Nestlé's sale of infant formula in developing countries called for a boycott of all Nestlé products. The boycott was coordinated with congressional hearings and pressure on the World Health Organization to condemn Nestlé's practices.[18]

Corporations that find themselves the target of a boycott are far from powerless. Boycotts are difficult to organize and even more difficult to sustain. Corporations can ignore them, assuming that they will dissipate over time. Or they can mount their own public information campaigns to explain their positions and try to reassure the buying public, thereby diluting the effectiveness of the boycott.[19] Procter & Gamble's experience (discussed in chapter 6) producing studies that contradicted growing evidence that disposable diapers caused environmental damage is one example of a corporation directly addressing consumer concerns.

Sometimes it is not necessary to mobilize consumers to boycott a corporation. Negative publicity about a company's (or an industry's) practices may be enough to accomplish the goal. The Center for Science in the Public Interest (CSPI) published a series of reports on the fat content of different foods and cuisines, notably movie theater popcorn.[20] The disclosure that popcorn, often considered a nutritious snack, was being popped in unhealthful saturated oils caused a public outcry that led many theater owners to use other fats and oils. Public pressure was focused by the media attention drawn to this issue by the CSPI study.[21] Theater owners changed their practices without waiting for popcorn sales to fall.

Negative publicity (and the pressure it puts on corporate images and, by extension, the bottom line) can come in "awards" for deceptive advertising, such as the Hubbard awards CSPI issues to "shame" those it believes are the worst offenders.[22] Environmental organizations frequently publish "dirty dozen" lists of corporate polluters, hoping that public pressure—and a business's desire to avoid the negative publicity—will prompt the business to change its policies and eliminate the activities that caused them to make the list in the first place.[23] When DuPont Chemical touted its environmentally friendly practices in a series of television advertisements, an environmental organization prepared a detailed report—"Hold the Applause"—to rebut DuPont's claims and to give the public and the media an alternative view of the company's practices.[24]

Advocates concerned with excessive sex and violence on television organized letter-writing campaigns to express their displeasure directly to the networks. When that failed to get results, they turned their attention to the corporate advertisers who sponsored the programs. With only the threat of a boycott, advocates successfully convinced the advertisers that their hard-won corporate images were being tarnished by association with the objectionable content of the programs they supported. Company after company decided to spend its advertising dollars elsewhere, causing television networks to reconsider their programming decisions.[25]

Accentuating the Positive

Advocates can influence corporate behavior by accentuating the positive, by providing incentives for corporations to conform their practices to issue advocates' goals, and to receive praise for so doing.

Environmental organizations created Green Seal and Green Cross labels, which environmentally responsible corporations could affix to their products to alert consumers that they meet standards established by environmental organizations.[26] An environmental organization published a small book to enable grocery shoppers to ascertain whether their favorite brand of cereal is made by a "socially responsible corporation," as measured by the corporation's policies on a range of issues including its hiring of women and minorities and its disposal of hazardous substances.[27]

Cooperation between interest groups and corporations can lead to win/win solutions. Rug manufacturers in Germany have cooperated with children's rights groups to label rugs as made without child labor.[28] Still another environmental organization, the Environmental Defense Fund, works with businesses to develop practices that will reduce waste and pollution while lowering costs.[29]

Shareholder Actions

Corporations are ultimately responsible to their shareholders. Large and small shareholders, including unions, pension funds, religious groups, and universities, can seek changes in corporate policies either directly, by meeting with and persuading corporate management; or indirectly, by placing a proposal before the shareholders at the corporation's annual meeting.

One of the most powerful tools available to interest groups is to influence large shareholders to divest their ownership in corporations engaged in practices offensive to the interest group. Universities, state-run public employee pension plans, and religious organizations all have considerable stock portfolios. They may be susceptible to pressure to sell their holdings in companies that pollute the environment or employ child labor, for example.

Public corporations subject to the jurisdiction of the Securities and Exchange Commission are required to permit a shareholder with $1,000 in stock to place certain matters before all shareholders for a binding vote.[30] Proposals often fail to win the support of a majority of shareholders, but the accompanying publicity and public debate frequently help accomplish their ultimate goal. Religious organizations, first prompted by efforts to force corporations to stop doing business in segregated South Africa, formed the Interfaith Center on Corporate

Responsibility, to coordinate stockholder activity to influence corporate policy on a range of human and civil rights issues.[31]

Business Interests Fight Back

When interest groups attempt to influence corporate policies by organizing boycotts, mounting media and public relations campaigns to damage a corporation's image, or even opposing business or corporate interests in zoning or other governmental proceedings, businesses can fight back. They can mount their own media and public relations campaigns and can employ all the advocacy techniques at their disposal to counter the interest group.

Some business interests have adopted an even more aggressive tactic to fight back. They sue. These lawsuits typically accuse citizen or community groups of defamation, product disparagement, restraint of trade, or abuse of legal process. Most often they arise in connection with real estate development and zoning, environmental protection, and wetlands and wildlife preservation. Organized groups and individual citizens can be sued for contacting government officials, circulating petitions, writing letters to the editor, or even making public statements on a referendum or initiative.

When C. Delores Tucker and William Bennett joined forces to oppose gangsta rap—music that glorifies violence and degrades women—they targeted companies that produced and distributed music they found offensive.[32] The companies chose to fight back, suing the advocates for extortion and conspiracy to damage the companies' reputations.[33]

These lawsuits have been termed SLAPP suits: "strategic lawsuits against public participation."[34] The suits typically seek large monetary damages, but their real purpose is to inhibit, or "chill," citizen advocacy, including testimony before governmental bodies, that damages a business's interests. While most of these suits are ultimately dismissed by the courts, the costs of defending against them may be an effective deterrent to citizen action and free speech. Recognizing this, several states have enacted laws to protect citizens who make statements or appear before public bodies, such as zoning commissions, in connection with public policy issues.[35]

Business interests often think twice before "SLAPPing back" citizen advocates. The negative publicity from suing citizens participating in

public policymaking may or may not outweigh the benefits from inhibiting citizen participation in this and other matters.

Money, Politics, and Lobbying

When Congress considered the Telecommunications Reform Act, it
was inundated with lobbyists. The final shape of the bill would have a
large effect on the bottom line of some of the biggest corporations in
the country, and they spared no expense in lobbying to get their way.
Among the biggest spenders were the "baby bells," the regional bell
operating companies that were created after the breakup of AT&T.
One observer noted:

> The bells hire the most influential legal talent, and have been known to
> steal away well-connected [Capitol] Hill staffers before their rivals can.
> They recruit such visible political figures as former defense secretary
> Dick Cheney, former labor secretary Lynn Martin, and former attorney
> general Griffin Bell to lobby for them.
>   All that lobbying costs money. . . . [T]he bells' . . . spent $64 million
> on state and federal lobbying expenses in 1993. . . . Political contribu-
> tions are part of the bells' clout. . . . [T]he bells donated $14 million to
> political action committees from 1983–1984.[36]

The Telecommunications Act illustrates how money, politics, and
lobbying interact. First, moneyed interests can hire more and better
lobbyists, lawyers, public relations, and media experts to mount extensive advocacy campaigns. Second, they can contribute money to legislators, their reelection campaigns, legal defense funds, favorite
charities and foundations (particularly those within the legislator's own
state or district), even a legislator's own political action committee.

Political action committees—PACs—allow individuals to combine
their campaign contributions for maximum impact. Doctors, teachers,
and real estate agents all join together to form PACs to multiply their
individual impact on legislators. The money comes labeled from an
identifiable interest, rather than from individuals who do not have a
clear way of expressing their policy concerns. PACs, and campaign
contributions in general, allow issue advocates to support the election
(or more often reelection) of legislators with whom they agree, or
those who they seek to persuade. Money can be used to reward legisla-

tive supporters or punish legislative opponents.[37] Contributions to opponents can lessen or mute their opposition.[38]

Money most often finds its way to legislators who fall into two categories: those whose seats are "vulnerable" and those who sit on powerful committees and subcommittees.[39] One result is that committee members tend to represent the interests inherent in their committee work as much or more than their constituents.[40] That was precisely the intent of Charles Keating, the principal in the Lincoln Savings and Loan scandal, who made significant campaign contributions to five members of the Senate Banking Committee.[41]

Money builds relationships between lobbyists and legislators. It also provides "access," at least allowing a lobbyist to get a foot in the legislator's door. While information has increasingly dominated lobbying, money can still play an important role. As we saw in chapter 6, money can buy the necessary studies or surveys, or expert witnesses to support a position. And as we see in the next chapter, money can even buy grassroots supporters.

10

Grassroots Mobilization

Bill Gradison knows that the most effective tool in his advocacy arsenal is not his overstuffed Rolodex or his political action committee's war chest. It is his ability to mobilize the grassroots. Real power does not reside in Washington; it exists "outside the Beltway," where people like Myra Rosenbloom, Frank MacConnell, and Donna Rosenbaum live. Every advocacy campaign ultimately depends for its success on the support of the people: the grassroots.

While some issue campaigns arise directly out of grassroots passion and indignation, many more are conceived and directed centrally, often by Washington-based organizations. Today's campaigns are most often the result of research, analysis, and advocacy begun at the top of interest groups. Those organizations face a difficult, dual challenge. They must involve their membership—their own grassroots—in the formulation of the campaign and its goals, and they must mobilize them and the general public to achieve success.

All Power to the People

The days are long gone when all lobbyists had to do to succeed was work quietly behind the scenes on Capitol Hill and in statehouses and city councils across the country. Politicians and lobbyists have traditionally paid lip service to the idea that all power resided in the people, while continuing to do "business as usual," relying on a combination of money and power to influence public policy. But for the reasons we have analyzed in the preceding chapters, times have changed and politicians, lobbyists, and interest groups now look to the people as the real source of power. All power is with the people, and the people know it.

They know it because they find themselves in the cross-hairs, targeted by interest groups that seek their support and by politicians who compete for their votes. Legislators now look to the people for support and guidance, not just on election day, but throughout the year. Every legislator looks over his or her shoulder on every vote to learn where the people are.

And where they are is often where interest groups have urged them to be. While legislators read their mail or answer their phones to assess the breadth and depth of public opinion, interest groups are busily working to motivate their members and the public to communicate their views to legislators.

Even President Clinton knew that all his "inside" lobbying efforts could not accomplish health-care reform without the support of the people. Lobbying—legislative arm twisting, even agreements to support legislators' pet projects—could get his proposal only so far. So, taking direction from the White House, reform proponents arranged a cross-country bus caravan to bring the issue to the people and, through them, to Congress. The tour was intended to "generate enough grassroots pressure on members of Congress."[1] To persuade Congress, the president first had to persuade the public.

Congress's Ear to the Ground

In our representative democracy legislators are expected to reflect the views of their constituents. While members of Congress can, and often do, "vote their conscience," they cannot stray too far from the electorate lest they be voted out of office by a disenchanted public at the next election.[2]

How do legislators determine what the people who elected them want? It is one thing to campaign on a platform that supports the military *and* increased aid to education. But governing requires making hard choices to allocate scarce resources between worthy, competing alternatives. Should we build more Stealth bombers *or* more schools? What does the public think about *that*?

Polls, focus groups, even constituent surveys provide some information. But when issues arise in the heat of legislative debate or take unexpected twists and turns as proposals evolve, and alternatives and compromises surface, legislators put their ear to the ground and listen to the rustling of the grassroots. The noise they hear will be a combination of phone calls, postcards, faxes, telegrams, e-mail messages, and letters. They will also hear opinions expressed through issue advertisements and newspaper editorials, op-eds, letters to the editor, and a host of personal visits and meetings at home and in the capital.

On important, well-publicized issues there is never a dearth of voices to heed. But are those voices reliable indicators of the strength and depth of thoughtful constituent opinions? How can legislators discern clear expressions of public judgment amid all the background noise?

Legislators try to separate reliable from unreliable public opinion for all the reasons discussed in chapter 5. Before elected representatives take a position they believe the public supports, they must be satisfied that the public's views are well considered and take into account all the relevant information, including facts that may later emerge in the crucible of public debate and discussion on the issue. The last thing a legislator wants is to take a position based on constituent opinions only to discover, as more information is disclosed and better alternatives surface, that the public's opinion has abruptly changed.

Interest groups can provide legislators with some insight into how people view issues. Interest groups, by virtue of their expertise and long-term issue commitment can be expected to reflect more thoughtful issue judgments than the general public. A senator may turn to a statewide union or a trade association to assess how its members might react to health-care reform. The public may want price controls on prescription drugs, but what effect will controls have on the industry? Will they result in less money for research and development or less money devoted to developing important drugs that may have very small markets? Small business owners may support exemptions from certain worker safety rules, but what will be the effect on union members and employee safety?

Members also need to know how an issue affects the larger public interest. Doctors may favor malpractice law reform and lawyers may oppose it, but how will it affect the quality of health care? Welfare reform engenders strong feelings, both pro and con, but how will it affect poor people and minorities? And, if those people do not write or call their elected representatives, then who speaks for them? Interest groups can reflect the views of the voiceless or disenfranchised, whether small businesses or immigrants or welfare recipients.

Communications that Work

Every legislator knows that relatively few citizens will ever communicate with government policymakers, no matter what the issue. To do so requires time, energy, resources, knowledge, involvement, and commitment. The public must know and care enough about an issue to make time in a busy day to pick up a pen or use a computer keyboard, telephone, or fax machine. Citizens must know the name and address or phone number of their legislator. They must believe the communication will make a difference.

Despite the obstacles, people do call and write their representatives. But do those calls and letters reflect widespread constituent views? How deeply do the callers feel about the issue? Will the legislator's vote on this bill influence the citizen's vote in the next election?

Advocates and legislators are constantly looking for "communications that work." They "work" for legislators if they are reliable indicators of deeply felt, broad-based public judgment. And they work for advocates if they convince legislators that they reflect that same considered public judgment.

Over time, legislators have learned that the best gauges of reliable, considered public opinion are personal, thoughtful, spontaneous, hand-written letters.[3] The depth of issue support reflected by personal letters is as important as its breadth, since those letters are believed to come from people who have considered the consequences of their positions and are firmly committed to them. And when lawmakers receive even a handful of such letters, each one appearing to express independent judgment, informed thought, deep and passionate concern, and a focused demand for action, they correctly assume that for every one spontaneous letter, hundreds remain uncommitted to paper yet are still deeply felt.

Members of Congress often dismiss postcards and form letters as being more representative of the interest group that generated them than the individuals who transmitted them. One former member explained that Congress is "moved more by individual letters than by orchestrated campaigns. . . . [Interest groups] are under this delusion that we weigh our mail and phone calls."[4] Members of Congress appear to have learned that even if the National Rifle Association can generate 3 million telegrams or the American Association of Retired Persons 15 million postcards on issues, they are not necessarily reliable guides to the breadth and depth of public opinion.[5] And some of those letters and postcards might not even have been sent by the people whose names appear on them.[6] Still, 15 million citizen communications on any issue may be difficult to ignore.

If personal, thoughtful letters are good predictors of reliable public opinion, personal meetings—in the capital or the district—are also very effective. They too reflect considerable time, effort, and thought. People who show up at town meetings (or the legislator's office door) with knowledge of an issue and questions in hand can make a lasting impression. As can letters to the editor or opinion pieces published in the member's local and state newspapers.

Identifying the Grassroots in Your Own Backyard

The grassroots may be all-powerful, but how can interest groups mobilize them? Every interest has grassroots; the first challenge is to identify them.

Citizen Interest Groups

Organizations that represent a broad base of individuals, such as the American Association of Retired Persons, Common Cause, the Sierra Club, the American Medical Association, or the AFL-CIO start with a powerful asset: their membership. Their members presumably share many of the interest group's goals. They are readily identifiable, easy to reach, and require little or no convincing to recognize their common interest in affecting public policy. Because they have joined an interest group, they are more likely than the average citizen to understand public policymaking, how to influence the process, and the reasons why their voices are important.

Sometimes the grassroots is simply unorganized, as it often is at the local level. There may be no existing interest group opposing (or supporting) the licensing of a new nuclear power plant or taking a stand on state or local welfare or education reform plans. Grassroots organizing, particularly at the local level, is akin to "retail politics," where organizers, like politicians, seek to meet and persuade the public (or small business owners) individually and in small groups. Organizers go door to door, distributing educational literature, seeking donations, and recruiting grassroots members. They hold demonstrations, rallies, and meetings in church basements, schools, libraries, and civic clubs, all designed to organize the hitherto unorganized public.

Business Interests

While citizen membership groups have an inherent advantage in their large grassroots base, business interest groups have their own potential grassroots supporters. For some, such as the chamber of commerce or the National Federation of Independent Businesses, their grassroots start with the large and small businesses that constitute their membership. But by digging deeper, even individual businesses can unearth significant grassroots power.

When Philip Morris, a major cigarette manufacturer, sought to display its grassroots power in a Capitol Hill demonstration against higher cigarette taxes, it was able to mobilize a large and diverse presence. With its corporate headquarters and a large manufacturing plant just 100 miles south of Washington, in Richmond, Virginia, it first looked inward. There it found its own workers, who quickly joined the demonstration out of concern that increased taxes would lower cigarette sales and production, thus costing workers their jobs.[7]

Next, Philip Morris turned to its major suppliers: tobacco farmers in nearby Virginia, Maryland, and North Carolina. The farmers shared the workers' concern that higher taxes would mean less demand for cigarettes, which would lead to lower prices for their tobacco.

Richmond itself provided another source of grassroots power. Tobacco is part of Richmond's heritage; cigarette manufacturers' names adorn tall downtown buildings. Tobacco has been good to Richmond, not just by creating jobs and providing tax revenues, but by charitable contributions to schools, hospitals, and museums. City leaders, businesspersons, and merchants who depend on the large Philip Morris corporate presence were persuaded that fewer jobs would hurt the city's economy and its tax base.

Like any corporation, Philip Morris could have tapped into its shareholders, alerting them to the harmful effect higher taxes would have on the company's bottom line, and eventually its stock price. It could have turned to convenience stores whose sales might suffer if cigarette taxes were raised, or contractors and subcontractors who make cigarette paper or print package labels, and whose employees might lose their jobs if cigarette sales decreased.

A broad base of grassroots supporters allows Philip Morris to frame its opposition to higher taxes in terms of jobs, farmers, and the local economy, rather than its own economic self-interest. Like any good advocate, the company would benefit from having others make its case for it, and doing it in a way that appeals to the largest number of decision makers.

Borrowing Your Neighbor's Grassroots

Many interest groups have few, if any, members. To demonstrate widespread public support, they often turn to existing or potential coalition partners who can complement their own interest and expertise in the issue with a formidable grassroots presence. Interest groups without a grassroots presence can lobby those with a membership base, urging them to mobilize their grassroots in support of an issue.

Mobilizing Your Grassroots

Much of an issue advocate's work is building the outside grassroots pressure to support inside lobbying activities. If lobbyists are the field generals, the grassroots are the troops.

Grassroots power is a function of both the sheer number of concerned individuals and the strength and depth of their concern. The two questions every decision maker wants answered are: how many people care about the issue, and how much do they care about it? It is the issue advocate's job to mobilize the grassroots in a way that demonstrates to decision makers that many people care deeply about the issue.

Lobbyists cannot rely for their persuasive power solely on the claim that they represent an interest group whose many members support (or oppose) a bill; instead, they must mobilize their organization's members, one member at a time. Legislators know, as we learned in chapter 3, that individuals join interest groups for many different reasons, most having nothing to do with influencing public policy. They know that no lobbyist can speak for all the members of any interest group, particularly if it is a large, broad-based group, with many issues on its agenda.

Once Philip Morris, or any interest group, identifies and educates its grassroots base about an issue and its impact on them, the next step is to mobilize them to demonstrate a broad base of popular support. The advocates' task is to convince decision makers that for every letter or phone call they receive, many more supporters are waiting in the wings, and each call or letter represents the firm, reliable judgment of an individual who has thought the issue through and is firmly convinced of his or her position.

To accomplish this goal, advocates must first overcome the resistances individuals have to communicating with decision makers: failing to understand an issue, how it affects them, and how they can influence the decision-making process. Interest groups also have to deal with the problem (discussed in chapter 3) that their members join their organization for many different reasons, only a few of which may be to change public policy. People are busy and fully engaged, yet they do make time for advocacy when they care about an issue and feel they can have an impact. Grassroots supporters must be educated about the issue, motivated to communicate, and have the tools necessary to become effective advocates in their own right.

"The Chicken Little" strategy—telling grassroots supporters that unless they act immediately, the sky will fall—might work once. Individuals might sign a petition or fill out a postcard or even make a phone call. But when the sky does not fall and the time comes to go back to the grassroots, the same strategy probably will not work a second time. What does work is building an advocacy infrastructure, complete with an internal communications network and a feedback mechanism.

Newsletters and Education

Before people can be mobilized, they must first be energized. Interest groups cannot expect their members to respond to alarm bells and calls to action without first understanding how an issue affects them. Members want and need to know why they should be involved in making change. What is at stake for them? How will change affect, for better or for worse, their environment, freedom, health, or financial well-being?

The most effective communication networks try to answer these questions by focusing on long-term education of the grassroots. Just as public policy issues are rarely addressed and resolved in a single effort, the best grassroots advocates will understand an issue and its history and be committed to it for the long term. That is as true for business interests pursuing regulatory relief as it is for environmentalists seeking clean air or union members fighting for greater workplace safety.

There is no substitute for an interactive communications infrastructure that builds grassroots capacity to change public policy. A cornerstone of such a structure is regular communications with the grassroots, beginning with newsletters or magazines that analyze public policy issues and their dynamics. They help the grassroots understand the issue and how it affects the organization and its members, how and where the issue is being addressed, who holds the power to affect the issue, and how the grassroots can be involved in the public policymaking process.

The best communication networks build on the trust that exists between members and the organizations or groups they have elected to join. Their goal is to build a cadre of informed, committed grassroots advocates who understand and pay regular attention to issues and the public policymaking process. Educated and informed grassroots members will understand the significance of an urgent call to action and be responsive even after a crucial vote or an interim battle is lost. They will understand an issue's shifting dynamics as well as the intricacies of the legislative or the administrative process.

Action Alerts

Newsletters or magazines can educate the organization's members about issues, build momentum, and occasionally prod them to take specific actions. But when the focus turns to influencing decision makers, advocates employ a system of "action alerts." These alerts can be disseminated by mail, phone, fax, e-mail, satellite conferences, or even in person at meetings and conferences.

Action alerts are typically addressed to people already informed about an issue and the policymaking process and predisposed to take the action described, usually contacting a decision maker. Alerts combine a sense of urgency ("act now") with a description of what is at stake ("to keep the water supply clean and safe"). They provide recipients with what they need to know about the action and the targeted decision maker and make taking the action as simple as possible.

Larger and wealthier organizations can do more than merely transmit an action alert to their grassroots and wait for something to happen. Organizations can establish networks or "trees" of core activists. They can assign a national "field" director to mobilize state directors, who in turn mobilize county or local directors. At each level, field directors are responsible for getting the word out to members and the grassroots about the urgency of taking the action described in the alert.[8] They may even follow up to make sure members take action and to analyze the decision makers' responses.

When the Christian Coalition opposed the 1994 lobby reform bill, fearing it would limit its ability to lobby Congress, it mobilized nearly 250,000 people to communicate their opposition to Congress using a combination of telephone trees, faxes, computer bulletin boards, and talk radio. It did it all in twenty-four hours, and Congress shelved the bill.[9]

Different kinds of alerts can be tailored to different types of members or grassroots supporters. A pharmaceutical manufacturer opposing price controls on prescription drugs described the negative effect of price controls on its stock price in an alert addressed to shareholders and included with shareholders' quarterly dividend checks to emphasize its message.[10] An insurance company sent a memorandum to its employees and insurance agents asking them to oppose health-care reform because of its economic effect on the company.[11] A hospital association sent each of its 4,900 hospital administrator-members a lobbying kit, with advice on how to mobilize the approximately 4 million hospital employees and volunteers to oppose health-care reform.[12]

Targeted alerts might ask different members to take particular actions, based on their commitment to or perspective on an issue. A trade association might have one message for its large business members and another for its small business members. Not only can it target members' most immediate concerns, but it can generate a broader base of communications to decision makers.

Some grassroots members may be asked to visit a decision maker with whom they have a personal, professional, or campaign relationship (such as by being a financial contributor). Others may be asked to write a letter to the editor or meet with a local or national newspaper's editorial board. The most activist grassroots members could be educated and trained to teach advocacy techniques to others.

Computer and telephone technology are useful tools to mobilize the grassroots. The Internet, with its gopher and worldwide web sites, is replete with electronic action alerts. Cheap and readily available technology allows organizations to transmit electronic messages instantaneously to thousands of on-line grassroots activists. Organizations such as the National Association of Manufacturers maintain their own private electronic networks, providing public policy information and grassroots alerts to interested members.[13] Computer databases allow issue advocates to select grassroots members in key legislative districts and mobilize them with carefully tailored alerts.

A final but often neglected element of alert networks is feedback and coordination. Just as "inside" lobbying requires careful targeting of decision makers and collecting and sharing information and "political intelligence," mobilizing the grassroots requires feedback and information exchange. What responses are grassroots members receiving to their communications with lawmakers? Which decision makers appear receptive to which arguments? Who still needs to be persuaded?

And because grassroots activists need constant reassurance and a sense that they are making a difference, grassroots mobilizers provide supporters with information about how their actions affect policy decisions. While successes can be empowering, interim setbacks can lay the groundwork for more intensive future efforts.

Which Way is Up?

In 1988 the American Association of Retired Persons (AARP), the nation's second-largest interest group and the main lobbying arm for seniors, celebrated the passage of legislation to provide seniors with additional Medicare benefits, including coverage for "catastrophic" health problems. AARP had lobbied long and hard for the law, and its efforts were largely responsible for its enactment.

But there was one minor problem: senior citizens, whom the law was intended to benefit, wanted no part of it. They objected to paying additional taxes for benefits many of them did not think they needed or for which they were already insured. Seniors rose up in protest, nearly assaulting Congressman Dan Rostenkowski, who chaired the House Ways and Means Committee, which drafted the bill, at a town meeting. In 1989, just sixteen months after the law was passed overwhelmingly, Congress heeded the grassroots voices and repealed it.[14]

How did the largest and most powerful senior citizens' lobby find itself in such an awkward position? By ignoring its grassroots and running its organization from the top down, rather than from the bottom up. Senator Phil Gramm (D-Tex) described the AARP's role as the "boy scout who sees a little old lady standing on the corner who happens to be going the other way, but he decides he is taking her across the street whether she wants to go or not."[15]

The AARP ignored a fundamental principle of grassroots mobilization. The group's leaders assumed that the organization could speak for its members.

Individuals join together in voluntary associations for many different reasons. Just as a coalition brings together individuals and organizations whose sole common ground is their support for the objectives of the coalition, so too an interest group such as the AARP often attracts as members individuals with diverse interests whose only point of agreement is their affiliation with the organization. Each new campaign the organization undertakes requires many of the same skills needed to form and manage a coalition. There is no assurance that an organization's members will all agree on the objectives of the campaign, at least not without a concerted effort to educate them and keep them focused on the campaign's objectives.

The AARP is not alone in failing to engage in an ongoing consultative process to craft positions on public policy. The process begins with listening attentively to members' voices and their concerns and then setting short- and long-term policy objectives accordingly.

Not only do supporters want to be heard, they want to listen and learn. An effective, organic, consultative process rewards and refreshes the inside advocate at the same time as it educates and invigorates the grassroots. It gives the organization's members a stake in the policy goals of the organization and an opportunity to shape them. Too often, interest groups are perceived as setting policy goals from the top down, with little or no prior consultation with the grassroots.

Many grassroots organizations send their lobbyists into the field to share their experiences with their members, as well as to listen and answer questions. Large organizations have an opportunity to become "real people" in the eyes of their members, and lobbyists get a first-hand opportunity to gauge the breadth and depth of grassroots concern on an issue.

The best grassroots mobilizers constantly check and recheck their positions with the grassroots, particularly in the final stages of the policymaking process, when alternatives and compromises are accepted or rejected. Grassroots members often have valuable information about how to influence and persuade their representatives, since they will inevitably know the member and the state or district as well or better than the Washington-based lobbyist. Still other organizations "connect" their grassroots activists electronically, taking advantage of the latest computer networking technology to connect activists to each other and to Washington-based advocates.

Member surveys, regional conferences (in-person or by satellite), field visits, polls, focus groups, newsletters, and reader responses can all supplement the information-gathering activities of issue advocates who represent—and therefore must be in touch with—the grassroots. Mobilizing the grassroots means making sure they get the information they need in a timely fashion to make intelligent choices. It means cultivating and developing the same high-quality opinion in one's own grassroots that legislators and decision makers seek in those they represent. It means resisting the tendency to believe that interest-group leaders know what is best for those they represent. It means respecting and encouraging the democratic voices of the interest-group's members. But it does not mean merely polling members and then taking positions. Interest groups, like elected and appointed political leaders, have an obligation to educate and lead their members.

Yet interest groups are rarely models of democracy. Policy is often determined by a small directorate of individuals, whether businesspeople acting for a trade association or an unelected board of directors deciding what is best for seniors or consumers. Although many organizations consult member surveys to get a general idea of their concerns, and all are careful not to stray too far from their membership base, in most cases policy is set in the national office by an appointed staff or an elected or appointed board. The AARP's experience should give many organizations pause, however, and convince them that policy setting works best when interest-group leaders are in close touch with their members and their concerns.

Mobilizing the Grass Tops

The greenest grassroots are the "grass tops": especially persuasive or powerful people who have a special relationship with, or power over, decision makers. As we discussed in chapter 2, these individuals include campaign contributors; business, community, or interest-group leaders; local or state legislators; or academic or other experts.

Grassroots mobilizers can identify and recruit the grass tops to help arrange one-on-one meetings and calls with congresspersons, organize town meetings, place op-ed pieces, and sponsor community-related events that showcase these individuals' views. One consulting firm reportedly charges $350 to $500 for each letter or call generated by a community leader. Actual meetings cost $5,000 to $9,000, or more, per meeting.[16] Grass-tops mobilization is expensive because it is time-consuming and highly selective.

Mobilizing the grass tops requires an in-depth knowledge of the targeted decision maker—who and what makes him or her tick. For health-care reform, grass tops may be hospital trustees, who are "respected business and community leaders."[17] For "unfunded mandates" or other "states' rights" issues, it may be state legislators or even the governor.

Effective grass-tops campaigns can use respected local or community voices to bolster national issue advocacy. While members of Congress are elected by state or district, their work (particularly in committees) has a national focus. A national debate may rage over litigation reform, with large interest groups lobbying Congress and advertising for grassroots support, but a key business leader in the member's district may have more influence over the member's vote than all the national interest-group lobbyists and generated faxes and phone calls.

Marketing the Issue to the Public

An advocate's own grassroots are always the first mobilization target because they are easier to identify and persuade than the general public. But to succeed, advocates need to build the broadest possible base of public support. For that, they turn to the general public.

Mobilizing the public amounts to issue marketing. Just as any consumer product company combines a range of tactics (direct mail, in-store displays, media advertising, and discounting and couponing) as incentives to purchase a product, issue advocates employ a variety of strategies to get the public to "buy" their product.

Going Door to Door

The most effective method to reach beyond an organization's own members or grassroots is through one-on-one contacts: one committed individual persuades another. Grassroots citizen groups post flyers in libraries, community centers, bowling alleys, supermarkets, or church basements (and increasingly on the Internet); neighbors go door to door handing out materials and informing the community about local or national issues; groups hold informal civic meetings and invite experts and local leaders to discuss issues with the public.

Citizen interest groups look for supporters in likely places. Environmentalists set up tables at Earth Day concerts and hold rallies and distribute literature at toxic waste dumps. They ask manufacturers of organic products to include inserts in their packaging asking customers—likely supporters—to write Congress to support environmentally friendly legislation.

Business interests employ the same tactics to identify likely supporters. Beer and wine companies approach restaurants and liquor stores asking them to post signs asking their customers to oppose increases in alcohol taxes. An airline prints the address of the state's senators on the back of its boarding passes to get passengers to urge Congress to support airline subsidies for rural areas.[18]

When Congress required banks to withhold income tax from bank interest, banks distributed postcards in their lobbies and at teller windows, and included them in customer statements, asking depositors to write to Congress urging it to repeal the withholding law. Twenty-two million people responded, and Congress repealed the withholding requirement.[19]

Expanding the Base

Having exhausted the opportunities for one-on-one contacts with potential grassroots supporters, issue advocates turn from "retail" to "wholesale" grassroots mobilization. They search for supporters amid the mass of citizens.

Identifying the Target

"Targeted issue marketing" relies on direct communications with potential grassroots supporters, by mail or by telephone. The twin principles of targeted issue marketing are that advocates cannot reach everyone and that they do not have to. No one, no matter how wealthy, can reach every citizen. Fortunately, effective grassroots advocacy depends only on finding and mobilizing a representatives sampling of supporters. A small number of carefully chosen, articulate advocates in the state or legislative district of a "swing vote" or powerful legislative committee chair can suffice. (Of course, it does not hurt to inundate decision makers with phone calls, letters, faxes, telegrams, and e-mails. "Mass issue marketing," usually conducted through advertising and discussed later in this chapter, often goes hand in hand with more narrowly targeted issue marketing.)

Advocates can acquire huge databases of names and addresses that combine public information culled from voter registration records (such as age, gender, and party affiliation) with proprietary data about consumer preferences, income level, marital status, motor vehicle ownership, and a host of other personal and social characteristics. The power of computers and databases to maintain information and sort it by dozens of variables can provide issue advocates with a targeted list of grassroots prospects that match a series of criteria.[20]

With hundreds of variables potentially included in a database, there are endless possibilities for targeting grassroots prospects and tailoring messages to each. Only time and money limit the choices. Advocates could, for example, target married women between the ages of thirty-five and forty who live in the first congressional district in Georgia, drive Volvos, have no children, own their own home, and did not vote in the last presidential election. But why would they? Because their focus groups and polling data reveal that they are likely supporters.

Focusing the Aim

Polling data and focus groups enable grassroots advocates to decide who to target and how to appeal to them. Even if advocates had the necessary resources, it would be foolish to try to reach individually every citizen in every legislative district. And when they do not target, advocates risk reaching more grassroots opponents than supporters, particularly when advocates represent an inherently narrow interest or viewpoint.

That is why advocates begin to build a grassroots campaign by learning as much as they can about the characteristics of their supporters from polling and focus-group data. Proponents of health-care re-form—or opponents of welfare reform—can identify categories and subcategories of likely supporters by age, gender, social, geographic, consumer, and other characteristics. They can then use that informa-tion to extract a list of targets who match those characteristics from an extensive database of names and addresses.

There will likely be many targeted groups and subgroups. While 55 percent of all women may, hypothetically, support health-care reform, a more refined analysis might reveal that 60 percent of women over thirty support it. Further refinements could allow precision targeting of increasingly narrower categories of citizens, where support could be expected to approach 90 percent. Theoretically, nine out of every ten individuals targeted could be expected to be supporters.

But focus groups allow advocates to go one step further. By testing themes and messages with different groups and subgroups, it is possi-ble to "narrowcast" messages to meet particular citizens' concerns and predispositions. Focus groups might reveal that women may respond better to health-care-reform arguments framed in terms of caring for children and the elderly poor, while men might be more concerned about coverage for preexisting medical conditions. Carefully targeted and crafted appeals could use different messages to appeal to different audiences.

Focus-group and polling data might reveal that a certain group is generally unsupportive of a position. For example, seniors might be unlikely to support health-care reform. Legislators representing dis-tricts or states with substantial senior citizen populations might be expected, therefore, to oppose reform. A grassroots supporter of re-form could, however, target particular subgroups of seniors known to contain unusually high percentages of supporters, such as men who have never married or women who are registered as political indepen-dents. After convening appropriate focus groups, advocates could use messages that appeal to those audiences. The resulting communica-tions to decision makers from even a small number of unlikely sup-porters could cause decision makers to rethink their positions.

Applying the results of focus groups to information in their databases enables grassroots mobilizers to target those they seek to persuade and craft the messages most likely to do the job. In addition to letters sent to targets, grassroots advocates increasingly employ tele-phone solicitors to reach their targets. Armed with a carefully constructed list of "prospects," they are often able personally to persuade the caller to take action. And to make sure that the caller does not put off writing a letter or lose the address, telephone "patch throughs" or "direct connects" enable the grassroots advocate to connect the caller directly and immediately with his or her legislator at no cost or effort to the caller.[21] The legislator may never know that the citizen did not take the time and go to the expense to make the call himself or herself.

Whether by mail or phone, advocates can generate a seemingly spontaneous outpouring of public support or opposition. For example, in 1991 the American Bankers' Association opposed legislation that would have forced its members to lower their credit card rates. By hiring a Washington-based grassroots lobbying firm, the association was able, over just a four-day period, to generate nearly 10,000 citizen calls to members of Congress, effectively killing the bill.[22]

While the American Bankers' Association paid $400,000 to the firm that generated those calls, that number pales in comparison to recent estimates of money spent on grassroots lobbying. In 1993–94, approximately $790 million was spent at the local, state, and federal levels.[23]

Painting the Grass Green

Astroturf has the look and feel of real grass, but it is a synthetic compound with no roots and no organic structure. In our noisy and crowded democracy, officials elected and appointed to represent the public may be unable to discern real grassroots support from manufactured Astroturf.

Decision makers understand that few individuals know or care enough about an issue to articulate their views. They therefore rely on thoughtful, handwritten letters as important predictors of underlying grassroots sentiment. Of course, grassroots advocates know this too, and those without genuine grassroots of their own attempt to mobilize popular support with the look and feel of real grassroots. It is no surprise, therefore, that they now generate a torrent of manufactured public support designed to resemble personal, thoughtful, handwritten letters. Grassroots mobilizers and the decision makers they seek to influence are engaged in an elaborate and expensive game of cat and mouse. Advocates try to mobilize citizens in such numbers and in such a manner as to give decision makers the illusion that there is broad and deep support for an issue. Both sides know that relatively few people will ever communicate with decision makers. If advocates can mobilize a large proportion of a small minority of supporters, they can give the impression that support is deeper and broader than it actually is.

For instance, suppose advocates' polls reveal that only 30 percent of the public supports their position, while 70 percent oppose it. On most issues, fewer than 1 percent of the public will ever write or call their elected representative to express their views. One percent of the opposition's 70 percent amounts to .7 percent of the general population who could be expected to express their views.

Now suppose advocates conduct a targeted grassroots campaign and mobilize 10 percent of the 30 percent who support their position. The result (as long as the opposition does not use the same tactics) is that 3 percent of the population will communicate their support to decision makers, giving the impression that more than four times as many people—3 percent versus .7 percent—support the position than oppose it. In fact, the public opposes it by more than two to one.

There are several ways to give the impression that support is broader and deeper than it actually is. Grassroots mobilizers stimulate different kinds of communications—letters, e-mail, phone calls, telegrams, postcards (with an emphasis on thoughtful, personal letters)—to give the illusion of randomness and dispel the impression that communications are generated, rather than spontaneous. Mobilization is often conducted in waves separated by days or weeks so that all communications do not arrive in legislators' offices at the same time.

Citizens can be encouraged to send letters to members of Congress in Washington or in their district offices. Some people can be enlisted to carry signs or ask questions at town hall meetings or on radio call-in shows where the member is a guest. Taken together, these tactics are designed to give the member the impression that "everyone back home" is talking about your issue, from your perspective.

Issue advocates can generate letters from constituents of different ages, races, sexes, and political affiliations, with those characteristics prominently mentioned in the letter. Opponents of health-care reform might stimulate letters from students, seniors, and small businesspeople. Each group or subgroup could be targeted with arguments that meet its particular concerns (as revealed through polls and focus groups) about health-care reform. And each could be asked to articulate its concerns—to frame them—in different ways. Seniors might be asked to argue that reform would eliminate their choice of doctors.

Small businesspeople could be recruited to express their concerns that reform would cause them to eliminate jobs. Students could be enlisted to complain about the impending decline in the quality of medical care.

Advocates try to make it difficult for decision makers to pigeonhole their grassroots supporters. When a large, well-known environmental organization, such as the Sierra Club, asks its members to tell Congress to support clean-air legislation, it instructs them not to mention their organizational affiliation. The Sierra Club's Washington lobbyists can make the organization's position clear "inside the Beltway." But the congressperson who receives thousands of letters from people who do not disclose that the Sierra Club asked them to write, may never know that the communications were not spontaneous outpourings from a broadly representative sampling of "ordinary citizens."

Deloitte & Touche, an accounting firm, urged its employees to write to Congress opposing a particular bill. The firm told its employees to use their home addresses "with no indication of your firm affiliation" so that the mailing would appear to be "an outpouring of constituent requests."[24] In that way the firm hoped to "paint the grass green," giving the impression of spontaneous, random constituent concern, rather than an orchestrated and generated campaign on the part of one narrow interest. Deloitte knew that no matter how many letters it generated from its own employees, customers, and suppliers, they would be much less effective—and more easily pigeonholed and ignored—if they were written on the firm's stationery.[25]

The latest computer software programs can effectively emulate personal hand written letters, attach signatures, and then print out thousands of "originals" in a matter of hours. In addition, decision makers at the state and national levels are moving toward full Internet accessibility. In the near future, grassroots advocates will be able to flood legislative computer systems with thousands of generated e-mail messages.

All these techniques are designed to minimize the "Astroturf effect" of grassroots lobbying.

Sometimes, grassroots members are inadvertent or even reluctant advocates. For example, a supporter of economic reform held a "contest," offering dinner and drinks as a prize. Entrants had to write a letter to a member of Congress expressing support for the issue to enter. They were encouraged to "use different stationery—change the words—and mail one every few days." Workers at a Pittsburgh steel plant were ordered to write letters to Congress supporting steel import quotas. When one worker refused, he was told he would lose his job unless he complied.[26]

Sometimes, grassroots supporters do not exist at all. In 1995, congressional offices were besieged with nearly identical telegrams from citizens purportedly supporting telecommunications law reform. Some congressional aides doubted that so many people could care so passionately about such an obscure issue, so they randomly contacted people who sent the telegrams. Few remembered sending or authorizing the telegrams. One aide even noticed her own name on a telegram addressed to her boss.[27] One observer speculated that "as many as half of 600,000 telegrams sent to Congress to support long-distance telephone companies were sent without proper authorization."[28]

In another example, congressional aides were surprised by the torrent of telegrams from seniors supporting the congressional Republicans' 1995 Medicare cuts. After all, most senior citizens' organizations had opposed the cuts. When the aides called a sample of seniors whose names appeared on telegrams, less than 15 percent endorsed the position described in the telegram. The telegrams had been prepared and sent by the United Seniors' Association, which was a creature of a direct-mail fund raiser.[29]

Advertising for Advocates: The Truth, The Half Truth, and Anything Else That Works

With so much as stake, and so much money at their disposal, it is not surprising that many issue advocates have turned to advertising as the grassroots mobilization tool of choice. Unlike direct issue marketing, advertising can reach a broad segment of the public. And advertisers can still target their markets by choosing appropriate media outlets, programs, and times of day that have "desirable demographics," and then matching the message to the expected audience.

Advertising for grassroots supporters is often no different from businesses advertising for customers. Each typically employs a range of media including billboards, radio, television, newspapers, and magazines. All the creativity, production values, and focus-group testing that go into selling toothpaste or beer go into advertisements for or against public policy initiatives. Instead of imploring the audience to purchase a product, issue advertisements include "tear off coupons," 800 telephone numbers, or congressional addresses and phone numbers. Instead of making a product appealing, issue advocates make a policy choice attractive. Like all advertisers, their goal is to get the public to "just do it."

Full-page newspaper advertisements (or thirty- to sixty-second radio or television commercials) are carefully tested for their impact on targeted audiences. Most often, issue advertisements funded, directly or indirectly, by economic interests are produced under the aegis of a public interest-sounding organization. They use appealing, citizen-friendly characters to importune the audience to contact a decision maker. They combine a public interest-sounding argument with a tug on the heartstrings. And they play to emotions such as fear, anger, and outrage, giving the public a sense of hope and possibilities if only citizens contact their legislators immediately to support or oppose the bill[30] (see Figure 6).

The most famous issue advertisements are the "Harry and Louise" ads funded by the Health Insurance Association of America (HIAA) to oppose President Clinton's health-care-reform plan.[31]

In a memorable exchange, that folksy couple discussed their concerns with the Clinton plan:

Louise: This plan forces us to buy our insurance through these new mandatory Government alliances.
Harry: Run by tens of thousands of new bureaucrats.
Louise: Another billion dollar bureaucracy.[32]

Other "Harry and Louise" advertisements found the couple complaining that the plan would take away their right to choose their own doctor. The advertisements noted that they were produced by the Coalition for Health Insurance Choices (CHIC). They asked the public to call CHIC for more information and gave the impression that CHIC was a broad-based citizens' group. But CHIC was funded by the HIAA and most of its members were insurance companies (and their representatives), facts not disclosed in the advertisements.[33]

Grassroots issue advertisements such as the "Harry and Louise" ads succeed in part because the public does not know, until the end, who produced them, and even then, the identity of the real interested parties is often obscured by inclusive-sounding organizational names. Viewers or readers may be unsure of the economic interest that produced the ad, solicited their participation, and stands to benefit from the actions citizens take.

Figure 6.

Is it reasonable for families in Lancaster, Parma and Spartanburg to pay more in taxes just so residents of Aspen, Hilton Head and Marco Island can have cheaper light bills?

L AST NOVEMBER, America turned Congress upside down. Voters had had enough of politicians who waste their tax money on programs that don't make sense — such as corporate welfare that gives subsidies to profitable companies.

Who benefits from these subsidies? The residents of Aspen, Colorado; Hilton Head, South Carolina; and Marco Island, Florida — to name a few. How does this happen? Year after year, the federal government gives away more than $1 billion in direct subsidies to electric cooperatives and government-owned utilities that operate in such communities.

Today, these subsidies are outdated and wasteful. Middle-class taxpayers in Lancaster, Parma and Spartanburg — and across the nation, for that matter — can't afford to pick up the tab any longer. Congress can and should prove to them that it means business by ending these welfare subsidies. It's time for the electric cooperatives and government-owned utilities to compete for business the way the rest of America competes: by standing on their own.

Citizens for a Sound Economy Foundation
~ The marketplace for market-based thinking ~
1250 H Street, N.W. • Suite 700 • Washington, D.C. 20005-3908 • Tel: 202/783-3870

Reprinted with permission

As tort reform reached the floor of the House of Representatives, supporters aired a television commercial showing boys and girls playing Little League baseball, warning that liability lawsuits could take away their baseball fields. The ad ended with an impassioned plea from a young girl saying, "Please, Congress, protect us all" from lawsuit abuse.[34] Briefly appearing fine print at the start of the advertisement disclosed that it was paid for by the Chamber of Commerce and the National Federation of Independent Businesses. But the ad ended with a plea for the public to call an 800 number to register their approval for tort reform. Bold print announced that the ad was produced on behalf of "Citizens for Lawsuit Sanity."

Citizens for a Sound Economy, funded in part by Cigna (an insurance company) and R.J. Reynolds (a tobacco company), produced advertisements supporting tort reform, with an "affable-looking old man who portrays the legal system as a circus controlled by lawyers and plaintiffs looking for easy money. 'I tell you the system is out of whack,' he says." But the ad does not disclose that it was funded by tobacco and insurance companies.[35]

Issue advertisements can play fast and loose with the truth, misleading the public or distorting the facts.[36] Unlike toothpaste purveyors whose advertisements are policed for accuracy and fairness by federal and state governmental agencies, no government agency monitors issue ads. While political campaign commercials increasingly undergo media scrutiny for accuracy (and are required to disclose who paid for the ad), only recently have the media examined the accuracy of claims made in issue ads.[37] The public is left to its own devices to sort out misleading, contradictory claims and discern the real interests behind issue advertisements.

Potemkin Interest Groups

When is an interest group not what it seems? More often than one would suspect, judging from the proliferation of "consumer-friendly" organizational names that business interests create to advance their interests.

The Coalition for Vehicle Choice, Alliance for Environment and Resources, Committee for a Constructive Tomorrow, Citizens for the Defense of Free Enterprise, Defenders of Property Rights, Mothers' Watch, Multiple Use Land Alliance, Oregonians for Food and Shelter,

People for the West!, Putting People First, Coalition for Health Insurance Choices, Citizens for a Sound Economy, Citizens for Lawsuit Sanity, and the Alliance for Energy Security were all created, funded, and promoted by business interests.[38] Despite their inclusive-sounding names, they typically have few, if any, citizen members.

Potemkin villages were nothing more than false fronts attached to dilapidated structures erected to convince the czar that prosperous peasants existed. Potemkin interest groups appear to represent the broad public interest, but in reality they are little more than fronts for the business interests that created them. They are created and promoted to give the public and decision makers the false impression of broad-based public support for an issue.

Creating False Fronts

The dark and stealthy nature of lobbying did not, on first blush, transfer well to mass media advertisements and grassroots mobilization. At least not until powerful (yet unpopular) moneyed interests learned to cloak themselves in the guise of citizen groups. Advertisements designed to make the case for Superfund reform portray mom and pop businesses as the victims of an overzealous law. But the prime movers behind reform are large companies and their equally powerful insurance companies. Tort reform carries the same message, with Girl Scouts and Little League teams portrayed as the victims of a legal system run amok, when the real beneficiaries of tort reform are more likely to be large pharmaceutical manufacturers and automobile companies.

False-front groups are a way for inherently narrow interests—usually businesses—to broaden their appeal to the general public. Instead of advocating on behalf of their own narrow self-interest, they attempt to build support by reframing the issue: *away* from requiring higher mileage automobiles *toward* affording car buyers "vehicle choice"; *away* from eliminating price controls on natural gas *toward* "energy security"; *away* from making health care affordable and available *toward* "choice" of doctors and insurers. In each case, it is *away* from an economic benefit to a small group and *toward* a public benefit for a large group.

Front groups mimic the success of more representative citizen groups. They frequently arise to counteract the power of citizen groups, such as the environmental movement's ability to win popular and legislative support for its policy agenda. Opposition forces formed front groups, collectively identified as the "wise use" or "property rights" movement. Using a combination of think tanks, legal foundations, and Potemkin interest groups, they advance farming, fishing, logging, oil and gas, real estate, and other business interests. They do so with a message calculated to appeal to a broad public interest.

Many of the groups involved in the "wise use" movement provide a counterweight to the growing influence of the grassroots environmental movement. They appeal broadly to citizens by invoking concepts such as wise use (who can oppose "wise use" of land?) or sustainable development or property rights.[39] They often adopt names that are confusingly similar to citizen groups, such as the Sahara (rather than the Sierra) Club.

For example, The Alliance for Energy Security was created by the Natural Gas Suppliers' Association to lobby for industry deregulation. But many members of the alliance did not know it was an industry-sponsored group, and none of its materials identified its backers. Representative Philip R. Sharp's (D-Ind.) comments on the alliance are broadly applicable to all such fronts: "It appears that there was a deliberate attempt to mislead citizens about the sponsors of this effort and a lack of integrity about defining clearly the funding and interests of the sponsors."[40]

The Coalition for Health Insurance Choices was a construct of the public relations arm of the Health Insurance Association of America. Almost all its listed members were employees and family members of health insurance companies. They did not elect or endorse the group's leaders, who were selected and hired by the insurance companies' trade association. The organization's positions were dictated by the trade association; its money came, not from individual donations, but from the trade association's war chest.[41] Families USA, an independent consumer advocacy organization, labeled the coalition "a puppet front created, funded and fully controlled [by the insurance industry to] tear the guts out of health reform."[42]

The Pharmaceutical Manufacturers' Association (PMA), which opposed price controls on prescription drugs, created the Physician's Committee for Quality Medical Care, to lobby against controls. Congressman Pete Stark (D-Calif.), who chaired the House Ways and Means Subcommittee on Health, said "no one has ever heard of the group, which is a phony front for the PMA." He told his colleagues that "you will probably have to spend hours of staff time answering angry letters from concerned retired persons in your district because the PMA has misled and scared them into writing." PMA denied that the doctor who set up the group was a "front," although it admitted that PMA underwrote the cost of the group's mailing.[43]

The Coalition for Vehicle Choice (CVC), created by automakers in 1990, purports to be a diverse organization made up of "automotive, insurance, and other business, consumer, farm and safety organizations." The group lobbies against increased federal fuel efficiency (Corporate Average Fuel Economy) standards. However, at least one quarter of its 4,600 members work for the auto industry and ten of its state chapters are run by public relations or lobbying firms receiving their funding from automobile manufacturers.[44]

In 1983, utility companies, hoping to defeat a Clean Air Act acid rain amendment, formed Citizens for Sensible Control of Acid Rain (CSCAR). Over a period of months, CSCAR deluged Congress with mail and phone calls urging that the amendment be defeated. But CSCAR had no citizen members at all: the entire group was funded and operated by at least ten electric and coal utilities. The money for its lobbying campaign came indirectly from utility consumers through their utility bills, but, of course, CSCAR did not poll those consumers on their views of acid rain.[45]

Tobacco companies created the National Coalition Against Crime and Tobacco Smuggling, which issued a report predicting rising crime because higher tobacco taxes would lead to cigarette smuggling from Mexico.[46] With money from tobacco companies and support from a tobacco company public relations firm, they created the National Smokers' Alliance, a "smokers' rights" organization that capitalized on popular support for citizen "rights," while advancing tobacco companies' economic interests.[47]

* * *

By creating front groups, moneyed interests attempt to convince citizens and decision makers that there is genuine grassroots sentiment for the causes they espouse. Citizens become confused about who is truly working in their interest (and where the real public interest lies) and may be less likely to participate at all. False fronts, flush with cash, can drown out more credible and truly representative grassroots organizations. These organizations can use the patina of a genuine grassroots group to legitimize their participation in public debates as representatives of the "public interest." Finally, they can confuse decision makers by muddying the waters, giving the appearance that public opinion is more divided than it actually is.[48]

Recruiting Grassroots Organizations

Moneyed interests recognize that it is to their advantage to have their views represented by other interests that do not appear to have a direct, financial interest in the outcome of the debate or are more appealing to decision makers and the public. We have seen the value in citizens or small businesses—mom and pop grocers, for example—advocating on behalf of large, moneyed interests.[49]

To this end, narrow, moneyed interests try to enlist other, more credible interest groups to support their cause. And the most effective groups are genuine grassroots organizations.

- When the Clinton administration proposed imposing a retaliatory excise tax on imported Japanese luxury automobiles in 1995, the automobile manufacturers did not approach the public for support directly. Instead, they attempted to mobilize public support to oppose the tax using as spokespeople "blue collar" automobile mechanics in American-owned Toyota dealerships.[50]
- In the California alcohol tax initiative, the alcoholic beverage industry was able to recruit teachers and a small branch of the police force to its side. Although the latter represented a tiny minority of all police officers, the appearance of law enforcement support was enough to confuse and mislead the public, which ultimately defeated the initiative.[51]
- In the 1990 congressional battle over clean-air legislation, the automobile industry contended that requiring higher-mileage cars would eliminate larger vans used to transport, among others, senior citizens and those suffering from multiple sclerosis. Mass mailings to genuine citizen groups resulted in letters to Congress supporting the automobile companies' position from a number of grassroots organizations representing those constituencies, including the Easter Seal Society of South Dakota and the Delaware Paralyzed Veterans Association. Family farmers, represented by

the Nebraska Farm Bureau, were recruited to oppose the bill out of fear that farmers could not do their jobs with smaller cars.[52]

- In its 1993 campaign against controls on prescription drug prices, the pharmaceutical industry recruited as supporters the National Medical Association, the National Multiple Sclerosis Society, the Cystic Fibrosis Foundation, and the National Coalition of Hispanic Health and Human Services Organizations. By tapping into their fears (probably unjustified and certainly fostered by the pharmaceutical industry) of pharmaceutical research cutbacks that could affect their members, these organizations became vocal and effective advocates for the drug industry's position.[53]

Were the grassroots concerns prompted by business or industry advocates real or imagined? Did citizens have reason to fear that higher fuel-efficiency standards would actually eliminate large cars or prescription drug price controls would cause research cutbacks? Did the grassroots organizations that supported the industry positions have all the necessary facts to make informed judgments about the issues? Were their actions in the best interest of their citizen members and those whose interests they sought to represent? Unfortunately, these key questions remain unanswered for now, but true citizen groups, who are responsive to their membership base, will eventually have to address them.

Buying Silence: Philanthropy and Grassroots

Business and economic interests attempt to influence public policy debates through their charitable giving. While there is no doubt that corporations, like individuals, often support worthy causes simply because it is the "right thing to do," both individuals and corporations also use their philanthropy to affect public policy. They do that in two ways.

First, a corporation such as Kraft General Foods can fund a study of childhood hunger in America prepared by the nonprofit Food Research and Action Center, a public interest group that sought to use the study results to build public support for increased food stamp funding.[54] Not coincidentally, more federal money spent on food stamps would benefit the corporation's bottom line.

Second, and less obviously, business interests can fund charities where there is no immediate connection between the corporation's economic interests and the charities' public service activities. No doubt the great majority of this type of funding is bereft of any corporate intent to influence public policy—funding libraries or orchestras or hospitals. But corporate money can have public policy strings. While citizen organizations do not automatically lose their independence and integrity by accepting money from economic interests, they may find it much more difficult to take independent positions on public policy issues.

In 1994, the New York City Council considered legislation severely restricting smoking in public places. Philip Morris, a major cigarette manufacturer headquartered in New York City, was a frequent contributor to arts groups in the city. As part of its lobbying effort to oppose the legislation, Philip Morris asked arts groups it supported to contact the City Council and express their opposition to the legislation. Philip Morris did not ask the arts groups to support smoking. It did not have to. Philip Morris had threatened to move its corporate headquarters out of New York City if the law passed, taking its corporate philanthropy with it. Arts groups were asked only to impress on the City Council the contribution Philip Morris makes to the cultural life of New York City—and the effect its move would have on that life. Arts groups struggled with Philip Morris's request, and while some declined to lobby the City Council, others did.[55]

California wineries, which had traditionally provided complimentary wine to charities for auctions and fund-raising events, decided they could use those donations to advance their public policy goals. Concerned with efforts to raise federal and state taxes on wine, the wineries asked the charities to provide something in return: a letter stating "we believe that the moderate enjoyment of table wine is socially beneficial, medically healthful, and culturally significant." While some charities declined, the Dallas Opera Guild and Beaux Arts Société of Boise, Idaho, among others, obliged. The wineries, of course, intended to use the letters to lobby against higher taxes.[56]

Proposition 134, the 1990 alcohol tax initiative in California, provides an excellent example of the power of philanthropy: "Particularly in areas surrounding Napa Valley, but also throughout California, small charities and community organizations of all kinds were accustomed to receiving support from wineries, sometimes in the form of money, but also donations of wines to be used for fundraising events. When some of these organizations expressed support for the alcohol tax initiative, the industry moved to deter what it considered to be disloyalty. A half dozen Napa wineries rescinded their donations to the Napa Emergency Women's Services after the non-profit [organization], which was neutral on the alcohol tax issue refused to allow vintners to distribute anti-tax literature at its facility."[57]

Charitable philanthropy, while often innocuous, can influence the participation of grassroots organizations in public policy issues, either by directly inducing the organizations to participate where they otherwise would not or by inhibiting them from taking positions on public policy issues out of justifiable concern that they might jeopardize their funding.

11

Initiatives and Referenda:
The Public Takes Charge

It had to happen sooner or later. From the nomination of Zoe Baird to health-care reform, citizens were making their views known loudly and clearly to their legislators. Time after time, they have been telling their representatives how to vote. Why not simply dispense with the middle-man and let the public vote directly on legislation? That is exactly what happened as citizens rediscovered the "ballot initiative" and trans-formed it into what some have called a "fourth branch of government."

Initiatives (where citizens obtain signatures to qualify measures for the general election ballot) and referenda (where legislatures "refer" matters to the electorate for decision)[1] are the logical outcomes of increased public and interest-group participation in public policymak-ing. They follow directly on issue advocates' efforts to convince the public, through advertising and issue marketing, to contact its legisla-tors to support or oppose policy actions.

In this chapter we discuss the origins, operation, uses, and abuses of initiatives; in the final chapter we explore what the explosion in the number of "direct democracy" initiatives means for issue advocacy, public policymaking, and our representative democracy.

Origins of Initiatives and Referenda

A disenchanted public is fed up with state legislatures in the grip of powerful, moneyed interests. Legislators are widely perceived as corrupt and unresponsive to the wishes of the people they are elected to represent. A popular uprising, led by labor, farmers', women's, and other citizen interest groups, convinces state after state to adopt provisions to return control to the people.

It may sound like a 1990s movement of which Ross Perot would be proud, but in fact it describes events that occurred in the Populist (and later the Progressive) era of the late nineteenth and early twentieth centuries. And the resulting reforms were not limits on legislative terms or campaign financing, but initiatives and referenda. Citizens could now vote to adopt laws or repeal those enacted by the legislature.[2]

The political landscape of the Populist and Progressive eras was characterized by legislatures controlled by railroad, mining, oil, banking, and large landowner interests. Business was largely unregulated, with monopolies and trusts carving up markets to the detriment of small businesses and consumers. The political parties were dominated by "party bosses," often corrupt leaders with strong financial ties (legal and illegal) to the same business interests. The party bosses and their "political machines" nominated candidates for state legislatures, often leaving citizens with a choice between two hand-picked candidates, neither of whom would be beholden to the people who elected them. Who would speak for the people and how would the public's voice be heard?[3]

In 1898, South Dakota became the first state to allow citizen ballot initiatives. Today, twenty-six states, the District of Columbia, and many localities allow initiatives.[4]

Giving citizens the power to enact legislation was originally intended to cure the perceived unresponsiveness and undemocratic nature of supposedly representative democracy. If legislators refused to act in the people's interest, then the people would do the job for them. Of course, initiatives were never intended to supplant representative democracy; no one seriously believed that citizens have the time or resources to consider *every* legislative proposal. But giving them the *power* to do so gives the people an important tool to hold legislators accountable to the electorate, rather than to moneyed interests and party bosses.

Initiatives can provide a safety valve to ensure that citizens have an opportunity to bypass the legislature when it does not or cannot act in their interest. Just the possibility that citizens can occasionally take legislative matters into their own hands can make legislators more responsive to citizen views on issues. But as we soon see, nearly a century after their birth, citizen initiatives finally reached maturity in a form their forbears could not have envisioned.

Recent Developments: What Goes Around Comes Around

In 1978, Howard Jarvis, a California antitax advocate, championed the popular cause of property tax relief. Instead of taking his case to an unresponsive legislature, he and an army of grassroots supporters succeeded in placing the issue on the ballot as an initiative. With overwhelming support for lower taxes, Proposition 13 passed and became law. Of course Howard Jarvis did not invent ballot initiatives. He (and the California voters seeking tax relief) just adapted an old concept to a new time.

Proposition 13 had immediate and predictable effects. First, it sounded a loud alarm throughout the legislative corridors of Sacramento. Legislators were forced to ask themselves whether they were really so far out of touch with the citizenry and to readjust their priorities to accommodate public opinion.

Second, its passage spurred action in other states, where legislators "read the handwriting on the wall" and enacted property tax cuts without waiting for citizens to use the initiative process.

Third, and most important, the success of Proposition 13 inspired other interest groups to use the initiative process to further their own policy goals. In California alone, the number of ballot initiatives in the 1980s was more than twice the number of the previous decade.[5] California voters approved initiatives lowering automobile insurance rates, requiring labels on products containing toxic substances, increasing cigarette excise taxes, imposing term limits for state elected officials, and reforming the criminal justice system.

Issue advocates in other states were equally active in the 1980s and 1990s, with initiatives in Maryland (handguns and abortion rights), Idaho ("right to work"), Michigan (abortion rights), the District of Columbia (campaign finance reform, death penalty), Oregon (anti-gay rights), Arizona (property rights), Massachusetts (rent control), and numerous other states and cities on issues including term limits, taxes, gambling, school prayer, and bottle deposit.

Success inspired and empowered issue advocates. When antismoking advocates were still celebrating their 1988 ballot initiative victory raising tobacco taxes, alcohol policy advocates were already planning an initiative campaign (ultimately defeated by the voters) to raise alcohol taxes. California alcohol tax proponents turned to the ballot initiative because the legislature had not raised the tax on wine since 1937, a result in large part of the power, money, and lobbying resources of the California wine industry.[6] The California alcohol tax initiative was defeated by the voters, largely due to the clout of the wine industry, this time directed not at lobbying the legislature but at mobilizing grassroots opposition to the initiative.

Contemporary initiatives are the result of the very citizen empowerment we have been chronicling, beginning as a reaction to isolated and unresponsive legislators and continuing as an outgrowth of rising citizen activism and grassroots empowerment. And what could better typify citizen reaction to recalcitrant legislators and moneyed interests than initiatives imposing term limits on California state legislators or limiting campaign contributions to $100 for elected officials in the District of Columbia?

The recent popularity of initiatives confirms that the public cares about issues. As public participation in candidate elections declines, growing interest in initiative campaigns provides a hopeful sign. People who stay home on election day may be disillusioned about politics as usual or may not perceive much difference between two major-party candidates. But they do care about issues, and they eagerly vote on initiatives they understand. A 1986 Idaho right-to-work initiative, for example, generated more interest than a Senate race. Ballot initiatives in Colorado and Oregon generated higher voter turnout than statewide or congressional races.[7] Initiatives have at least the potential for renewing citizen interest and participation in public policymaking.

The Initiative Process

Initiative campaigns give advocates a guaranteed opportunity to have their proposal considered by the voters. Once it qualifies for the ballot, an initiative will proceed to a vote: no powerful legislator can bottle it up in committee; no governor can veto it.

But taking an issue directly to the voters through an initiative is rarely an advocate's first choice. Initiatives are time-consuming and expensive. Advocates must draft the initiative, gather the necessary signatures to qualify it for the ballot, and conduct a full-scale advocacy campaign to win a majority of the votes cast on election day. Initiative campaigns are a microcosm of issue campaigns, yet they are compressed into an election cycle. Initiatives, then, are most often an advocacy tool of last resort, to be used only if all efforts to persuade the legislature fail.

Initiatives begin with an idea, usually one that has been tested and explored in previous issue campaigns. Citizen or business interest groups seek higher (or lower) taxes, greater (or lesser) environmental regulation, more (or fewer) rights for gays, increased (or decreased) availability of abortion. Because initiative campaigns are expensive, particularly in large states such as California, where even qualifying for the ballot can cost millions, good ideas alone will get advocates only so far. They must first test potential support for their idea among likely interest-group supporters ("campaign insiders"), using all the networking tools at their disposal to raise the issue in formal and informal meetings and casual conversations.

If advocates find the necessary support among campaign insiders, they then assess their strength with the public. Polling data and focus-group information will later help in drafting an initiative and constructing a campaign, but at this early stage they are essential in assessing the feasibility of going forward.

Finally, if all signs look favorable, advocates will test their ability to raise the funds necessary to mount an initiative campaign. Interest groups will be asked to pledge resources, funding sources will be tapped, and a campaign plan (complete with budget) will be drafted.

If issue advocates discover they have a committed and capable group of inside supporters, potential public backing, and access to financial resources, their next step is to draft an initiative for placement on the ballot. No matter how well advocates have prepared and how early they have started, once the decision to proceed is made, the clock begins ticking. The countdown has begun to election day.

Writing the Law

With their sights firmly fixed on the calendar, issue advocates begin to draft the language of the initiative. Getting general agreement on an initiative is one thing; working out all the details and language of the initiative is quite another.

It is at this stage that initiative proponents face an unusual challenge. If they are accustomed to lobbying legislators or bureaucrats and supporting or opposing legislation or administrative rules, they have probably had little or no experience drafting precise legislative language. It usually suffices to support or oppose insurance reform and leave the drafting to the experts. And even the experts, legislators and their experienced staffs, do not face what the initiative proponents face. No legislative proposal—no bill—must be written in indelible ink before the first hearing is held, the first lobbyist visits, the first interest group suggests a modification, and the first legislative colleague suggests an amendment or compromise.

But that is precisely the problem facing initiative proponents. Their draft will be submitted to the voters for approval. It cannot be amended or negotiated. Minor or major drafting mistakes cannot be corrected, nor can accommodations be reached with opponents. That is why advocates pay particular attention to the details of drafting the initiative, including enlisting support from legislative and legal experts. Even with the best advice, advocates will inevitably make mistakes, include language they will come to regret, or create loopholes through which their opponents can drive trucks.[8] And opponents need only point out drafting flaws, inconsistencies, or unintended consequences to raise public doubts about the initiative.

Qualifying for the Ballot: Signing Up Supporters

Once the initiative language is approved by the campaign insiders, the next step is to qualify it for the ballot. Supporters must obtain signatures from registered voters on petitions. The number of signatures is set by state law and is usually a percentage of those who voted for governor in the previous election. In California, for example, qualifying an initiative for the ballot requires a relatively low 5 percent of the number who voted in the last gubernatorial election. But that can amount to more than 385,000 signatures.[9]

It is not surprising, therefore, that signature gathering is no longer a task for volunteers. In California, as elsewhere, initiative proponents routinely hire professional signature gatherers who, for a million dollars or more, "guarantee" they will obtain the necessary signatures, with enough to spare to account for unregistered voters and duplicate names.[10]

Professional signature gatherers operate on the assembly-line principle, setting up tables at shopping malls, busy downtown corners, and mass transit stations. Their only goal is to obtain the necessary signatures, not to educate the public or persuade individual signers about the merits of the initiative. People are not encouraged to read the petition, just to sign it.[11]

Building a Campaign: Money, Media, and Grassroots

Once the necessary signatures are obtained and the initiative is approved by the appropriate state officials, advocates begin to build a campaign. While many issue campaigns operate for long periods in relative obscurity, struggling to get public recognition and media attention, qualifying an initiative for the ballot guarantees advocates will draw attention to their issue. Once the initiative qualifies (and usually much earlier), opposition will surface and the issue will be joined.

The mere act of qualifying for the ballot attracts public and media attention for two reasons: a significant percentage of the public has indicated its interest in the issue by signing petitions, and the entire electorate will soon have the opportunity to vote on the initiative. The media typically seek out campaign spokespersons and experts and conduct public opinion polls to gauge popular support for the initiative. As election day approaches, newspapers will frequently express their editorial views on the initiative, just as they do on candidates.

No matter how much time and energy proponents have spent formulating, drafting, and qualifying an initiative, they will usually find themselves unprepared for the campaign that follows. Advocates, who may have spent years discussing and contemplating an issue campaign, have little time to enjoy the "success" of qualifying for the ballot. Along with that success comes the realization that they have suddenly lost the luxury of time; their timetable is no longer their own. They cannot regroup after an interim legislative loss or retreat to consider accepting a compromise solution. They no longer have the time to test their message, develop public support, or assemble the necessary resources. The clock is ticking toward election day.

Initiative proponents must devise and execute a well-prepared and funded issue campaign, building and maintaining broad coalitions, educating and persuading the public, mobilizing supporters, and battling for media attention and favorable coverage. Initiative campaigns combine the elements of a traditional electoral campaign with the unpredictable elements of an issue campaign. Proponents and opponents vie for newspaper editorial support, enlist volunteers to take the issue door to door, and find and promote articulate spokespersons who can engage the opposition in the media and in community forums all across the city or state.

Too often an initiative campaign is organized by dedicated citizen activists, with more commitment than money. They may seek a deposit on beverage containers or a hike in the cigarette tax and may be cheered by preinitiative polls showing public support for their campaign. But they will soon encounter active, well-funded opposition from beverage or tobacco companies and find themselves outgunned by superior resources and campaign expertise. That is why proponents, particularly citizen interest groups, will find it necessary to recruit and hire experienced professional staff to manage the initiative campaign. Volunteers and "loaned" coalition staff will be no match for a well-funded opposition with much riding on the outcome.

As in any electoral campaign, money is crucial, and raising it can be a full-time preoccupation. Paid advertising can tilt the balance, and opponents can use media messages skillfully to raise questions and doubts, pointing out drafting errors and unintended consequences. Advertisements must be countered, and arguments must be rebutted. In a large state such as California, more money can easily be spent on ballot initiatives than on electoral campaigns. In 1988, for example, $80 million was spent by both sides on a citizen initiative that sought to lower automobile insurance rates.[12]

It should come as no surprise that money can have a decisive impact on initiative campaigns. But while the side with more financial resources historically has about a 75 percent chance of defeating an initiative, moneyed interests have only about a 25 percent success rate in promoting ballot issues.[13] About 20 percent of the time, the more weakly financed side wins.[14] The sources of money can themselves become a campaign issue, especially if money is funneled into campaigns from out-of-state business interests. Thanks to a 1978 Supreme Court decision, states have little or no power to limit expenditures on ballot initiatives.[15]

While money can certainly help defeat initiatives (and cannot hurt in advancing them), opponents have other strategies at their disposal. Lawsuits to invalidate initiatives on state constitutional grounds are common. Even when they have little or no merit, suits can be effective at tying up proponents in depositions and court hearings and siphoning resources away from the issue campaign and into the pockets of lawyers.

Opponents can also qualify alternative or counterinitiatives for the ballot. For example, alcohol industry opponents of the California nickel-a-drink initiative (Proposition 134 in 1990) qualified a counterinitiative that would have raised the tax much less than Proposition 134 and diverted the funds for other purposes. It was intended, of course, to siphon support away from the original proposition. Proponents of Proposition 134 were then forced to campaign *for* their initiative and *against* the competing initiative. To make matters even worse, the counterinitiative contained a "poison pill," which provided that if voters approved both initiatives, Proposition 134 would be invalidated. The wine, beer, and alcohol industry could then concentrate on seeking approval for their own, lower tax initiative, confident in the knowledge that, thanks to their poison pill, they would prevail even if both initiatives passed.[16]

As initiative campaigns progress, opponents need only raise public doubt and confusion, poking holes in the initiative, and suggesting more "popular" alternatives. When the consequences of an initiative are in doubt, a single strategic study can call into question proponents' predictions of environmental benefits or lower insurance costs. Opponents can capitalize on the voters' propensity to vote no, or at least not to disturb the status quo.[17] Cracks in the proponent's coalition can be exploited, just as opponents of Proposition 134 successfully recruited teachers and a small group of police officers to oppose the alcohol tax increase.

Often initiative proponents seal their own doom by reaching too far and formulating complex solutions with unpredictable, long-range consequences. Successful initiatives are uncomplicated and easy to explain and understand. No matter how sympathetic California voters may have been toward protecting the environment, when Proposition 120 (known as "Big Green") appeared on the initiative ballot in 1990, it was resoundingly defeated, largely because it attempted a comprehensive solution to far-reaching environmental problems such as global warming, oil spills, water pollution, and preserving redwood forests.

Initiatives are costly, time-consuming, resource-draining, and fail more often than they succeed. Proponents have all the burdens of legislating without the advantages of access to drafting expertise or the ability to compromise or adjust proposals as the legislative process proceeds. But even when initiatives lose, advocates can win.

Winning While Losing

An initiative that wins is a reason to celebrate on election day. Proponents can cheer a victory that successfully overcame legislative deadlock or inaction and achieved an important goal. Of course, a loss is still a loss. A poorly planned and underfunded campaign that results in an overwhelming loss might deal a serious setback to advocates and their issue, which would have lasting impact. Unsympathetic legislators will have still another reason to reject advocates' positions: they have already been rejected at the polls.

But even supporters of initiatives that lose can find some consolation. Unlike losing candidates who fold up their tents and recede into the background on election night, issue advocates can build on their initiative defeats. Ballot initiatives may be the culmination of a long issue advocacy campaign, but more often they are just one step in a long journey for or against property rights, gun control, abortion, environmental protection, or gay rights.

A highly visible initiative campaign can draw public attention to an issue and a problem. Advocates can take advantage of the media spotlight to educate the public about their issue. The campaign can be an organizing tool, serving as a way to recruit new supporters, motivate and sustain existing interest-group members, and identify new sources of financial and other support.

Issues that languish on the social and political back burner can ripen, in one initiative campaign, from Stage 1 or 2 to Stage 3. Raising the profile of an issue can help set the agenda, leading to greater public and decision maker attention to the issue. The defeat of Proposition 134 nevertheless put alcohol tax issues "on California's political map." A legislature that many viewed as captive of the state's wine industry (and its campaign contributions) sat up and paid attention to the electorate. For the first time in more than thirty years, the legislature increased the tax on alcohol the year after the initiative lost.[18]

The alliances and coalitions that form in an initiative campaign can lead to ongoing coalitions, fostering working relationships among interest groups and organizations who have not previously worked together. In California, Proposition 134 brought together individuals and groups who discovered a common interest in alcohol policy issues, including emergency physicians, highway patrol officers, and child abuse prevention advocates.

Initiatives and the resulting public discussion of the underlying issues can be an opportunity to frame (or reframe) issues so they resonate more broadly with prevailing public concerns. A gun-control initiative can be an opportunity to talk about gun violence and suicide prevention as a public health issue; or an alcohol excise tax initiative can draw attention to child abuse and domestic violence as products of alcohol misuse.

Action in one state can be a way to attract national attention and build momentum for an issue. Gay rights initiatives (both for and against) have drawn national attention to an issue that was not yet ripe for action on the national agenda.[19] Voters in several states, most notably California, have enacted term limits for their state legislators, providing impetus for congressional term limits. Property rights advocates qualified an initiative that failed in Arizona in 1994, but drew considerable attention to the issue and inspired advocates in other states (and at the federal level) to consider action.

Every losing initiative campaign yields a series of lessons that advocates can learn and put to use in subsequent issue advocacy campaigns, whether an initiative or legislative effort. Skills can be acquired and shared, and a leadership base built.

Even the Public Doesn't Have All the Answers

Citizen initiatives have the reassuring feel of pure democracy, with echoes of Thomas Jefferson and Populism. In theory at least, initiatives can provide the public with a way to remind their elected representatives—whenever they need reminding—that they represent the people, not large and powerful interest groups.

But just as letters and phone calls from the public to decision makers have evolved from spontaneous outpourings of public concerns into generated letter-writing campaigns by moneyed interest, initiatives may have strayed from their populist incarnation into just another issue advocacy strategy, subject to manipulation and distortion. Among the questions raised by the contemporary explosion of initiatives are the following:

Ballot Access

"Qualification by petition is too easy with money and too difficult without," concluded a California commission appointed to examine the consequences of initiatives in that state.[20] The median cost of obtaining the necessary signatures in California in 1990 was more than a million dollars.[21] Money, rather than popular support, has become the threshold for qualification. The image of concerned neighbors knocking on doors and circulating petitions at community meetings is belied by the need for even the greenest of grassroots campaigns to hire professional signature gatherers.

Nor is the signature-gathering process a means for educating the public about issues or even the initiative process. "Why try to educate the world when you're trying to get signatures?" asked an experienced initiative proponent who admits that most of the time people do not bother to read the petition, and signature gatherers do not bother to explain the issue. Why should they, when they are likely to be paid signature gatherers, not citizen advocates?[22] And signature gathering can take the form of direct mail solicitations, replete with all the deception and misinformation that plague grassroots mobilization.[23]

Money and Disclosure

Not surprisingly, where computerized direct-mail solicitations abound, money is not far behind. As we have seen, money—lots of it—can often make the difference between success and failure for an initiative campaign. Direct democracy, which was designed in part to overcome moneyed interests dominating state legislatures to the detriment of ordinary citizens, may just have shifted the arena of action. As soon as citizen initiatives proved an effective way to bypass legislatures, large economic interests simply redirected their attention and resources to oppose (or support) initiatives. This shift in resources in response to changing tactics and strategies parallels the movement away from "inside" lobbying and campaign contributions and toward mobilizing the grassroots, real or synthetic. The problem is compounded because the funding disclosure and limitation laws applicable to many electoral campaigns generally do not apply to initiatives.[24]

Misleading and Deceptive Campaigns

Mix money, advertising, and powerful interests with much at stake, and you inevitably get deception. Wild predictions of dire consequences are disseminated through expensive advertising campaigns designed to convince the public to support or oppose an initiative. False-front groups with comforting, public-interest-oriented names that we identified in chapter 10 proliferate in initiative campaigns.

When environmental groups qualified a bottle-deposit initiative as California Proposition 11 in 1982, opponents—bottlers, container manufacturers, soft drink and beer companies—organized Californians for Sensible Laws.

> Californians for Sensible Laws consistently claimed the bottle bill could destroy California's voluntary recycling industry, even though recycling levels in each of the states with bottle bills were triple those of California. The group ran a television advertisement with a uniformed Boy Scout asking his father why "the grown-ups" behind Proposition 11 were shutting down "Mr. Erickson's recycling center and putting us scouts out of business." Despite protests from Boy Scouts of America . . . , the advertisements continued. Another advertisement presented five Oregonians who claimed the bottle bill did not work in their state, even though polls have shown that Oregonians overwhelmingly favor their law. The advertising firm for the opponents merely hired four Oregon beer distributors and one Safeway employee and paid them to pose as typical Oregonians on the street.[25]

Voter Turnout and Expertise: The Quality and Fairness of Initiative Decisions

Adams, Madison, and the early Federalists espoused representative democracy as a way to avoid giving too much power to an uninformed and self-interested public. Representative democracy is designed both to deal with the logistical problems of requiring all decisions to be made by the entire electorate and to interpose a body of "experts" charged with considering the larger public interest when legislating.

Initiatives reject the representative model in favor of "direct democracy." But how democratic is the initiative process? Does it just replace elected representatives with a larger but self-selecting body of voters? One observer notes that those who vote on ballot issues "may be less representative of the general population, and even less representative of those who vote for partisan elected officials, [but] they are surely more representative, in a variety of ways, than the members of state legislatures."[26] Unquestionably, those who vote on initiatives tend to be better educated than those who do not.

Representative, legislative bodies provide an opportunity for thoughtful deliberations and the balancing of the rights of minorities and unpopular causes. Can the citizenry be expected to look beyond their individual interests and biases to protect the rights of minorities, the underrepresented, and those with unpopular views? (Of course, even elected representative from time to time deny the rights of minorities, and courts can be unresponsive as well. It took the Supreme Court fifty-eight years to reverse its early decision that "separate but equal" education permitted one school for whites and one for blacks.)

Most recently, the proliferation of antigay initiatives raises complex questions of allowing the majority of citizens to impose its views and beliefs on others, as do initiatives to deny immigrants and aliens public services and to make English the "official language." When resources are scarce and public tempers are short, will voters give in to their "baser" instincts? Will they opt for short-term gains, such as more jobs and college openings for the majority by eliminating affirmative action at the longer-term expense of creating a more polarized society and denying opportunities to minorities? Initiatives provide that opportunity with few checks on the will of the majority.

Do the voters understand the dynamics of complex issues and the effect of particular initiatives? Do they know and accept the consequences of their decisions? Do they look beyond their immediate self-interest and take into consideration the larger public interest? In all these and other ways, does the electorate make "better" decisions than those they elect to represent them? Does the mere existence of initiatives make the legislature more responsive to public views? Does the initiative process increase government accountability, produce better decisions, and stimulate citizen involvement in public policy?

Those who vote on initiatives believe they have the necessary information to make an appropriate judgment on the issue. This is true despite ballot complexity; initiatives drafted in the turgid legalese required of legislation; competing, often contradictory initiatives on the same issue; the absence of reassuring party labels; and the oft-encountered problem of a no vote meaning yes, and a yes vote meaning no.[27]

While initiatives may make legislators "sit up and take notice," the process rarely leads to significant policy change. Voters may be as easily manipulated by moneyed interests as legislators, and more likely to be confused by misleading initiative campaigns. But the very existence of the ballot initiative process—and the rare initiative that succeeds—gives legislators an added incentive to pay attention to citizen voices.

The next chapter explores the implications of rising citizen activism for all our public policy decisions.

12

Issues and Advocacy Strategies for the Twenty-First Century

The science and art we have been exploring is issue advocacy. Too often, however, issue advocates function as passive issue managers, waiting for issues to appear on their radar screens and then devising appropriate strategies to deal with them. They become reactive, only recognizing an issue so late in its life cycle that they have few options and limited opportunities to influence its course. On issue after issue, they are forced to play defense and catch-up. Success is too often defined as "minimizing one's losses."

Instead, issue advocates should take control of the agenda, identifying issues early in their life cycles and planning their campaigns while the opposition is still celebrating its victory (or licking its wounds) from the last campaign. As discussed in chapter 2, a relatively modest amount of resources can have a dramatic effect on an issue if it is applied early in the issue's life cycle, before public opinion is fully formed, opposing coalitions are built, grassroots and lobbying campaigns begin, and decision makers line up to declare their support or opposition.

Effective issue advocacy requires constant vigilance and foresight. Advocates need to use every tool at their disposal to anticipate the future course of issues and society. While few could have predicted the bombing in Oklahoma City, attentive advocates had long been tracking the growing separatist, antigovernment militia movement. Unlike most of the public, they were not surprised to learn of the extent of that movement and its disaffection with government. They had been tracking the movement and assessing its implications for civil rights, crime, law enforcement funding, and its larger message about citizen disaffection with, and distrust for, government.

Peering into the Future

The issue landscape is constantly changing as society marches inexorably onward, encountering new obstacles and opportunities. Issue advocates look for early signs of change in the issue terrain, searching out the highest observation points from which to get the best possible view.

National newspapers and magazines, radio and television news reports, and the Internet are the obvious places to start. So too are local and community newspapers and obscure newsletters tracking industries and issues. But issues do not emerge full-blown and ready for action. Initial issue sightings usually occur in specialized or "fringe" publications or even in academic discussions. Environmentalists may discuss their concerns first in *Buzzworm* or *Rolling Stone* before they hit the cover of *Newsweek* or *Time*; businesspeople share their thoughts with each other through trade publications that few outsiders read.

Advocates should expand their horizons to identify public concerns long before they become problems for policymakers to solve. Many times that requires reading and learning from sources with whose views we often disagree. It is an understandable human tendency to seek out those with whose opinions we agree. We seek support and reassurance for our own views, and we avoid conflict and confrontation. At the same time, real knowledge comes only from challenging our assumptions and beliefs. We grow stronger as we learn from our opponents, listening with open minds to other perspectives. We learn best by exploring what we do not initially understand, extracting the nuggets of truth buried deep within competing arguments and viewpoints. Advocates who are comfortable with the editorial views of the *New York Times* and the *Nation* should force themselves to read the *Wall Street Journal* and the *National Review*, even to listen to Rush Limbaugh, and vice versa.

Advocates can learn most by watching what their opposition does and says. Sitting through still another trade association meeting where colleagues share strategies and nod in agreement at shared issue concerns is only a base on which work must be done to build a solid foundation. Too often, issue advocates dismiss their opponents' positions as lacking in merit or even mean-spirited. Instead, they should be looking for the germ of truth in their positions, from which they can learn more about their own strengths and weaknesses.

Environmentalists in the 1980s could have foretold the rise of the property rights and wise-use movements had they paid greater attention to their opponents' arguments and claims. Oil companies could have anticipated environmentalists' concerns about global warming and the greenhouse effect had they carefully monitored their words and deeds. More important, each side could have tailored its issue campaigns to meet the real concerns buried within the opponents' arguments. Had environmental protection run roughshod over the rights of businesses and property owners, imposing excessive costs leading to lost jobs? Was America's profligate use of energy causing long-term problems? The answer in both instances was yes, but each side pointed an accusatory finger at the other; lines were drawn in the sand, and the public was encouraged to choose sides. The debate consisted of charges and countercharges, rather than thoughtful, constructive arguments that addressed real concerns.

Leaders, whether in business, academia, arts, politics, or the world of interest groups, also provide valuable clues to future issues. What is on the mind of corporate heads? Or union leaders? What is on the agenda of the AARP or the Sierra Club or the National Association of Manufacturers? Here too, issues will most often surface first at the local level. What concerns state and regional business, labor or public interest-group leaders? What do they say in their speeches or articles or at their annual meetings?

The states are increasingly becoming important arenas for issue action. Not only are states (and localities) addressing issues such as health care, immigration, education reform, and crime, but public demand for action often surfaces first in the states. The most promising, or popular, solutions often make their way quickly from state to state and then to the national agenda.

"Three strikes and you're out" was a popular slogan and then a law in California. Soon thereafter, it became the law of the land. Any state (or city or local school board) can provide important issue clues, but some states provide better early warnings than others. California, for example, is often in the forefront on environmental and immigration issues. New Jersey and Pennsylvania are early indicators of developments on insurance reform. Minnesota often leads other states on worker protection and employment issues. Oregon and Hawaii are already implementing innovative health-care-reform plans. Advocates need to understand the forces behind change in the states and the states' experiences living with them. What problems do state administrators have? Is the public satisfied with the solutions?

There are many sources of information to track issue developments in the states. Elected and appointed state and local officials all have associations that conduct national and regional meetings and publish newsletters and issue papers. Advocates can easily learn what issues are on the agenda of the annual meeting of the National Governor's Association, the National Association of Attorneys' General, the National League of Cities, or even the National Association of Chief State School Officers. *Governing* magazine provides insightful information about issue developments at the state level.

An issue, like grass, usually grows from the ground up. But when advocates listen to the grassroots, they often hear contradictory public opinion based on incomplete or incorrect assumptions. Advocates can look beyond and beneath the latest poll data to identify fundamental public and social concerns. They can constantly look for clues to emerging trends. And clues abound: they are in the books people read, the music they play, the movies they see. They are in the frequency with which people attend church or commit crimes or get divorced; in the foods they eat, the jobs they hold, and the sports they play. Advocates can pay attention to what people think and say, but closer attention to what they do. They can employ the tools of psychology, sociology, history, and political science to temper "expert" predictions, based on elaborate computer models, with the concerns of real people.

Issues for the Next Century

Specific issues often arise out of broad trends. Issue advocates who seek to prepare themselves for the future begin by identifying broad trends—the forest—as a way to anticipate future issues—the trees.

From Global Security to Economic and Personal Security

The world is changing, and the speed at which change is occurring is increasing. The Cold War ends, the Soviet Union dissolves, the Berlin Wall falls, Europe unites in a true economic community, and democracy erupts in Eastern Europe. At the same time, stock markets emerge in socialist India and communist China, and U.S. corporations sell increasingly larger percentages of their goods and services in other countries. NATO no longer faces Soviet expansionism and the Warsaw Pact. Now it must deal with Bosnia and decide whether to admit as members former adversaries such as Hungary and Russia. Instead of war with the Soviets, new threats emerge from more focused military exigencies in Kuwait, Haiti, and Bosnia. A "new world order" in which America is the only superpower places new and different demands on a U.S. military unprepared for peacemaking or peacekeeping operations.

All threats to global peace are not on the scale of Haiti. As Israel makes peace with some of its neighbors, others, such as Iran, Iraq, and Libya, continue to defy international norms of behavior, developing weapons of mass destruction and fostering terrorism throughout the world. South Korea threatens North Korea; China physically intimidates Taiwan, raising concerns about the future of human and civil rights in Hong Kong, which reverts to China in 1997.

With the demise of America's most formidable enemy, we have lost our clear international focus: it is difficult to tell friend from foe. Americans know they live in a global village, yet without a coherent explanation of our foreign policy role and international obligations, people seem most comfortable in isolationism. They are satisfied with the outcome of the Cold War and now express their disapproval with foreign aid, viewing it as global welfare. They support a strong military and high defense spending, but agonize over every effort by our leaders to use troops to solve international crises, from Somalia to Haiti to Bosnia.

As nuclear weapons are dismantled in the large and small republics that once comprised the Soviet Union, concerns arise about the proliferation of nuclear weapons in the Middle East. Declining economies in former Soviet states shift concern to the underground trade in nuclear warhead components.

Terrorism becomes a real threat to America, with the specter of chemical and nuclear weapons falling into the hands of dangerous individuals, rather than nations. The United States, once blissfully thought to be immune from terrorism, watches the conflict in the Middle East spill into the streets around New York's World Trade Center. Angry, antigovernment militants attempt to destroy their own government in Oklahoma City. Legislation to make America less vulnerable to terrorism is opposed by civil libertarians who question whether giving up some freedoms make us safer. The White House and the Capitol are surrounded by fences and concrete barriers; visitors to government buildings are required to pass through metal detectors and display identification.

The American economy may depend on international trade, but the public distrusts internationalism, whether in the shape of the United Nations or the World Trade Organization created by the General Agreement on Tariffs and Trade (GATT). Workers and their unions favor protection for American jobs and oppose tariff-free trade agreements, such as NAFTA, while their bosses in industry seek competitive advantages in international trade.

The United States may no longer be vulnerable to physical attack from abroad, but the invasion of foreign automobiles, televisions, and semiconductors constitutes a real threat to American jobs and prosperity. Fewer American troops are stationed abroad, and those who guard the home front are unable to stem the rising tide of imported goods and exported jobs. The U.S. dollar, whose stability was once the envy of the world, now rises and falls like any other currency.

Capital flows freely across international borders, especially in an era of fewer trade barriers and more "common markets." With capital goes jobs. From clothing to semiconductors, manufacturers maximize their profits by minimizing labor costs. If it is cheaper to make chips in India, rather than Indiana, then India is where the jobs go. American consumers are hard pressed to find shirts or VCRs made in this country.

American companies participate in a global market, where stiff competition is provided not just by Japan but by a European union and the burgeoning markets of South America, China, India, Taiwan, the Philippines, and even Indonesia. It is not very surprising, therefore, that the CIA reportedly used its espionage technology to spy on Japanese trade negotiators in a dispute with the United States over access to Japanese markets by American companies.[1]

Safety and security now have less to do with national security than with an individual's ability to walk safely in his or her own neighborhood or get and hold a job and maintain a reasonable standard of living. Losing one's job to layoffs or one's life to crime has replaced fear of annihilation by nuclear weapons or international conflict. The Pentagon is forced to accept additional B-2 bombers, for which it professes no need, by a Congress seeking to preserve defense industry jobs in members' states and districts.

A generation of baby boomers finds itself sandwiched between the demands of children ready for college and elderly parents needing expensive care and attention. At the same time, they are concerned about their own retirement (and the diminishing prospect that social security will provide substantial benefits for them). If that is not enough, as they approach middle age they face the real possibility of being laid off or restructured out of a job in an economy that discards experienced, middle-aged workers like outdated weapons systems.

And the boomers' children—Generation X—are assured of living decades longer than their grandparents. Yet they worry if they will have decent jobs and a lifestyle even close to that of their parents. Unlike the boomers, who crawled under their schoolroom desks in air-raid drills designed to allow them to survive a nuclear attack, their children worry about random shootings and finding a job. They worry that they will never own their own homes or receive social security. Will their parents' generation consume all the world's environmental and financial resources?

Even as high-paying jobs disappear, corporate layoffs and "downsizing" take their toll among mid-level workers.[2] At the same time, corporate CEOs see their pay reach astronomical levels amid calls for "corporate responsibility" and efforts to use the tax code to reward companies that treat their workers fairly by providing health care, pensions, and job retraining.

The first generation that came of age driving down the information highway at 28,000 bps before they were old enough to drive a car at 55 mph must face the realities of an economy shifting away from manufacturing jobs to an information-based economy. High-paying, low-skill jobs have largely disappeared, leaving the undereducated with few options and little hope for the future. The economic boom that accompanied the population explosion occasioned by the boomers has become a "slow growth" economy creating fewer jobs.

Radical changes are occurring in American demographics. The large baby-boom generation is wending its way through the population pipeline, where it will soon claim its share of retirement and Medicare benefits. A once relatively homogeneous population that was predominantly white and European in its heritage will soon look very different. The Census Bureau estimates that "by 2050 immigration patterns and differences in birth rates, combined with an overall slowdown in growth of the country's population, will produce a United States in which 53 percent of the people will be non-Hispanic whites, down from 74 percent today."[3] By 2030, the non-Hispanic white population is projected to make up less than half of the people under the age of eighteen, but three-fourths of those over sixty-five. Will generational and racial conflicts arise as resources are divided among competing needs such as social security and education?

Government and Its Discontents: Taxes Are Too High and Government Is Too Big

The rising tide of conservatism, the backlash against high taxes, the growing federal deficit, and the Republican congressional victory in 1994 combined to occasion a reexamination of the role of government. Is government the solution to our national problems, or is government itself the problem? The public appears to reject "big government," yet it wants the services government provides. The public wants more aggressive law enforcement to rid its neighborhoods of crime, but it wants less aggressive law enforcement by the FBI and the Bureau of Alcohol, Tobacco, and Firearms.

The public believes government officials wield too much power over citizens and businesses. Congressional hearings on Ruby Ridge and Waco feed distrust of centralized power. The IRS is often described as a bureaucracy run amok. OSHA and the EPA are seen as imposing burdensome requirements on businesses, particularly small businesses, who seek only to create jobs and make money.

Whenever government tries to make a difference, the underlying assumption is no longer that government help is well intentioned. Now government action is often seen as causing more problems than it solves. Has teen pregnancy exploded because of welfare? Have medical costs skyrocketed because of government involvement through Medicare? Does the FDA prevent lifesaving drugs from reaching the market? Increasingly, the answer is yes, and the solution is less government action and regulation. The public looks at government spending on welfare, the environment, even health care, and questions whether it is money well spent.

Big government may be bad, but state government is seen as good and local government as better. Congress and the public look at new and existing programs and now ask: are federal bureaucrats really better at making decisions than state and local officials who are more in touch with the needs of the people? The answer is most often no.

Not only is the federal government not the answer, it often creates problems for the states by imposing requirements without providing funds. "Unfunded mandates" has become a watchword to stop federal programs that place burdens on states, such as the Brady bill, which requires states to conduct background checks on prospective gun owners but fails to provide states with the money to do the checks. The argument against unfunded mandates is reminiscent of the property rights movement, which demands compensation for government "takings" of property through environmental restrictions on land use. Limited resources will likely prevent the federal government from paying the states for enforcing federal mandates or paying landowners for environmental restrictions on property use.

With less federal government, more problems will perforce be addressed at the state or local level. And with fewer federal standards imposed on the states (for along with standards come costs), states will have more flexibility to act. States will have to determine how to spend "block grants" of federal funds, deciding for themselves how to allocate funds for housing, education, health care, and public welfare. Fewer federal standards will yield a greater diversity of state experiments: states may truly become Brandeis's laboratories of democracy. Along with experimentation will come real solutions and real failures.

The locus of issue advocacy will follow the programs and the money to state and local governments. Will the states be prepared for the new demands placed on them? Will their citizens support developing the governmental infrastructure necessary to accomplish new and important tasks?[4] As issue forums shift, advocates must be prepared to influence the implementation of fifty different state environmental and public welfare programs. Corporations, newly freed from many government regulations and capable of moving jobs and capital to "favorable" states or countries, will be less accountable to any government's control. If government at all levels will not or cannot protect public health, safety, and consumers, issue advocates must employ their tools of persuasion to influence corporations and other nongovernmental institutions.

The Republicans may have swept into congressional power in 1994, but government itself still demands to be fixed. The public is not satisfied with the progress it made in 1994 in "throwing the bums out"; it wants to save itself from itself, by adopting term limits for elected officials. California has already done so.

But neither elections nor term limits will voluntarily separate elected representatives from the money they need to get elected and reelected. Reforming the process of funding electoral campaigns, at all levels of government, is an issue that will not disappear. When and if it happens, it will have important consequences for issue advocates, as it forces elected representatives to look for support and guidance directly from the electorate.

Congress has enacted a line-item veto, enabling the president to pick and choose among the provisions in most appropriations bills Congress passes, signing those he likes and vetoing those he does not.[5] Appropriations bills have become opportunities for interest groups to "slip in" provisions without a full hearing. The public and other interest groups are often unaware that an issue is being addressed through the appropriations process. A line-item veto might shed more light on the process, by allowing the president to veto, and thus highlight, offending provisions, forcing Congress to consider them fully and openly. That might represent a loss for "inside" lobbyists who flourish best in low light, but a victory for those who represent broader interests who depend on grassroots support.

Problems Persist as Resources and Public Patience Dwindle

As individuals struggle to make ends meet, so do all levels of government. The trillion-dollar federal debt, which grows larger with each unbalanced national budget, demands more and more resources just to pay interest to willing lenders, often from Europe and Japan. With national resources in short supply, America faces hard choices. People want lower taxes and a balanced budget, but they demand more police protection, better schools, and cleaner water. Will we build new prisons or new schools? Although we need new prisons *and* new schools, we seemingly lack the resources to build both. How do we make choices between worthy public needs, and who and what suffers when we do?

A growing faith in free-market forces and "personal responsibility" leads to new ways to solve old problems: let the free market preserve the environment; let charities and volunteers solve hunger and homelessness; let people take personal responsibility for their actions, rather than seek public assistance. In an era of selfishness that does not encourage individual sacrifices to meet community or national needs, the public is having second thoughts on providing welfare, education, housing, even civil rights for those in need. Compassion, like charity, seems to begin at home.

The majority in our democracy has always had the power to impose its will on the minority, as long as the minority's constitutional rights are not violated. Religious organizations who have found a new home in the politics of the Republican Party now raise issues such as school prayer and question library books and school curriculums that portray gays in a favorable light or religion in an unfavorable one.

How will the majority—those with political power—deal with the minority—those without it? The first sign that resources would not be provided to those who need them came in California in 1992, with the enactment of Proposition 187. That initiative denied nonemergency medical care and education to illegal immigrants in California. The majority's attitude appears to be not to share scarce resources when it can find an excuse not to do so. In that instance, it was immigrants who, by virtue of being "illegal," were somehow to blame for their own predicament. Never mind that children would not be educated and the sick would be denied "nonemergency" medical care. California taxpayers voted not to share their resources with a powerless minority.

The next hot issue on the nation's agenda is affirmative action. No one disputes the evils of racism, but the public increasingly believes that those evils are in the distant past and that affirmative action now acts to penalize meritorious whites. While California voters approved Proposition 209 in 1996, eliminating most state affirmative action programs, it remains undeniable that minorities are disproportionately poorer than whites. Minorities, particularly African Americans, are less likely than whites to be employed and are more likely to be in jail.

If affirmative action, welfare, and poverty programs have not accomplished their goals, should they merely be discarded and replaced by the invisible, and indifferent, hand of the free market? Have Americans lost patience with programs designed to create a level playing field? Are they tired of paying today for the evils of previous generations? From minority contracting with government agencies to affirmative action admission programs at public universities, the public is registering its dissatisfaction with the current system.

Welfare has come to mean government handouts, dependency, and a cycle of poverty. Just as the public does not want to spend its tax dollars educating the children of illegal aliens, it appears reluctant to use those resources to help those in need. Instead, it appears all to eager to blame those in need for their own predicament, not pausing to understand the economic or social plight of those with whom the majority rarely associates and into whose neighborhoods and homes they never venture. Cutting off government benefits from poor women who have children while receiving welfare, or forcing individuals off welfare after a period of time, even if their economic and social situation does not change, may satisfy some, but who will suffer? Will Americans be comfortable with the consequences of their choices? It is easier and cheaper to blame the poor and the homeless for their own condition than to devote public resources to solving them.

Clean air and clean water are admirable goals, but at what cost? Should burdens be placed on businesses and property owners for the benefit of the larger public and future generations? Is it really necessary to protect every endangered species, especially when jobs are lost in the process? Once again, the contest is between those with power and resources and those without, as society searches for solutions that work.

On a whole range of issues, debate proceeds, decision makers act, and the problems persist. Health-care costs rise, pricing some out of the market. Crime increases, despite restrictions on gun ownership and the availability of the death penalty. How will we solve persistent problems when we are running out of resources and patience?

Emerging Advocacy Strategies

Just as new issues constantly emerge, and old issues rise and fall on our public policy agenda, advocacy tactics and strategies evolve to meet new challenges and take advantage of new opportunities. Like good generals, issue advocates quickly learn not to fight the last war. But there are lessons to be learned from studying the last war.

Using and Abusing the Grassroots

Moneyed interests have turned their attention and resources away from highly visible and questionable campaign contributions and toward developing the appearance of grassroots support. This movement parallels the rising public scrutiny of campaign contributions, the openness of public policymaking deliberations, and decision makers' increased reliance on public input.

Gucci-shoed lobbyists carrying satchels of money for honorariums and campaign contributions are out; television advertising appeals urging the public to contact their legislators are in. Money can buy grassroots support by purchasing databases and polls, and by conducting mail and telephone campaigns. Money can buy expensively produced advertisements and the air time to show them. "Harry and Louise" advertisements, which helped shape the health-care-reform debate, are likely to proliferate. They have already been used effectively on issues as diverse as tort and telecommunications reform and the effort to balance the federal budget.

Money can also buy studies and surveys and the scientists and experts to produce the desired results. The move toward a better understanding of the costs and benefits of potential government actions leads advocates to pay greater attention to information that can make their case. Dueling experts, rather than competing lobbyists, are now at the front of most public policy debates, as each side pours money and resources into identifying and supplying putatively persuasive and reliable information to the public and decision makers.

As the public is subjected to more intense issue advertisements and more competing studies reaching plausible, but opposite, conclusions, it will undoubtedly become more skeptical of all issue claims. How long will it be before a public, already suspicious of products that advertise that they are the "best" or "improved," applies that same skepticism to issue claims and scientific-sounding "truth"?

Manufactured grassroots campaigns succeed because they give the illusion that a majority supports a position, when in fact the grassroots voices have been bought and paid for. Yet generated grassroots communications and false fronts are already beginning to backfire. Decision makers have learned to recognize the telltale signs of callers who are unfamiliar with an issue or letters that fall into predictable patterns. Which means that advocates and interest groups must constantly invent techniques (and spend money) to produce grassroots communications that look and feel even more genuine. Grassroots mobilization strategies cannot afford to stand still: "grassroots campaigns must constantly change, lest they appear manufactured and lose their clout."[6]

If legislators know the mail and calls are generated, will they discount or ignore them? And if they do, how will the voice of the average concerned citizen get through? Will members take the extra steps necessary to weed out the real from the manufactured, the sincere from the bought? What criteria will they use? Or will they turn to other indicators of public sentiment in an effort to determine what the public wants and what is the best solution to public problems? Will elected representatives be forced to lead, rather than follow, the public?

Reinventing Interest Groups and Coalitions

Interest groups, like lobbyists, once held great power. Groups representing seniors, doctors, or environmentalists needed only proclaim that their million-strong membership supported or opposed a bill. Their public or private pronouncement of support or opposition was sufficient to convince lawmakers. But the day is long gone when seniors or doctors or environmentalists (or even large or small businesspersons) could speak with one clear voice. Lawmakers rightfully question whether those positions reflect the considered judgment of interest-groups' diverse memberships.

Membership numbers remain important, but an interest-group's effectiveness is now gauged by its ability to demonstrate that large numbers of its members care deeply about an issue. This change is partly the result of the disconnect between interest-group members and their leaders, who are only now becoming accustomed to consulting and representing their membership, instead of taking positions formulated in Washington conference rooms.

But it is mostly the result of the recent proliferation of interest groups. Interest groups have grown in three directions. Some, such as the American Association of Retired Persons or the Sierra Club, have amassed huge membership rolls in relatively short periods of time. At the same time, subinterest groups have mushroomed, each seeking to speak for some defined subgroup of seniors or environmentalists or businesses. New and varied interest groups now advocate on behalf of narrower and more limited interests. Medical professionals are no longer represented in public policy debates by a single interest group; instead, there are nearly as many interest groups as there are medical specialties. Finally, the growth of "front groups," whose membership and sponsorship are intentionally obscured by inclusive-sounding names or campaign themes, calls into question the legitimacy of all interest groups.

More interest groups, some with confusing names and large, disparate membership bases, may ultimately spell less influence for all interest groups. Elected and appointed representatives may look to the polls or the mailbag more often than to interest-group leaders to divine public opinion. It is ironic that more and better-funded interest groups, each with a thorough command of grassroots mobilization and message development strategies, may ultimately decentralize power, devolving it back into the hands of the people.

Political parties are adding their voices to the issue dialogue, historically led by interest groups. On health care, welfare reform, the balanced budget, and other issues, political parties have weighed in with advertisements and grassroots mobilization campaigns. Electoral and issue campaigns have converged as hotly contested issue campaigns cross the line between issue advocacy and electoral politics. President Clinton assured that result when he rode the public's perceived desire for health-care reform into office and proceeded to attempt to implement his campaign promises. So it was only to be expected that political parties, both the Republican and Democratic National Campaign Committees, would air their own issue advertisements. This confluence of issues and electoral campaigns bodes ill for issue advocates and public policymaking, if the public debate on issues sinks to the level of electoral campaign attack ads.

Interest groups and coalitions will be most effective if they are broad based, representing as many different and unlikely allies as possible, without alienating their core constituency. Effective coalitions will find ways to unite interests that cross traditional lines of geography, generations, issues, ethnicity, ideology, and politics, thereby compelling the public and decision makers to view problems in new and different ways. The most powerful coalitions will bring in new resources and new interest groups to enliven old debates. They will link disparate interests in the search for workable solutions built on common ground. And they will use unifying themes (derived from polls, focus groups, and a sound understanding of social and political forces) that transcend the narrow boundaries of individual issues to communicate their message.

Issue advocates should also learn from their opponents. Environmentalists, for instance, must recognize that the public will no longer blindly agree to preserve the environment without regard to the cost in lost jobs and business profits. "Property rights" and "wise use" are more than fronts behind which business interests can hide to oppose environmental regulation. They are themes that resonate with the public because they address underlying public concerns. As sure as environmentalists may be that the environment needs protecting, they must recognize the concerns of property owners and workers and businesses.

If interest-group leaders and lobbyists can no longer be counted on to represent the uniform views of their members, they may still be able to use their "inside" influence and political action committees to advance their organization's interests. They may not be able to deliver their membership, but they can still deliver their money.

Money that distorts every other aspect of the political process distorts interest groups. It buys grassroots supporters, it creates new grassroots interest groups, and it has the potential to undermine existing grassroots groups through targeted corporate philanthropy. With more competition for members and financial support, citizen interest groups may be all too willing to accept money from interests with whom they may eventually have to do battle in the public policy arena. An environmental group may reject contributions from an oil company, but it may join with that same company to establish a fund to save endangered tigers. A minority rights organization may be on opposite sides from large corporations on affirmative action, but it may accept charitable contributions from tobacco or beer companies.

What happens when the issue is not affirmative action but tobacco advertising to minorities? A citizens' food-safety group opposes grocery manufacturers on nutrition labeling while accepting contributions to fund studies and conferences. Can interest groups maintain their independence when money is on the table? Will interest groups represent the views of their members or their funders?

Doing Better: The Search for Lasting Solutions

Everyone—every citizen activist, businessperson, or elected official—gets involved in public life to solve problems. Issues should be at the heart of politics. Yet too often politics is more about partisanship and elections than solving problems. In this section we explore ways to return politics to its problem-solving roots.

Tackling Tough Issues

Politics encourages polarization and labels. In the process, issues become partisan. Republicans have firmly held positions on crime, environmental protection, education, taxes, health care, social security, and welfare. Democrats have equally firmly held, but opposite, positions on each of those issues. While the parties wrestle for power and preeminence, the public cares only about solutions.

The obvious accommodation or middle ground on most issues eludes us, in part because our system does not set out to find them. The lack of unifying solutions, and a system that seems to disdain even the search for them, frustrates and discourages the public. It leads to a constantly swinging pendulum, where the ascendant political party capitalizes on the latest expression of offhand public opinion to implement its solutions. When the pendulum swings and another party is in power and public opinion shifts, so too do the solutions. The rise and fall and rise again of the death penalty as a "solution" to crime is a prime example.

After a heated national discussion about crime in 1992, we embraced "three strikes and you're out" and the death penalty, while rejecting strict gun control and "midnight basketball." Midnight basketball programs give energetic inner-city young people something constructive to do other than to inhabit drug-laden city streets. But in the heat of the crime bill debate they were quickly labeled "social spending" and "pork" by congressional republicans and attacked by, among others, the National Rifle Association.

Could midnight basketball programs have reduced crime and violence? Had they done so in cities and states where they already existed? What did sociologists and criminologists say? Former gang members? Police? Unfortunately, we will never know. The debate was driven by ideologies and hardened positions, with predictable political allies lined up in their expected positions. Crime statistics may gyrate, but politics has not solved the problem of crime, and few individuals feel safer in their homes or on their streets because of the death penalty.

This might be an appropriate way to conduct politics, but not to solve public problems. Our most heated public policy arguments are not designed to identify the most pressing public problems or to look for solutions that accommodate the greatest good for the greatest number. Interest groups seek what is best for their members, leaving it to their opponents to argue the opposite position. Politicians pander to their constituencies, partisan politics, and the polls, leaving the public to choose between polar positions with little room for reconciliation and accommodation. In the process, real solutions, even real problems, become obscured by rhetoric and political posturing.

People care about crime and education and employment opportunities, but politicians prefer to argue about the gas tax, gay marriages, the death penalty, and regulatory reform. They seemingly measure an issue's importance by how amenable it is to discussion in thirty-second sound bites on CNN's *Crossfire* or how well the public responds to it in polls and focus groups, rather than how its resolution can benefit the public. Politicians seem especially adept at finding solutions to problems that do not concern most people, while ignoring underlying issues that have no easy, obvious answers.

Most public problems are persistent and resist easy solutions. Yet politicians often avoid difficult issues entirely because finding and implementing solutions will likely be costly and painful. When they do address them, politicians frequently embrace simplistic solutions that test well in public opinion polls but do little to solve problems.

Rather than upset large and powerful constituencies, politicians prefer patchwork, short-term solutions, confronting a problem only when absolutely necessary. Health-care reform could proceed only when termed a "crisis," and then the debate over reform turned in large part on whether or not a "crisis" actually existed. How will we fix problems before they become crises, when choices are limited, there is little margin for error, and minor adjustments will no longer suffice?

Politics is too often an exercise in pain avoidance and a search for a magic bullet. (Remember the Laffer curve and supply-side economics? All we had to do was lower taxes and the economy would improve and the budget deficit disappear.) The temptation is for elected leaders to find answers that appeal to the greatest number of voters. That is why tax cuts are always popular, even when real needs exist. It is easier to appease the majority than to educate the public about why the easy and popular solutions will not work. It is hard work to create a public consensus to make the necessary sacrifices that will ensure lasting solutions.

Individuals understand the connection between short-term sacrifices and long-term gains in their private lives. They save money today to pay for a college education or a new home later. They "set money aside for a rainy day"; they invest small sums in maintaining a house or car with the expectation that they will gain in the long run. They change their diet or quit smoking to improve their long-term health. But they balk at investing public resources in educating and training the poor and disadvantaged to enable them to get jobs, pay taxes, and contribute to society. They, and their leaders, fail to make the connection between expenditures to clean the air and water and the benefits of better public health and increased safety for all.

Global warming, discussed in chapter 6, illustrates this problem. Global warming as a scientific phenomenon is often described as the "greenhouse effect," whereby the earth's atmosphere traps gases generated by burning coal and oil. As the greenhouse effect it remained an interesting scientific theory. Environmental advocates viewed the scientific studies with alarm, however, particularly when initial findings seemed confirmed by subtle but perceptible climate changes recorded in the 1980s.

If, and it is a big if, the earth *is* slowly but inexorably warming because of humankind's rapid consumption of fossil fuels, the consequences would be devastating for life on earth. Temperatures would soar, seas would rise, and agriculture would disappear in many parts of the world. Starvation and death would surely ensue, sooner or later, for millions, perhaps billions.

Scientists do not agree on the inevitability or severity of the greenhouse effect; more recent weather data appear to contradict earlier findings; and more pressing problems demand solutions. The scientific debate continues, but the public policy focus has largely moved on.

But what if there had been a scientific consensus? What if nearly everyone agreed that continuing on the current path would lead, sooner or later, to disaster? What if Americans understood the need to reduce the greenhouse effect in the same way they appear to understand the need to balance their household budgets or to act now to save social security or Medicare? How would decision makers address the problem?

Dealing with the greenhouse effect would not be easy. Government could not simply throw money at the problem. Industry could not readily retool its manufacturing and production to ease the problem. The only "solution" that works would require fundamental shifts in lifestyles, energy use, and consumption patterns in the most heavily industrialized societies, particularly America, which consumes a vastly disproportionate share of the world's fossil fuels.

If politicians followed form, they would argue about costs and benefits. "Convert to nuclear power," some would say, but others would point to Three Mile Island and Chernobyl. "Require automobiles to get twice as many miles per gallon," some would argue, except Detroit automakers would produce their own studies that "demonstrated" that higher gas mileage would cost thousands of jobs, result in unsafe cars, and take a decade of time the scientists tell us we do not have. Interest groups would argue endlessly about how each proposed solution would harm their members or the interest they represent. Seniors would contend that they would be harmed by requiring public spaces to be cooler in winter and warmer in summer. Their grandchildren would argue that without radical change now, there would be nothing left for them. In the end, someone would unearth a study casting doubt on the conventional consensus, providing an excuse for leaders and the public to avoid making hard choices and painful, current sacrifices.

The search for a friendly "expert" or a "persuasive" study would yield, not answers, but a justification for avoiding painful and costly solutions. The sick man is thrilled to get a fifth opinion that, unlike the previous four, declares that surgery is not necessary. He is all too happy to ignore the expert consensus and accept the easy way out. But public policymaking requires resisting cheap and easy solutions that are popular (primarily because they are cheap) but do not work.

The alternative would be finding and implementing difficult, expensive, and unpopular solutions. It would require educating citizens about the problem and ways to deal with it. It would mean explaining and justifying the necessary government actions, and how individual and collective sacrifices are necessary to achieve long-term benefits. It would demand building, not just reflecting, a public consensus. And the ultimate solution would have to do more than put a temporary

Band-Aid on a problem, allowing decision makers to declare victory and move on to the next issue.

Solutions must actually work. They must serve the larger public interest and balance or accommodate competing interests. They must solve problems and be cost effective, even if the costs are short term and the benefits long term, as they most often are. And they must not create more problems than they solve. The public is tired of experimenting with solutions that do not work and often do more harm (albeit unintentionally) than good.

Welfare began as a well-intentioned effort to help the needy. Did it instead create disincentives to work and marriage, and incentives for women to have children while on welfare? Raising the minimum wage was a way to provide a decent living standard for working people. Did it cost jobs and force more people onto welfare? Public housing projects provided affordable living for lower-income citizens. Did they foster crime and urban decay? Welfare undoubtedly helps those in need, but overburdened taxpayers have seemingly tired of supporting a "permanent" underclass, perceived as unwilling to work and comfortable accepting government handouts.

Affirmative action was promoted as a solution to persistent discrimination, but support waned when it was depicted as unfairly favoring one group over another. Everyone wants cleaner air or water, but what good is air to breathe and water to drink if people lose jobs and are forced to move or to live in less comfortable surroundings?

Issues are becoming more complex, cutting across traditional lines: crime and violence are now a public health concern; health-care reform involves efforts by American companies to be competitive in international markets; environmental protection is analyzed according to its effect on job creation. With limited resources to solve public problems, solutions are expected to do more with less. They should preserve the environment *and* create jobs, provide health-care coverage for all *and* reduce costs, reduce crime *and* lower taxes.

People are concerned about meeting their personal, family, and community needs. They will not be satisfied with providing more money for education if it means less money for public safety. And they certainly will not tolerate clean-air regulations so strict that they force companies to close plants and lay off workers.

Yet we insist on addressing issues as if they are neatly compartmentalized. First we tackle health care, then welfare reform, then it is on to crime, even though the issues are inextricably intertwined. It is no surprise that Senate committees carve up legislative jurisdiction into ill-shaped boxes: energy and natural resources is separate from labor and human resources, which is distinct from environment and public works. Why do decision makers believe they can solve multifaceted problems by examining and addressing them as if they are unrelated?

While there is much to quibble with in the Republican's 1994 Contract with America, it represented a comprehensive effort to solve problems. It used consistent themes—freedom, enterprise, responsibility, family, security—to put problems and their solutions into a single framework. But the Contract did not stop with consistent themes; it advanced to consistent solutions, viewing issues in a larger context, as the public does, making a coherent whole out of seemingly inconsistent parts, showing how solutions in one area relate to solutions in another.

Lasting solutions are more likely to come from creative approaches that transcend artificial issue categories and solve problems comprehensively without creating new ones. To do that, we must avoid making public policymaking a zero-sum game where someone "wins" only when someone else "loses." If product-liability lawsuits remain unfettered and punitive damages unrestrained, will the economy suffer when businesses pass higher insurance costs on to consumers and lay off workers to save money? Or will manufacturers create safer products that will gain greater global market shares? Must every health, safety, or consumer regulation, every requirement that air or water be cleaner, inevitably impose an economic cost? Or can long-term economic "wealth" and societal benefits be created with "win-win" solutions that protect the environment and create jobs?

Innovative solutions might follow the example of the 1990 Clean Air Act, which allows polluters to buy, sell, or trade the right to pollute.[7] By creating wealth—pollution credits—government action attempts to clean the air without imposing undue costs. Wherever solutions come from, they will require new cooperation between the people and their leaders.

Everyone Must Pitch in To Do Better

Everyone shares blame for the current situation, and everyone must contribute to the solution. Interest groups, the media, government, business, and most of all the public must do their part to create and implement a forward-looking, problem-solving public policy agenda that meets real needs with effective solutions.

Too often, interest groups view the world as divided into supporters and opponents. Those with whom they disagree are painted as their "opponents"; yet they are fellow citizens (or businesses)—men and women of presumed goodwill—who may differ on allowing prayer in schools or raising or lowering the gasoline tax but share deep, fundamental concerns about jobs, health, and financial and personal security.

Oil companies are polluters, in the view of environmentalists, while environmentalists are antibusiness in the view of oil companies. With positions staked out at the extremes, it is difficult for environmentalists to remember that oil companies do not want oceans and beaches fouled with oil any more than environmentalists want pristine forests but no jobs for loggers or paper for newsprint. Welfare opponents do not want children to starve, nor do its supporters want more welfare cheats. On both sides of contentious issues, beneath the rhetoric and the anger lie real people (and interests) with genuine and legitimate concerns.

Interest groups that persist in demonizing the opposition only create a climate where public decisions result in winners and losers. Instead, opposing interest groups can search for common ground. Environmentalists and businesses can identify their core, shared values and search for solutions that accommodate mutual concerns. Every difference will not disappear, but a greater understanding of the opposition's motives can only make each side a more effective participant in public policy-making debates.

When choices have to be made between competing values, interest groups owe it to their members and the public to explain the consequences of the choices. Instead of staking out extreme positions (that are seemingly designed more to build membership and attract media attention than to solve problems), they should educate their members and the general public. In the brave new world of issues and advocacy, interest groups must recognize that their effectiveness will depend not just on their ability to mobilize supporters, but on their success in educating their members and the public about issues and their consequences, and ultimately in shifting public opinion. Instead of flitting from battle to battle, from thirty-second advertisements to 800 numbers to full-page newspaper ads, interest groups should raise the level of the dialogue by helping the public understand the issues. Interest groups that cultivate trust with the public and their members will be seen as responsible voices that can be relied on to represent their members'—and the public's—interest.

Senior citizens' groups should undertake to explain the effect of policy initiatives, not just on their core constituency but on society. Seniors have grandchildren, as do oil company executives. Both must recognize that progress will be made only when real solutions address the many dimensions of public problems. And the more the public understands and appreciates the legitimate concerns on both sides of an issue, the more easily it will accept the ultimate choice.

There is no excuse for "dirty tricks" in issue advocacy campaigns, and no room for misleading and deceptive advertisements that frighten the public with exaggerated predictions of catastrophic consequences. Advertising professionals and consultants who produce issue ads—and the interest groups and issue advocates who hire them—should hold themselves to the highest possible standards of truthfulness and full disclosure, rather than hide behind the First Amendment and the lack of government regulation of issue advertisements. The media, which have begun to scrutinize claims presented by candidates in their advertising and speeches, have shown recent signs of applying that same scrutiny to issue ads. With some help from the media, misstatements and exaggerations by both sides can be filtered out of the public policy debate.

The media have special privileges in our society, and along with those privileges come special responsibilities. That means when the debate turns to issues and public problems the media must go beyond reporting political slogans and rhetoric. The media have an obligation to help educate the public about issues, rather than report on them in the "horse race" mode they have adopted for electoral politics. Issues are much too important to be treated so cavalierly.[8]

The media should seek out impartial and unbiased experts to provide the public with the necessary information to make policy choices. They should avoid giving credence to paid policy experts, at least without exposing the interests that pay them. They should demand and analyze underlying data, rather than merely report paid conclusions. While it is futile to search for one reliable voice that will predict with certainty the consequences of choosing among competing public policy options, more and better information can only improve the process. By doing quick and dirty research, as they struggle to meet deadlines, the media all too eagerly quote any available, authoritative-sounding voice.[9] The public, which relies on the media for most of its information about issues, is inevitably poorer for it.

More attentive media may expose the real interests behind front groups. Even if the merits of each position remain unclear and unpredictable, at least the public and their representatives will know the real parties behind the messages.

Governing institutions at all levels must acknowledge the legitimate concern that tax money be well spent and that the money they do spend comes from the pockets of hard-working citizens. Governments should strive for excellence, always looking for ways to do more with less. They should be open and honest with the public, acknowledging and learning from their failures as well as touting their successes. They should be aggressive in eliminating waste, fraud, and abuse, and in so doing restore public confidence in the work they do.

Government should serve the people who pay the bills. It should not be an impenetrable bureaucracy, forcing citizens and businesses to make multiple calls or visits to get necessary licenses or permits. Government service should be a badge of honor, awarded to a few who meet and maintain the highest standards of excellence. Too often, government workers are dismissed as "bureaucrats" performing unseen and presumably useless tasks. How can we expect our best and brightest to aspire to government service? And if they do not, what kind of government will we have?

Clean air is a desirable result, but so too are regulations written by government officials who understand both the science of clean air and the business of those who, in the course of their activities, may create pollutants. Clear rules should take into account the best science and place reasonable restrictions on those whose activities the government seeks to regulate. Government should keep faith with all the people, providing thoughtful, thorough explanations for its actions or inactions, taking into account competing viewpoints and values, and basing its decision on reliable information, even when not required to do so.

Governments must cooperate. There is little room for duplication of effort and resources between federal and state governments. True meetings of the mind should occur, where regulators parcel out responsibility for public health, safety, welfare, and consumer protection based on competency and available resources. Governments need to be mindful of conflicting and burdensome requirements they impose on businesses and even on other governmental entities.

Businesses should understand that there are public policy goals that cannot be met by blind faith in the invisible hand of the free market. They should respect well-meaning government regulators, working to educate them about unnecessary or burdensome compliance requirements.

Just because they engage in job and wealth creation, businesses, and especially the men and women behind them, are not excused from the obligations of citizenry. If individuals are required to make sacrifices by paying higher taxes or getting fewer public services, businesses should share the pain. The fact that the free market justifies higher prices for goods or services, or higher pay for CEOs, does not mean responsible corporations cannot limit prices or pay in the name of a broader public interest.

No responsible business would knowingly dump hazardous materials into the water supply, even if the government did not make it illegal to do so. It is simply the wrong thing to do, and responsible businesspeople do not need the government to tell them not to do it. Corporations should recognize the greater societal good that goes beyond the bottom line. Increasingly, responsible corporations have recognized that meeting their workers' physical and psychological needs, and improving the extended community in which they exist, can reward them. With government doing less with fewer resources, corporate responsibility becomes even more important.

The people are at the center of every effort to improve public policymaking. They are the engine that drives the process and the ones who have to live with the choices made. It is the public's money that government spends. It is the public's views that are solicited by decision makers, interest groups, and pollsters, and duly reported in the media.

The public cannot be blamed for spending little time thinking about public problems. Family, work, finances, health, and a host of daily problems will always take precedence. But the public deserves more and better opportunities to make its views known to decision makers, and more and better information on which to formulate those views.

The public must be more patient with policy experiments, accepting the fact that failures will occur. The public must have tolerance for ambiguity; even the best scientific minds and careful planning cannot avoid disasters like the *Challenger* explosion. How, then, can we approach certainty when so many public policy decisions depend on much less precise social sciences?

The public must also accept that nothing is free. After a major airplane or train crash, the public demands safer air and train travel. One horrific crime creates a hue and cry for stricter gun-control laws or more police and prisons. But the public must learn to accept the painful truth that easy answers to difficult problems—crime, education, welfare—are illusory; real problems are persistent and resist short-term solutions.

That sounds like a lot to ask of busy citizens, many of whom do not even take the time to vote. While many organizations, including both political parties, expend considerable resources registering individuals to vote, few if any spend the time to educate the public about how to make its views known to policymakers as they make the difficult, day-to-day choices necessary for governing. Politicians concentrate on elections; interest groups narrowly focus on their members' interests; the media have too many other concerns.

Citizens need and deserve new institutions that go beyond traditional interest groups to provide them with accurate, timely information about public policymaking and how they can influence the process. These new institutions can and should concentrate on educating the public about the root causes of public problems, the costs and benefits of proposed solutions, and the likelihood that solutions will work as claimed.

They should also be dedicated to "getting out voices," in the same way that voter registration and education organizations "get out the vote." That means not just providing information to those already familiar with the policymaking process and ways to affect it, or "mobilizing" the grassroots to support or oppose a position, but encouraging and enabling those whose voices have traditionally not been heard to be full participants in public policy debates.

Everyone is affected by public policymaking, but without every voice being heard we cannot be confident that we are making the best policy choices that will provide the greatest benefits for all.

Leaders and the People: Toward a New Relationship

Money and technology now allow wealthy interests to "buy" grassroots support with mass media and direct marketing in much the same way they once "bought" legislative votes with campaign contributions. Democracy can be easily manipulated by money and resources to produce an active and vocal minority with sufficient influence to control policy. "Direct democracy" is no longer limited to ballot initiatives. Legislators get instantaneous feedback, sometimes just after they speak on the floor of Congress.[10] They constantly monitor the pulse of the public, like an intensive-care patient whose every physical response is registered. The technology and the political climate exist to govern by electronic plebiscite.[11]

But the loudest and most powerful are not always the clearest and most representative voices. How do decision makers distinguish meaningful, thoughtful opinions from shifting background noise? Or do they not bother? Who speaks for those who do not choose, or know enough, to participate? Who searches for the best solutions for the greatest number while protecting the rights of the minorities and ensuring society cares for those who are needy and voiceless?

It is a national shame that our leaders, who are elected by the people, are more dependent on support from their campaign contributors than from the voters. And how can legislators be expected to concentrate on the important tasks at hand when they must constantly raise money for the next election? In 1994, the average successful campaigns for the House of Representatives spent $516,126; for Senate races, the average winner spent an astounding $4,569,940.[12]

Legislators who sit on powerful congressional committees attract significant attention and financial support, not from their own constituents, but from interests affected by the committee's jurisdiction. Weaning legislators from their dependence on money and the interests that provide it will restore public confidence in the integrity of public policymaking. It might even lead to policy decisions that benefit the public more than narrow, well-heeled financial interests.

When students were testifying in support of reauthorization of the Higher Education Act in 1992, they were asked by Senator Simon what programs the students would cut to provide more money for college aid. Their naive, but perceptive answer, was: "Senator, that's for you to decide." How would we expect our senators to make that choice? Probably by examining the list of possible program cuts, then deciding which cuts will produce the least "political fallout:" which programs have the most popular support, or, more cynically, which programs have the support of the wealthiest campaign contributors. That would be business as usual in issue politics. But business as usual produces the same old gridlock and "popular," but ineffective, programs.

We deserve more from our leaders. They must go beyond weighing the mail, faxes, e-mail, and phone calls. They must do more than read the latest polls and count the political action committee checks. They cannot merely see which way the wind is blowing and cast their vote in that direction. They have an obligation to lead the people, helping them arrive at the best possible decision for all the people. To do that, they must resist the urge to do what is popular and instead do what is right. They must foster an interactive dialogue between government and the people, one that is inclusive, frank, and avoids playing to fears and emotions.

Our leaders must have the courage to reject the expressed will of the public when it is based on flawed assumptions or angry, emotional reactions. They must educate the public about choices and their consequences, forcing the public to face, and accept, the facts, even when the facts are not pretty and turning one's back on them is easier and more popular. They must force us all to face difficult issues and convince us to make unpopular sacrifices.

With few incentives to look beyond their immediate and personal concerns, citizens can sometimes be forgiven for viewing issues narrowly and seeking instant gratification: "what's in it for me" is an understandable public response. Californians can be excused for being disgusted by the murder of Polly Klaas and channeling their anger and frustration with crime into support for a counterproductive "three strikes and you're out" law. But what excuse do our leaders have?

* * *

Our nation's problems are legion, and they are mounting. Education, crime, health care, race relations, AIDS, homelessness, downsizing and layoffs, the plight of children in poverty, to name the most obvious, defy easy answers. To begin to solve them we must involve all our nation's multifaceted resources, and all its people. Lasting solutions can be found only if citizens and their leaders are willing and able to work together in the public interest.

Notes

Chapter 1

1. Megan Garvey, "Widow Makes Hospitals Change Their Ways," *Washington Post,* September 14, 1994, A3.

Chapter 2

1. *Well-Healed: Inside Lobbying for Health Care Reform,* (Washington, DC: Center for Public Integrity, 1994), 12–16.
2. "The Man Behind the Microsoft Miracle," interview in the *Washington Post,* December 3, 1995, H1.
3. Peter W. Huber and Robert E. Litan, *The Liability Maze* (Washington, DC: Brookings Institution, 1991).
4. Sandra Torrey and Mark Stencel, "Bush, Quayle Put Lawyers in Election Year Docket," *Washington Post,* August 28, 1992, A16.

Chapter 3

1. Jack L. Walker Jr., *Mobilizing Interest Groups in America* (Ann Arbor: University of Michigan Press, 1991); Robert H. Salisbury, ed., *Interest Group Politics in America* (New York: Harper & Row, 1970); Ronald Hrebenar, *Interest Group Politics in America,* 3d ed. (Armonk, NY: M.E. Sharpe, 1997); Mancur Olson, *The Logic of Collective Action.* (Cambridge: Harvard University Press, 1965); Jeffrey M. Berry, *The Interest Group Society* (Glenview, IL: Scott, Foresman, 1989); Mark Petracca, ed., *The Politics of Interests* (Boulder, CO: Westview Press, 1992).

2. *Well-Healed,* Appendix I.

3. There may be as many as 25,000 recognized interest groups today, with many more small local and regional groups, both formal and informal. Jonathan Rauch, *Demosclerosis* (New York: Times Books, 1994), 39–44.

4. William Greider, *Who Will Tell the People?* (New York: Simon and Schuster, 1992), 177–80; David Plotke, "The Mobilization of Business," in Petracca, *Politics of Interests,* 175–200.

5. David Hilzenrath, "AARP's Nonprofit Status Comes under Scrutiny," *Washington Post,* May 22, 1995, A1.

6. Jack Anderson and Michael Binstein, "AARP's Medicare Debate Quandary," *Washington Post,* July 6, 1995, B8.

7. For a general discussion of the theory of interest-group power, see Andrew S. McFarland, "Interest Groups and the Policymaking Process: Sources of Countervailing Power in America," in Petracca, *Politics of Interests,* 58–79.

Chapter 4

1. William Greider, *Who Will Tell the People?* (New York: Simon and Schuster, 1992), 134.

2. The Federal Cigarette Labeling and Advertising Act, 15 U.S.C. § 1331.

3. Larry Rohter, "Florida Prepares New Basis to Sue Tobacco Industry," *New York Times,* May 27, 1994, A1.

4. *New State Ice Co.* v. *Liebmann,* 285 U.S. 262 (1932).

5. Don Phillips, "Federal Speed Limit, Set in 1974, Repealed," *Washington Post,* November 29, 1995, A1.

6. Michael Kramer, "Fixing Welfare Right," *Time,* August 14, 1995, 30.

7. This principle also extends down to the state level, where localities are increasingly unhappy living with mandates imposed by the states. In fact, many states limit the ability of their legislatures to impose unfunded mandates on cities and towns. "Since the 1970's, at least 17 states have either amended their constitutions or enacted statutes that limit the ability of their legislatures to foist so-called unfunded mandates on counties, cities and towns." For example, Kansas requires dog kennels, including those operated by the police, to be "climate controlled," effectively requiring them to be air conditioned, where no similar requirement exists for public housing or schools. Keith Schneider, "Many States Are Limiting the Power to Pass the Buck," *New York Times,* February 5, 1995, 18.

8. 29 U.S.C. § 2601.

9. Richard Harris and Stanley M. Milkis, *The Politics of Regulatory Change* (New York: Oxford University Press, 1989), 140–224.

10. Ibid., 128–39.

11. In addition, the Commerce Clause of the Constitution, Art. I, Sec. 8, Clause 3, grants Congress the power to regulate interstate commerce and imposes limits on state actions that discriminate against interstate, or in favor of intrastate, economic interests.

12. Ellen Perlman, "The Gorilla That Swallows State Laws," *Governing,* August 1994, 46. Most often, the real reason industry opposes preemption is that it doesn't want to be bothered with another level of government having the potential

to act. In some instances we have seen the comical situation of "forum shopping," where franchisors, for instance, first endorsed the authority of the FTC to act (and preempt state action), then decided that the federal government might actually do something, so switched their focus to the states and decided that they are the best forum to enforce the law, backing efforts to take away the FTC's authority to regulate franchisors. Then franchisors became frightened by the prospect of active state regulators and decided to support the FTC's regulatory authority. This sorry tale is aptly chronicled in the *Wall Street Journal,* which first reported it under the headline "Franchisors Flip Flop on Choice for Regulators" (August 7, 1989). At that time, franchisors believed they would get a better deal from the FTC, couching their arguments in terms of it "making sense to work under the same rules nationwide." But three months later a reawakened FTC threatened to act and franchisors changed their minds, prompting another *Wall Street Journal* headline: "Turf Battle Over Regulation of Franchisors" (November 15, 1989). But the battle was never between the states and the federal government; it was a search by franchisors for the "easiest" regulator.

13. E.J. Dionne, "The New, New, New Federalism," *Washington Post,* March 7, 1995, A17.

14. 42 U.S.C. § 7416.

15. Greider, *Who Will Tell the People?,* 26.

16. For example, *Yakus* v. *United States,* 347 U.S. 483 (1944), *Vermont Yankee Nuclear Power Corp* v. *Natural Resources Defense Council,* 435 U.S. 519 (1978).

17. *Rust* v. *Sullivan,* 500 U.S. 173 (1991).

18. 5 U.S.C. § 751 et seq.

19. 16 C.F.R. Part 400.

20. 347 U.S. 483 (1954).

21. Timothy Egan, "A Year Later, Raw Meat Still Lacks Labels," *New York Times,* December 20, 1993, A1.

22. Nan Aron, *Liberty and Justice for All: Public Interest Law in the 1980's and Beyond* (Boulder, CO: Westview Press, 1988)

23. David Helvarg, *The War Against the Greens* (San Francisco: Sierra Club Books, 1994).

24. Margaret Kriz, "Land Mines," *National Journal,* October 23, 1993, 2531.

25. *Nollan* v. *California Coastal Commission,* 483 U.S. 825 (1987); *Dolan* v. *Tigard,* 114 S.Ct. 2481 (1994); *Lucas* v. *South Carolina Coastal Council,* 112 S.Ct. 2886 (1992).

Chapter 5

1. George F. Bishop et al., "Opinions on Fictitious Issues," *Public Opinion Quarterly,* Summer 1986, 240; Richard Morin, "The 1975 Public Affairs Act: Never Was—But Not Forgotten," *Washington Post,* February 26, 1995, C5.

2. Polls vary greatly, from brief telephone interviews to written questionnaires, "mall intercepts," and lengthy interviews. The bibliography contains sources for more information about how to conduct polls and evaluate their reliability.

3. A stark example of public misperceptions was illustrated by a survey that asked Americans what percentage of the population was African American. The answers ranged up to 25.9 percent for African Americans. The actual figure is closer to 12 percent. Richard Morin, "A Distorted Image of Minorities," *Washington Post,* October 8, 1995, A1.

4. "GOP Reading It Wrong; Polls Says Party's Agenda Doesn't Match Public's," *San Francisco Chronicle,* February 28, 1995, A3.

5. Daniel Yankelovich, *Coming to Public Judgment: Making Democracy Work in a Complex World* (Syracuse, NY: Syracuse University Press, 1991).

6. Margaret Carlson, "Order on the Court," *Time,* August 29, 1994, 35.

7. William Claiborne, " 'Three Strikes' Tough on Courts Too," *Washington Post,* March 8, 1995, A1 (quoting Robert A. Pugsley, Southwestern University School of Law: "The economic ramifications are going to be enormous, but I don't think people realize that yet").

8. David Johnston, "A Parting Shot at the Crime Bill Backed by Clinton," *New York Times,* February 16, 1994, A1.

9. Robert Morgenthau [U.S. attorney for the Southern District of New York], "What Prosecutors Won't Tell you," *New York Times,* February 7, 1995, A25; Patrick V. Murphy [former New York City police chief], "Death Penalty Useless," *USA Today,* February 23, 1995, 11A; Joan Biskupic, "Judges Attack the Death 'Machine,' " *Washington Post,* April 16, 1995, A16.

10. Gwen Ifill, "Spending in Crime Bill: Prevention or Just Pork," *New York Times,* August 16, 1994, B7.

11. Yankelovich, *Coming to Public Judgment,* Harwood Group, *Meaningful Chaos: How People form Relationships with Public Concerns* (Dayton, OH: Kettering Foundation, 1993).

12. How else can one explain New York Governor Pataki's 1995 budget proposal? In the words of one commentator, "the budget would reduce welfare grants, which could force poor people onto the streets, but also cut spending for shelters, prevention of homelessness, and transitional housing construction. It would place strict limits on Medicaid coverage for home health care, which could force some frail patients into nursing homes, but would declare a moratorium on the creation of new nursing home beds." Kevin Sack "Social Service Advocates Attack Pataki's Budget as Contradictory," *New York Times*, February 4, 1995, 21.

Chapter 6

1. FRAC's study, however, has been criticized for its methodology, which some believe skewed the results toward the answers FRAC sought. Cynthia Crossen, *Tainted Truth: The Manipulation of Fact in America* (New York: Simon and Schuster, 1994), 152–55; Robert Rector, "Food Fight: How Hungry Are America's Children?" *Policy Review,* Fall 1991, 38.

2. General Accounting Office, "Homelessness: Demand for Services to Homeless Veterans Exceeds VA Program Capacity" Report No. 94–98, February 23, 1994 (estimating that veterans constitute 250,000 of the nation's 600,000 homeless).

3. "Of Magic, Myth, and the Minimum Wage," *The Economist,* September

30, 1995, 94. The 1996 debate on raising the federal minimum wage produced dueling economists, analyzing the same data and reaching opposite conclusions. David E. Rosenbaum, "Analysis: Minimum Wage Debate—Much Bluster over 90 Cents," *New York Times,* April 30, 1996, A1.

4. Robert Pear, "Study Criticizes Subsidy for Insurance for Poor," *New York Times,* June 28, 1994, A14; Jason DeParle, "Clinton Planners Facing a Quiet Fight on Welfare," *New York Times,* March 18, 1994, A18.

5. Barbara Vobejda, "For 19 Million, There's No Father Home," *Washington Post,* April 24, 1995, A5, quoting "Kids Count," report of the Annie E. Casey Foundation.

6. Daniel Yankelovich, *Coming to Public Judgment: Making Democracy Work in a Complex World* (Syracuse, NY: Syracuse University Press, 1991), 15–55.

7. Christopher Jencks, *The Homeless* (Cambridge: Harvard University Press, 1994); Rick Fantasia and Maurice Isserman, *Homelessness: A Sourcebook* (New York: Facts on File, 1994); Susan Yeich, *Politics of Ending Homelessness,* (Lanham, MD: University Press of America, 1994).

8. Peter W. Huber and Robert E. Litan, eds., *The Liability Maze* (Washington, DC: Brookings Institution, 1991); Walter Olson, *The Litigation Explosion* (New York: Dutton, 1991).

9. Joe Queenan, "Birth of a Notion: How the Think Tank Industry Came Up with an Issue that Dan Quayle Could Call His Own," *Washington Post,* September 20, 1992, C1.

10. Liz Spayd, "America the Plaintiff," *Washington Post,* March 5, 1995, C1.

11. Letters to the Editor: Charles Allen, "The McDonald's Coffee Spill Case," *Washington Post,* April 4, 1995, A22 (written by the son-in-law of Stella Liebeck, the woman burned by the McDonald's coffee spill).

12. Stephanie Goldberg, "Tough Times for Victims?" *Chicago Tribune,* July 30, 1995, 14.

13. Richard Saul Wurman, *Information Anxiety,* (New York: Bantam Books, 1989).

14. Lawrence Wallack et al., *Media Advocacy and Public Health* (Newbury Park, CA: Sage, 1993).

15. Council for a Livable World Education Fund, 110 Maryland Avenue NE, Washington DC, 20002. (Action Alert, January 1995.)

16. Gary Lee, "Energy Secretary Faces Hill Fire on Consultant," *Washington Post,* November 16, 1995, A12 (quoting Representative Thomas Bliley Jr., R-VA).

17. Fox Butterfield, " 'Silent March' on Guns Talks Loudly: 40,000 Pairs of Shoes, and All Empty," *New York Times,* September 22, 1994, A18.

18. Jay Mathews, "Federal Rules Carry Weighty Responsibility," *Washington Post,* July 17, 1994, A1.

19. Richard B. Schmitt, "Truth is First Casualty of Tort-Reform Debate," *Wall Street Journal,* March 7, 1995, B1; Colman McCarthy, "House Zealots Serve Half-Baked Evidence," *Washington Post,* March 21, 1995, C9.

20. Stephen J. Simurda, "When Gambling Comes to Town," *Columbia Journalism Review,* January/February 1994, 36–38.

21. Howard Kurtz, "Dr. Whelan's Media Operation," *Columbia Journalism Review,* March/April 1990, 43–47.

22. Amy Schwartz, "Double Blow for the Tobacco Industry," *Washington Post,* May 27, 1994, A8.

23. Myron Levin, "Who's Behind the Building Doctor?" *The Nation,* August 9–16, 1993, 168; Philip J. Hilts, "Data on Secondhand Smoke Were Faked, Workers Say," *New York Times,* December 21, 1994, D23; Alix M. Freedman, "Grand Jury Probes Relationship between Tobacco Industry and Air Quality Firm," *Wall Street Journal,* February 15, 1996, A1.

24. Cynthia Crossen, "How 'Tactical Research' Muddied Diaper Debate," *Wall Street Journal,* May 17, 1994, B1.

25. Crossen, *Tainted Truth,* 133.

26. Peter Passell, "How Much for a Life? Try $3 Million to $5 Million," *New York Times,* January 29, 1995, F3.

27. The Republican's Contract with America included a requirement that federal agencies formally weight the costs and benefits of major regulatory actions, using risk assessment principles.

28. For a detailed analysis of making policy in the face of uncertainty, including proposals for elevating these decisions above the political process, see Stephen Breyer, *Breaking The Vicious Circle: Toward Effective Risk Regulation* (Cambridge: Harvard University Press, 1993); Kenneth R. Foster et al., *Phantom Risk: Scientific Interference and the Law* (Cambridge: MIT Press, 1993).

29. Philip H. Abelson, "Toxic Terror's Phantom Risks," *Science* 46 (July 23, 1993): 407.

30. Doug Haddix, "Alar as a Media Event," *Columbia Journalism Review,* March/April 1990, 44–45.

31. Eliot Marshall, "A Is for Apple, Alar, and . . . Alarmist," *Science,* October 4, 1991, 20.

Chapter 7

1. In chapter 12 we explore the implications of Internet discussions, electronic town halls, local-origination cable programs, and other "alternative media" for issue advocacy.

2. The media can also be used to change individual behavior, such as by urging people to wear seat belts or conserve energy. For our purposes, we confine our discussion of media advocacy to efforts to influence public policy. Of course some campaigns to change individual behavior are part of a broad-based advocacy campaign, such as alcohol and beer companies urging teenagers not to drink, which are intended, in part, to fend off additional government regulations.

3. William Greider, *Who Will Tell the People?* (New York: Simon and Schuster, 1992), 116.

4. Daniel Seligman, "Condiment Capers," *Fortune* 109 (June 25, 1984): 125–26.

5. Lance Marrow, "Video Warriors in Los Angeles," *Time* 139 (May 11, 1992): 68; "Video Vigilantes," *Newsweek* 118 (July 22, 1991): 42.

6. R. Lee Sullivan, "Leaner Menus," *Forbes* 155 (March 13, 1995): 154.

7. Kenneth Brower, "Save Our Sea Mammals," *Omni* 11 (June, 1989): 26.

8. Michael Clayton, "A Boycott to Kill a Seal Hunt," *Maclean's* 97 (March 26, 1984): 24.

9. Adam Clymer, "Pizza Chain Blocks Critical Commercial," *New York Times,* July 16, 1994, A9.

10. Michael Doan, "The Little Hostage to a Killer in the Blood," *U.S. News and World Report* 101 (September 8, 1986): 10.

11. Lawrence Wallack et al., *Media Advocacy and Public Health* (Newbury Park, CA: Sage, 1993), 92.

12. Ibid.

13. Guy Gugliotta, "Anti-Pesticide Coalition Finds Toxic Atmosphere at Most Government Sites," *Washington Post,* March 7, 1995, A5.

14. Amanda Spake, "When the Stars Come Marching In," *Washington Post,* January 12, 1992, W10.

15. Anna Borgman, "Garment Workers show U.S. the 'Child Behind the Label,' " *Washington Post,* July 24, 1995, D4. (The National Labor Committee, an interest group opposed to child labor, brought two teenage Central American garment workers to America to describe their experiences to American audiences and testify before Congress.)

16. "Deadly Burgers," *Time* 141 (February 8, 1993): 22.

17. Leon Dash, "A Difficult Journey: From Rural Hardship to Urban Adversity," *Washington Post,* September 18, 1994, A1.

18. Warren King, "Smoking Satire: Statue Opposes Tobacco Company's National Exhibit," *Seattle Times,* November 15, 1990, A1.

19. Wallack et al., *Media Advocacy and Public Health,* 183–88.

20. Howard Kurtz, "The GOP Finds an Ally in an Unexpected Paper," *Washington Post,* December 13, 1995, C1.

21. Amy Bernstein, "PC Comics," *U.S. News and World Report* 114 (May 7, 1993): 16; "Green Comics," *Buzzworm* 4 (January 1992): 12.

22. A representative of the National Coalition Against the Misuse of Pesticides worked with Senator Leahy's staff, who were drafting legislation to prohibit the sale of pesticides in other countries that are banned in the United States. Together they helped *L.A. Law* prepare the fact-based episode. Greg Ashford, "US Pesticide Exporters Outflanked by Greenpeace," *Legal Times* 14, no. 42 (March 9, 1992): 1, 16.

23. Sandra Torrey, "Lawyers—A Spoiled Salmon Turns into a Half-Baked Shark," *Washington Post,* December 12, 1994, F7.

24. Kathryn C. Montgomery, *Target: Prime Time. Advocacy Groups and the Struggle over Entertainment Television* (New York: Oxford University Press, 1988); Todd S. Purdum, "At Lunch with Ron Silver: Lights, Camera, Action! Ideas, Activism, Democracy!" *New York Times,* December 29, 1993, C1.

25. R. Kenneth Godwin, "Money, Technology, and Political Interests: The Direct Marketing of Politics," in *The Politics of Interest,* ed. Mark Petracca (Boulder, CO: Westview Press, 1992), 175–98.

26. Leon Jaroff, "A Crusader from the Heartland," *Time,* v. 137, March 25, 1991, 56.

27. Wallack et al., *Media Advocacy and Public Health,* 89–90.

28. Robert L. Heath, *Strategic Issues Management* (San Francisco: Jossey-Bass, 1988); William Renfro, *Issues Management in Strategic Planning* (Westport, CT: Quorum Books, 1993).

29. Tom Kenworthy, "Drive Begun to Protect Tiger Species," *Washington Post,* September 29, 1995, A3.

30. Jarol B. Manheim, *All of the People, All the Time: Strategic Communication and American Politics* (Armonk, NY: M.E. Sharpe, 1991), 111.

31. Ibid., 112

32. Kevin Sack, "Andrew Cuomo," *New York Times Magazine,* March 27, 1994, 40.

33. John F. Harris, "Correct Lingo Is Essential during Furlough," *Washington Post,* December 19, 1995, A10.

34. Memorandum from Frank Luntz to the Republican Conference, January 9, 1995; Ann Devroy, "House Republicans Get Talking Points," *Washington Post,* February 2, 1995, A9.

35. Adam Clymer, Robert Pear, and Robin Toner, "For Health Care, Time Was a Killer," *New York Times,* August 29, 1994, A1.

36. Neal Templin, "Detroit Girds for Fight over Fuel Economy," *Wall Street Journal,* October 18, 1994, B4.

37. Margaret Kriz, "Land Mine," *National Journal,* October 23, 1993, 2531.

38. Ann Devroy, "House Republicans Get Talking Points," *Washington Post,* February 2, 1995, A9.

39. Michael Pertschuk and Wendy Schaetzel, *The People Rising: The Campaign Against the Bork Nomination,* (New York: Thunder's Mouth Press, 1989), 117–45.

Chapter 8

1. For example, the Alliance for Jobs and Health was a coalition of retailers and restaurants that participated in health care reform, but kept a low profile. "It's one of those unique Washington things . . . very ad hoc." *Well-Healed: Inside Lobbying for Health Care Reform* (Washington, D.C.: Center for Public Integrity, 1994), 62.

2. As we explore the nature of coalitions, it's important to recognize that many entities call themselves "coalitions," probably because the term implies power and unity, although they do not function as coalitions as we describe them. Typically they are simply interest groups adopting the name coalition.

3. Examples include the work of the Industrial Areas Foundation, Communities Organized for Public Service (COPS) in San Antonio, Baltimoreans United in Leadership Development (BUILD), and the Association of Community Organizations for Reform Now (ACORN). William Greider, *Who Will Tell the People?* (New York: Simon and Schuster, 1992), 222–41; Saul D. Alinsky, *Rules for Radicals* (New York: Vintage Books, 1989); Si Kahn, *Organizing: A Guide for Grassroots Leaders* (New York: Mc-Graw Hill, 1982); Gary Delgado, *Organizing in the Movement: The Roots and Growth of ACORN* (Philadelphia: Temple University Press, 1985); Kim Bobo, Jackie Kendall, and Steve Max, *Organizing for Social Change: A Manual for Activists in the 1990's* (Cabin John, MD: Seven Lock's Press, 1991).

4. David Plotke, "The Political Mobilization of Business," in *The Politics of Interest,* ed. Mark Petracca (Boulder, CO: Westview Press, 1992), 175, 181–93.

5. David Gonzalez, "Religions Are Putting Faith in Environmentalism," *New York Times,* November 6, 1994, 34.

6. Michael Weisskopf, Health Care Lobbies Lobby Each Other, *Washington Post,* March 1, 1994, A8.

7. Steven A. Holmes, "The Strange Politics of Immigration," *New York Times,* December 31, 1995, E3.

8. Jill Lancelot, National Taxpayers Union Foundation, as quoted in Tom Kenworthy, "Green Scissors Coalition Seeks $33 Billion in Cuts," *Washington Post,* January 31, 1995, A13.

9. George Lardner Jr., "Coalition Urges Congress to Reject New Powers for Federal Law Enforcement," *Washington Post,* October 25, 1995, A7.

10. Tom Kenworthy, "Unlikely Alliance Finds Common Ground for Grizzlies," *Washington Post,* October 29, 1995, A3.

11. Robert L. Heath and Associates, *Strategic Issues Management* (San Francisco: Jossey-Bass, 1988), 190.

12. Steven A. Holmes, "Abortion Foes Reach Accord on Adoption," *New York Times,* August 18, 1995, A17.

Chapter 9

1. Michael Weisskopf, "An Exercise in Pain Avoidance," *Washington Post,* February 24, 1995, A19.

2. Michael Weisskopf, "Health Care Lobbies Lobby Each Other," *Washington Post,* March 1, 1994, A1.

3. Alison Mitchell, "Two Genteel Giants Meet in New Hampshire," *New York Times,* June 12, 1995, A1.

4. The tax laws restrict most nonprofit interest groups from participating directly in election campaigns, 26 U.S.C. § 501(c). The federal election laws prohibit corporations, including nonprofits from making campaign contributions, 2 U.S.C § 441(b), although they may establish separate political action committees.

5. Adam Clymer, Robert Pear, and Robin Toner, "For Health Care, Time Was a Killer," *New York Times,* August 29, 1994, A1.

6. Richard Harris and Stanley M. Milkis, *The Politics of Regulatory Change* (New York: Oxford University Press, 1989), 140–224.

7. Dan Morgan, "Pressure on NLRB Turns into a Doubled Budget Cut," *Washington Post,* July 2, 1995, A8.

8. Cindy Skrzycki, "Rulemakers Discover Hill's Power over the Purse Strings," *Washington Post,* September 15, 1995, F1.

9. Jane Fritsch, "Threat to Cut EPA Budget Reflects a New Political Shift," *New York Times,* August 24, 1995, A1.

10. See for example, the requirements imposed on Federal Trade Commission rulemaking by 15 U.S.C. § 57a.

11. Harris and Milkis, *Politics of Regulatory Change,* 184.

12. *Federal Register* 60 (August 11, 1995): 41314.

13. Barnaby J. Feder, "Weighing in on Tobacco at the FDA," *New York Times,* January 2, 1996, A7.

14. N. Craig Smith, *Morality and the Market: Consumer Pressure for Corpo-*

rate Accountability (New York: Routledge, 1990); Diane MacEachern, *Enough Is Enough: The Hell-Raiser's Guide to Community Activism* (New York: Avon Books, 1994).

15. A spokesman for Starkist explained his company's response to the boycott: "The idea that the company could be branded as the largest slaughterers of dolphins in the world seemed to us to be dramatically opposed to where the company wanted to position itself as health-conscious and caring." See Bernice Kanner, "Forcing the Issues," *New York Times,* February 11, 1991, A22 ("companies with low priced, frequently purchased items are especially vulnerable" to boycotts).

16. Bhushan Bahree, Kyle Pope, and Allanna Sullivan, "How Greenpeace Sank Shell's Plan to Dump Big Oil Rig in Atlantic," *Wall Street Journal,* July 7, 1995, A1.

17. "How to Make Lots of Money and Save the Planet Too," *The Economist,* June 3, 1995, 57–58.

18. Smith, *Morality and the Market,* 49–51.

19. Ibid., 266.

20. Jayne Hurley and Stephen Schmidt, "Movie Theater Snacks," *Nutrition Action Health Letter,* May 1994, 1.

21. William Grimes, "How about Some Popcorn with Your Fat," *New York Times,* May 1, 1994, 4:2. On May 4, 1994, the *New York Times* published an editorial entitled "Kernels of Truth," calling on theater owners to post signs disclosing the kind of oil used to cook their popcorn (A22).

22. See Peter W. Huber, "Publicize or Perish," *Forbes* 145 (June 11, 1990) 208, reacting to the awards from a business perspective.

23. Martha Hamilton, "Virginia Power Plant Called Major Polluter," *Washington Post,* November 30, 1995, B14.

24. Doyle, *Hold the Applause* (Washington, DC: Friends of the Earth, 1991).

25. Raymond L. Fischer, "Sex, Drugs, and TV: Stretching the Limits of Bad Taste," *USA Today* (Weekly) 118 (March 1990): 46–49.

26. "How Green Is My Label," *Time,* June 25, 1990, 44.

27. Rosalynn Will, *Shopping for a Better World: A Quick and Easy Guide to Socially Responsible Supermarket Shopping* (New York: Council on Economic Priorities, 1994).

28. "Ethical Shopping: Human Rights," *The Economist,* June 3, 1995, 58.

29. Keith Schneider, "For the Environment, Compassion Fatigue," *New York Times,* November 6, 1994, A3.

30. The Investor Responsibility Research Center tracks major corporations and shareholder proposals and reports that the number of proposals, and the number of winning proposals, are both increasing. "Silly Season Gets More Sensible as Gadflies Fight the Good Fight," *Barron's,* June 26, 1995, 10.

31. S. Prakash Sethi, *Interfaith Center on Corporate Responsibility: A Sponsored-Related Movement of the National Council of Churches* (Dallas, TX: University of Texas, 1980).

32. Mark Landler, "Coalition Challenges Time Warner over Gangsta Rap," *New York Times,* June,1 1995, B10.

33. Judith Weintraub, "Delores Tucker, Gangsta Buster," *Washington Post,* November 29, 1995, C1.

34. George W. Pring and Penelope Canan, "Symposium: Strategic Lawsuits

Against Public Participation," *Bridgeport Law Review* 12 (Summer 1992): 937.

35. See, for example, California Code of Civil Procedure Section 425.16, effective January 1, 1993.

36. Mike Mills, "The New Kings of Capitol Hill: Regional Bells Use Lobbying Clout to Push for New Markets," *Washington Post,* April 23, 1995, H1, H5.

37. Larry Sabato, *PAC Power: Inside the World of Political Action Committees* (New York: Norton, 1985).

38. M. Margaret Conway and Joanne Connor Green, "Political Action Committees and the Political Process in the 1990s," in *Interest Group Politics,* ed. Allen J. Cigler and Burdett A. Loomis (Washington, DC: CQ Press, 1995), 155–74.

39. Benjamin Sheffner, "House Committee Chairmanships Are More Lucrative Than Ever for Fundraising," *Roll Call,* September 11, 1995, A24.

40. William Greider, *Who Will Tell the People?* (New York: Simon and Schuster, 1992), 66.

41. Michael Waldman, *Who Robbed America: A Citizen's Guide to the Savings and Loan Scandal* (New York: Random House, 1990).

Chapter 10

1. "The Clinton Sales Campaign," *Newsweek,* November 8, 1993, 41–42.

2. Members in "safe" seats have more latitude than those in "vulnerable" districts. And congressional leaders, including many committee and subcommittee chairs, may have more loyalty to their party (or president) than to the voters who elected them.

3. Bonner & Associates/Gallup Poll, "Survey of Business Issues in the New Congress," December 1992; Western Union, "Survey of Congressional Staff," June 1993; Burston-Marsteller, "Communicating with Congress 1992," June 1992; 20/20 Vision, "Is Anyone Listening?" 1991. One survey of congressional members and staffs found that handwritten letters were rated "most effective" or "very effective" by 91 percent, while postcards or computer-generated letters were ranked "not very effective" or "not effective" by 87 percent. Ann Cooper, "Middleman Mail," *National Journal,* September 14, 1985, 2036, 2037.

4. Former Congressman Mike Synar, quoted in Peter H. Stone, "Green, Green Grass," *National Journal,* March 27, 1993, 755. But one grassroots lobbyist who specializes in generating large quantities of mail believes that lawmakers do "weigh their mail." "Special Interest Lobbyists Cultivate the 'Grass Roots' to Influence Capitol Hill," *Congressional Quarterly,* September 12, 1981, 1739, 1740.

5. Hedrick Smith, *The Power Game* (New York: Random House, 1988), 240.

6. David Segal, "Legislators Challenge Telegrams' Credibility," *Washington Post,* August 4, 1995, B1.

7. In another context, AT&T brought more than 2,000 of its corporate managers and employees to Washington to oppose telecommunications reform. Mike Mills, "Going the Distance to Block the Bells," *Washington Post,* July 28, 1995, C3.

8. Ron Faucheux, "The Grassroots Explosion," *Campaigns and Elections,* December/January 1995, 20.

9. Kathryn Seelye, "Hobbling of Lobbying Bill Shows Muscle Power of 'Grass Roots' Conservative Network," *New York Times,* October 7, 1994, A22.

10. Art Levine and Ken Silverstein, "How the Drug Lobby Cut Cost Controls," *The Nation,* December 13, 1993, 731.

11. *Well-Healed: Inside Lobbying for Health Care Reform* (Washington, DC: Center for Public Integrity, 1994), 46.

12. Ibid., 56.

13. "Cyber-lobbying has clearly arrived. Companies, especially those looking to cut costs, are finding the Internet an irresistible way to get out a message and mobilize consumers. Posting on the World Wide Web is vastly cheaper than using regular mail or broadcast faxes, and it reaches millions instantly. Copies, moreover, can be effortlessly forwarded to countless addresses. And once a company reaches and agitates an audience, the Internet allows that audience to rant and rave in bulk. If you e-mail your representative and want to make sure that every other legislator in the chamber gets a copy, a few choice keystrokes will do the job." David Segal, "Making Their Case in Cyberspace, *Washington Post,* April 24, 1995, H15.

14. William Aronson et al., "The Success and Repeal of the Medicare Catastrophic Coverage Act," *Journal of Health Politics, Policy, and Law* 19 (Winter 1994): 753–71; John Hess, "The Catastrophic Health Care Fiasco," *The Nation* 250 (May 21, 1993): 698. Bruce Wolpe, *Lobbying Congress* (Washington, DC: CQ Press, 1990), 67–83.

15. Wolpe, *Lobbying Congress,* 76.

16. Peter H. Stone, "Green, Green Grass," *National Journal,* March 27, 1993, 755.

17. *Well-Healed,* 56.

18. James Brooke, "Budget Cuts Threaten Air Links to Remote Areas," *New York Times,* September 6, 1995, A1.

19. Hedrick Smith, *The Power Game* (New York: Random House, 1988), 240; Fritz Elmendorf, "Generating Grass-Roots Campaigns and Public Involvement," in *Strategic Issues Management,* ed. Robert L. Heath and Associates (San Francisco: Jossey-Bass, 1988), 312.

20. Ann Cooper, "Lobbying in the '80s: High Tech Takes Hold," *National Journal,* September 14, 1985, 2030. Steven Waldman, "Watering the Grass Roots," *Newsweek,* May 6, 1991, 35; Burdett A. Loomis, "A New Era: Groups and the Grass Roots," in *Interest Group Politics,* ed. Allen J. Cigler and Burdett A. Loomis (Washington, DC: CQ Press, 1995), 169.

21. R. Kenneth Godwin, "Money, Technology, and Political Interests: The Direct Marketing of Politics," in *The Politics of Interests,* ed. Mark Petracca (Boulder, CO: Westview Press, 1992), 308–25; Jane Fritsch, "The Grassroots, Just a Phone Call Away," *New York Times,* June 23, 1995, A1.

22. Stone, "Green, Green Grass," 756.

23. Faucheux, "Grassroots Explosion," 21.

24. Richard B. Schmitt and Amy Stevens, "Deloitte Pushed for Anonymity in Lobby Effort," *Wall Street Journal,* April 1994, B1.

25. The same tactic can be employed in writing letters to the editor without revealing the writer's affiliation. Serge Kovaleski and John Mintz, "NRA Letter Writer Fiddles with Name to Get Published," *Washington Post,* July 25, 1995, A1.

26. Bill Keller, "Special-Interest Lobbyists Cultivate the 'Grass Roots' to In-

fluence Capitol Hill," *Congressional Quarterly Weekly Report,* September 12, 1981, 1739, 1742.

27. David Segal, "Unleashing the Lobbyists and More," *Washington Post,* August 3, 1995, A1.

28. David Segal, "PR Firm Retreats on Telegrams: Phone Companies' Lobbying Tarnished," *Washington Post,* September 16, 1995, C1.

29. Jack Anderson and Michael Binstein, "Fund Raiser Already a Medicare Winner," *Washington Post,* October 2, 1995, B8.

30. Elizabeth Kolbert, "Special Interests' Special Weapon," *New York Times,* March 26, 1995, 20.

31. *Well-Healed,* 47–51.

32. Adam Clymer, Robert Pear, and Robin Toner, "For Health Care, Time Was a Killer," *New York Times,* August 29, 1994, A1.

33. Michael Weisskopf, "Grassroots Health Lobby Financed by Insurers," *Washington Post,* October 20, 1993, A1.

34. Jay Mathews, "Torts and a Tug on the Heartstrings," *Washington Post,* May 10, 1995, F1.

35. Kolbert, "Special Interests' Special Weapon," 20.

36. Allan J. Cigler and Burdett A. Loomis, "Contemporary Interest Group Politics: More than 'More of the Same,' " in Cigler and Loomis, *Interest Group Politics,* 403.

37. For example, see Richard Schmitt, "Truth Is First Casualty of Tort-Reform Debate," *Wall Street Journal,* March 7, 1995, B1.

38. Carl Deal, *The Greenpeace Guide to Anti-Environmental Organizations* (Berkeley, CA: Odonian Press, 1993).

39. David Helvarg, *The War Against the Greens: The Wise-Use Movement, the New Right, and Anti-Environmental Violence* (San Francisco: Sierra Club Books, 1994); John Echeverria and Raymond Eby, *Let the People Judge: Wise Use and the Property Rights Movement* (Washington, DC: Island Press, 1995).

40. Cooper, "Middleman Mail," 2041.

41. Michael Weisskopf, "Grassroots Health Lobby Financed by Insurers," *Washington Post,* October 20, 1993, A1; *Well-Healed,* 41.

42. Quoted in Weisskopf, "Grassroots Health Lobby Financed by Insurers," A1.

43. Wolpe, *Lobbying Congress,* 69.

44. "Public Interest Pretenders," *Consumer Reports,* May 1994, 318

45. Mark Megalli, *Masks of Deception* (Washington, DC: Essential Information, 1991), 56.

46. Michael Weisskopf, "Invisibly, Tobacco Firms Back Campaign Against Higher Cigarette Taxes," *Washington Post,* August 26, 1994, A10.

47. Peter Stone, "Learning from Nader," *National Journal,* June 11, 1994, 1342.

48. Laurie McGinley, "Upstart Conservative Groups Split Seniors Lobby Opposed to Budget Amendment, Helping Odds," *Wall Street Journal,* February 23, 1995, A16.

49. "Important economic interests are sensitive to democratic attitudes and typically seek out allies that do not themselves seem so powerful. Community

bankers are recruited to speak for banking. Small town insurance agents lobby for mammoth insurance companies; independent drillers and gas-station operators defend big oil." William Greider, *Who Will Tell the People?* (New York: Simon and Schuster, 1992), 28.

50. Advertisement in the *Wall Street Journal,* June 12, 1995, B7B.

51. Advocacy Institute, *Taking Initiative: The 1990 Citizens' Movement to Raise California Alcohol Excise Taxes to Save Lives.* (Washington, DC: Advocacy Institute, 1992), 91–92.

52. Greider, *Who Will Tell the People?* 36–37.

53. Art Levine and Ken Silverstein, "How the Drug Lobby Cut Cost Controls," *The Nation,* December 13, 1993, 725, 731.

54. Peter Carlson, "The Truth . . . But Not the Whole Truth," *Washington Post Magazine,* June 4, 1995, 13.

55. Paul Goldberger, "Philip Morris Calls in I.O.U.'s in the Arts," *New York Times,* October 5, 1994, A1.

56. Pamela Sebastian, "Charitable Wineries Ask for More Than Thanks," *Wall Street Journal,* October 21, 1994, B1.

57. Advocacy Institute, *Taking Initiative,* 105.

Chapter 11

1. Throughout this chapter, we use the term *initiative* to refer to both referenda and initiatives, since initiatives are much more common and both share many of the same characteristics.

2. Thomas Cronin, *Direct Democracy* (Cambridge: Harvard University Press, 1989); David Schmidt, *Citizen Lawmakers: The Ballot Initiative Revolution* (Philadelphia: Temple University, 1989); Report and Recommendations of the California Commission on Campaign Financing, *Democracy by Initiative* (Los Angeles: Center for Responsive Government, 1992).

3. Lawrence Goodwyn, *Democratic Promise: The Populist Movement in America* (New York: Oxford University Press, 1976); George McKenna, ed., *American Populism* (New York: Putnam's, 1974).

4. Cronin, *Direct Democracy,* 3.

5. California Commission on Campaign Financing, *Democracy by Initiative,* 7.

6. Advocacy Institute, *Taking Initiative: The 1990s Citizens' Movement to Raise California Alcohol Excise Taxes to Save Lives* (Washington, DC: Advocacy Institute, 1992), 1.

7. Cronin, *Direct Democracy,* 68.

8. In most states initiatives must be submitted to the attorney general to ensure their legality and conformity with the state constitution.

9. California Commission on Campaign Financing, *Democracy by Initiative,* 6.

10. Ibid., 9.

11. Cronin, *Direct Democracy,* 62–66.

12. California Commission on Campaign Financing, *Democracy by Initiative,* 15.

13. Cronin, *Direct Democracy,* 108–16.

14. Betty Zisk, *Money, Media, and the Grass Roots: State Ballot Issues and the Electoral Process* (Newbury Park, CA: Sage, 1987), 90–110.

15. *First National Bank of Boston* v. *Bellotti,* 435 U.S. 765 (1978).

16. Advocacy Institute, *Taking Initiative,* 90–95.

17. "Voters will support the status quo unless they are given the arguments for changing it, especially if each side . . . presents a plausible case and challenges the veracity of the other side." Cronin, *Direct Democracy,* 86.

18. Advocacy Institute, *Taking Initiative,* 116.

19. Cronin, *Direct Democracy,* 94–96.

20. California Commission on Campaign Financing, *Democracy by Initiative,* 12.

21. Ibid., 13.

22. Ed Koupla, quoted in Cronin, *Direct Democracy,* 63.

23. Cronin, *Direct Democracy,* 64–65.

24. Ironically, California voters adopted, through the initiative process, Proposition 105, the Public's Right to Know Act, requiring disclosure of funding sources in initiative campaigns. The California law is the exception, rather than the rule, among the states.

25. " 'For Farmworkers' Rights . . . Yes on 22,' was a billboard message in 1972 portraying a measure as one whose adoption would help the farmworkers. But in fact the initiative was sponsored by farm and ranch owners and was explicitly intended to restrict farmworkers' rights." Cronin, *Direct Democracy,* 218.

26. Ibid., 77.

27. Ibid., 70–76.

Chapter 12

1. David Stern and Tim Weiner, "Emerging Role for the CIA: Economic Spy," *New York Times,* October 15, 1995, A1.

2. Louis Uchitelle and N.R. Kleinfield, "On the Battlefields of Business, Millions of Casualties," *New York Times,* March 3, 1996, A1 (start of a seven-part article, "The Downsizing of America").

3. Steven A. Holmes, "U.S. Undergoing Major Demographic Shift, Census Bureau Says," *New York Times,* March 15, 1996, A1.

4. Doubts are already being raised, even by state governmental officials. Sam Howe Verhover, "With Power Shift, State Lawmakers See New Demands," *New York Times,* September 24, 1995, A1; Charles Babbington, "Potholes on the Road to a New Federalism," *Washington Post,* October 15, 1995, A1; Albert Karr, "State Officials Ready to Take Control of More Programs, but Many See Risks," *Wall Street Journal,* October 23, 1995, C13.

5. The line-item veto is limited in its applicability and the Supreme Court has yet to rule on its constitutionality.

6. Peter H. Stone, "Green, Green Grass," *National Journal,* March 27, 1993, 755.

7. Jeffrey Taylor, "Smog Swapping: New Rules Harness Power of Free Markets to Curb Air Pollution," *Wall Street Journal,* April 14, 1992, A1.

8. Howard Kurtz, *Media Circus: The Trouble with America's Newspapers* (New York: Times Books, 1993); James Fallows, *Breaking the News: How the Media Undermine American Democracy,* (New York: Pantheon, 1996).

9. Joe Saltzman, "Journalism at Its Worst," *USA Today* 118 (May, 1990): 27.

10. R.W. Apple Jr., "Challenges from a Headstrong Public," *New York Times,* January 29, 1993, A1. ("With the whole country wired, ordinary voters in Kansas with time on their hands often have a better grip on events in Washington, through CNN or C-SPAN, than harried officials here. That is especially true when hearings are involved; so quick is the response that senatorial aides field telephone calls from home and rush to the hearing room to hand their bosses notes advising them not to look so prosecutorial or to change their posture as they ask questions.")

11. Jeffrey B. Abramson, F. Christopher Arterton, and Garry R. Orren, *The Electronic Commonwealth* (New York: Basic Books, 1988).

12. Larry Makinson, *The Price of Admission* (Center for Responsive Politics, Washington, DC: 1995), 1.

Bibliography

Abramson, Jeffrey B., F. Christopher Arterton, and Gary R. Orren. *The Electronic Commonwealth*. New York: Basic Books, 1988.

Alinsky, Saul D. *Rules for Radicals*. New York: Vintage Books, 1989.

Altschull, J. Herbert. *Agents of Power*. White Plains, NY: Longman, 1995.

Aron, Nan. *Liberty and Justice for All: Public Interest Law in the 1980's and Beyond*. Boulder, CO: Westview Press, 1988.

Asher, Herbert. *Polling and the Public: What Every Citizen Should Know*. Washington, DC: CQ Press, 1992.

Auerbach, Joel D. *Keeping a Watchful Eye: The Politics of Congressional Oversight*. Washington, DC: Brookings Institution, 1990.

Berry, Jeffrey M. *The Interest Group Society*. Glenview, IL: Scott, Foresman, 1989.

Birnbaum, Jeffrey H. *The Lobbyists: How Influence Peddlers Get Their Way in Washington*. New York: Times Books, 1992.

Birnbaum, Jeffrey H., and Alan S. Murray. *Showdown at Gucci Gulch: Lawmakers, Lobbyists, and the Unlikely Triumph of Tax Reform*. New York: Random House, 1987.

Bobo, Kim, Jackie Kendall, and Steve Max. *Organizing for Social Change: A Manual for Activists in the 1990's*. Cabin John, MD: Seven Lock's Press, 1991.

Boyte, Harry C., Heather Booth, and Steve Max. *Citizen Action and the New American Populism*. Philadelphia: Temple University Press, 1986.

Brecher, Jeremy, and Tim Costello, ed. *Building Bridges: The Emerging Grassroots Coalition of Labor and Community*. New York: Monthly Review Press, 1990.

Breyer, Stephen. *Breaking the Vicious Circle: Toward Effective Risk Regulation*. Cambridge: Harvard University Press, 1993.

Broder, David S. *Behind the Front Page: A Candid Look at How the News is Made*. New York: Simon and Schuster, 1987.

273

Carmines, Edward G., and James A. Stimson. *Issue Evolution: Race and the Transformation of American Politics*. Princeton, NJ: Princeton University Press, 1989.

Center for Public Integrity. *Well-Healed: Inside Lobbying for Health Care Reform*. Washington, DC: Center for Public Integrity, 1994.

Center for Responsive Government. *Democracy by Initiative, Report and Recommendations of the California Commission on Campaign Financing*. Los Angeles: Center for Responsive Government, 1992.

Cigler, Allan J., and Burdett A. Loomis, eds. *Interest Group Politics*. 4th ed. Washington, DC: CQ Press, 1995.

Clawson, Dan, Alan Neustadtl, and Denise Scott. *Money Talks: Corporate PACs and Political Influence*. New York: Basic Books, 1992.

Cobb, Roger, and Charles Elder. *Participation in American Politics: The Dynamics of Agenda-Building*. Boston: Allyn and Bacon, 1972.

Conway, M. Margaret. *Political Participation in the United States*. Washington, DC: CQ Press, 1991.

Cronin, Thomas. *Direct Democracy*. Cambridge: Harvard University Press, 1989.

Crossen, Cynthia. *Tainted Truth: The Manipulation of Fact in America*. New York: Simon and Schuster, 1994.

Crotty, William, Mildred A. Schwartz, and John C. Green, eds. *Representing Interests and Interest Group Representation*. Lanham, MD: University Press of America, 1994.

Davis, Kenneth C. *Discretionary Justice*. Baton Rouge: Louisiana State University Press, 1969.

Deal, Carl. *The Greenpeace Guide to Anti-Environmental Organizations*. Berkeley, CA: Odonian Press, 1993.

Delgado, Gary. *Organizing in the Movement: The Roots and Growth of ACORN*. Philadelphia: Temple University Press, 1985.

Dionne, E.J. *Why Americans Hate Politics*. New York: Simon and Schuster, 1991.

Dodd, Lawrence C., and Calvin Jillson, eds. *New Perspectives on American Politics*. Washington, DC: CQ Press, 1994.

Dodd, Lawrence C., and Bruce I. Oppenheimer, eds. *Congress Reconsidered*. 5th ed. Washington, DC: CQ Press 1993.

Drew, Elizabeth. *Showdown: The Struggle between the Gingrich Congress and the Clinton White House*. New York: Simon and Schuster, 1996.

Echeverria, John, and Raymond Eby. *Let the People Judge: Wise Use and the Property Rights Movement*. Washington, DC: Island Press, 1995.

Ehrenhalt, Alan. *The United States of Ambition: Politicians, Power, and the Pursuit of Office*. New York: Times Books, 1991.

Elving, Ronald D. *Conflict and Compromise: How Congress Makes the Law*. New York: Simon and Schuster, 1995.

Erickson, Robert S., Gerald C. Wright, and John P. McIver. *Statehouse Democracy*. New York: Cambridge University Press, 1993.

Ewing, Raymond. *Managing the New Bottom Line: Issues Management for Senior Executives*. Homewood, IL: Dow Jones-Irwin, 1987.

Fallows, James. *Breaking the News: How the Media Undermine American Democracy*. New York: Pantheon, 1996.

Fantasia, Rick, and Maurice Isserman. *Homelessness: A Sourcebook*. New York: Facts on File, 1994.

Fishkin, James. *The Voice of the People: Public Opinion and Democracy*. New Haven, CT: Yale University Press, 1995.

Foster Kenneth R., et al. *Phantom Risk: Scientific Interference and the Law*. Cambridge: MIT Press, 1993.

Gold, Philip. *Advertising, Politics, and American Culture*. New York: Paragon House, 1987.

Goodwyn, Lawrence. *Democratic Promise: The Populist Movement in America*. New York: Oxford University Press, 1976.

Graber, Doris A. *Mass Media and American Politics*. Washington, DC: CQ Press, 1993.

Grefe, Edward A., and Martin Linsky. *The New Corporate Activism: Harnessing the Power of Grassroots Tactics for Your Organization*. New York: McGraw-Hill, 1995.

Greider, William. *Who Will Tell the People?* New York: Simon and Schuster, 1992.

Harris, Fred R. *Deadlock or Decision: The U.S. Senate and the Rise of National Politics*. New York: Oxford University Press, 1993.

Harris, Richard A., and Sidney M. Milkis. *The Politics of Regulatory Change*. New York: Oxford University Press, 1989.

Harwood Group. *Meaningful Chaos: How People Form Relationships with Public Concerns*. Dayton, OH: Kettering Foundation, 1993.

Heath, Robert. *Issues Management: Corporate Public Policymaking in an Information Society*. Beverly Hills, CA: Sage, 1986.

——. *Strategic Issues Management*. San Francisco: Jossey-Bass, 1988.

Helvarg, David. *The War Against the Greens*. San Francisco: Sierra Club Books, 1994.

Hertzke, Allen D. *Representing God in Washington, DC: The Role of Religious Lobbies in the American Polity*. Knoxville: University of Tennessee Press, 1988.

Hess, Stephen. *Live from Capitol Hill!* Washington, DC: Brookings Institution, 1991.

Hirschman, Albert O. *Shifting Involvements: Private Interest and Public Action*. Princeton, NJ: Princeton University Press, 1982.

Hrebenar, Ronald. *Interest Group Politics in America*. 3d ed. (Armonk, NY: M.E. Sharpe, 1997).

Huber, Peter W., and Robert E. Litan, eds. *The Liability Maze*. Washington, DC: Brookings Institution, 1991.

Jamieson, Kathleen Hall, and Karlyn Campbell. *The Interplay of Influence: Mass Media and Their Publics in News, Advertising, Politics*. Belmont, CA: Wadsworth, 1988.

Jencks, Christopher. *The Homeless*. Cambridge: Harvard University Press, 1994.

Jones, Charles O. *The Presidency in a Separated System*. Washington, DC: Brookings Institution, 1994.

Kahn, Si. *Organizing: A Guide for Grassroots Leaders*. New York: McGraw-Hill, 1982.

Kazin, Michael. *The Populist Persuasion: An American History*. New York: Basic Books, 1995.

Kennamer, J. David, ed. *Public Opinion, the Press, and Public Policy*. Westport, CT: Praeger, 1992.

Kingdon, John W. *Agendas, Alternatives, and Public Policy*. Boston: Little, Brown, 1984.

Kurtz, Howard. *Media Circus: The Trouble with America's Newspapers*. New York: Times Books, 1993.

Lake, Celinda C. *Public Opinion Polling*. Washington, DC: Island Press, 1987.

Loftus, Tom. *The Art of Legislative Politics*. Washington, DC: CQ Press, 1994.

MacEachern, Diane. *Enough Is Enough: The Hell-Raiser's Guide to Community Activism*. New York: Avon Books, 1994.

McFarland, Andrew S. *Common Cause: Lobbying in the Public Interest*. Chatham, NJ: Chatham House, 1984.

McKenna, George, ed. *American Populism*. New York: Putnam's, 1974.

Mack, Charles S. *Lobbying and Government Relations: A Guide for Executives*. New York: Quorum Books, 1989.

Magleby, David. *Direct Legislation: Voting on Ballot Propositions in the US*. Baltimore: Johns Hopkins University, 1984.

Mahood, H.R. *Interest Group Politics in America*. Englewood Cliffs, NJ: Prentice Hall, 1990.

Makinson, Larry. *The Price of Admission: Campaign Spending in the 1994 Elections*. Washington, DC: Center for Responsive Politics, 1995.

Manheim, Jarol B. *All of the People, All the Time: Strategic Communication and American Politics*. Armonk, NY: M.E. Sharpe, 1991.

Mann, Thomas E., and Norman J. Ornstein, eds. *Congress, the Press, and the Public*. Washington, DC: American Enterprise Institute/Brookings Institution, 1994.

Mann, Thomas E. and Gary R. Orren. *Media Polls in American Politics*. Washington, DC: Brookings Institution, 1992.

Megalli, Mark. *Masks of Deception*. Washington, DC: Island Press, 1995.

Meredith, Judith C. *Lobbying on a Shoestring*. Dover, MA: Auburn House, 1989.

Miller, Charles. *Lobbying: Understanding and Influencing the Corridors of Power*. Cambridge, MA: Blackwell, 1990.

Montgomery, Kathryn C. *Target: Prime Time. Advocacy Groups and the Struggle over Entertainment Television*. New York: Oxford University Press, 1988.

Nagel, Jack H. *Participation*. Englewood Cliffs, NJ: Prentice Hall, 1987.

Olson, Mancur. *The Logic of Collective Action*. Cambridge: Harvard University Press, 1965.

Olson, Walter. *The Litigation Explosion*. New York: Dutton, 1991.

Patterson, Thomas E. *Out of Order*. New York: Knopf, 1993.

Pertschuk, Michael. *Giantkillers*. New York: Norton 1986.

Pertschuk, Michael, and Wendy Schaetzel. *The People Rising: The Campaign Against the Bork Nomination*. New York: Thunder's Mouth Press, 1989.

Peterson, Mark A. *Legislating Together: The White House and Capitol Hill from Eisenhower to Reagan*. Cambridge: Harvard University Press, 1990.

Petracca, Mark P., ed. *The Politics of Interests*. Boulder, CO: Westview Press, 1992.

Pinkerton, James P. *What Comes Next: The End of Big Government and the New Paradigm Ahead*. New York: Hyperion, 1995.

Price, David E. *The Congressional Experience: A View from the Hill*. Boulder, CO: Westview Press, 1992.

Pring, George, and Penelope Canan. *SLAPPs: Getting Sued for Speaking Out.* Philadelphia: Temple University Press, 1994.

Qualter, Terence. *Advertising and Democracy in the Mass Age.* New York: St. Martin's Press, 1991.

Rauch, Jonathan. *Demosclerosis.* New York: Times Books, 1994.

Renfro, William. *Issues Management in Strategic Planning.* Westport, CT: Quorum Books, 1993.

Rieselbach, Leroy N., ed. *Congressional Politics: The Evolving Legislative System.* 2nd ed. Boulder, CO: Westview Press, 1995.

Rosenthal, Alan. *The Third House: Lobbyists and Lobbying in the States.* Washington, DC: CQ Press, 1993.

Rosentone, Steven J., and John Mark Hansen. *Mobilization, Participation, and Democracy in America.* New York: MacMillan, 1993.

Ryan, Charlotte. *Prime Time Activism: Media Strategies for Grassroots Organizing.* Boston: South End Press, 1991.

Sabato, Larry J. *PAC Power: Inside the World of Political Action Committees.* New York: Norton, 1990.

Salisbury, Robert H., ed. *Interest Group Politics in America.* New York: Harper & Row, 1970.

Schattschnedier, E.E. *The Semisovereign People.* Hinsdale, IL: Dryden Press, 1975.

Schmidt, David. *Citizen Lawmakers: The Ballot Initiative Revolution.* Philadelphia: Temple University Press, 1989.

Schwartz, Tony. *The Responsive Chord.* New York: Anchor Press/Doubleday, 1973.

———. *Media: The Second God.* New York: Random House, 1981.

Sethi, S. Prakash. *Interfaith Center on Corporate Responsibility: A Sponsored-Related Movement of the National Council of Churches.* Dallas, TX: University of Texas, 1980.

Sinclair, Barbara. *Legislators, Leaders, and Lawmaking: The U.S. House of Representatives in the Postreform Era.* Baltimore, MD: Johns Hopkins University Press, 1995.

Smith, Hedrick. *The Power Game.* New York: Random House, 1988.

Smith, N. Craig. *Morality and the Market: Consumer Pressure for Corporate Accountability.* New York: Routledge, 1990.

Spitzer, Robert J., ed. *Media and Public Policy.* Westport, CT: Prager, 1993.

Stern, Philip M. *Still the Best Congress Money Can Buy.* Washington, DC: Regnery Gateway, 1992.

Truman, David B. *Governmental Process.* New York: Knopf, 1971.

Vogel, David. *Lobbying the Corporation.* New York: Basic Books, 1978.

Waldman, Michael. *Who Robbed America: A Citizen's Guide to the Savings and Loan Scandal.* New York: Random House, 1990.

Walker, Jack L., Jr. *Mobilizing Interest Groups in America: Patrons, Professions, and Social Movements.* Ann Arbor: University of Michigan Press, 1991.

Wallack, Lawrence, et al. *Media Advocacy and Public Health.* Newbury Park, CA: Sage, 1993.

Wattenberg, Martin P. *The Rise of Candidate-Centered Politics: Presidential Elections in the 1980s.* Cambridge: Harvard University Press, 1991.

Will, Rosalyn. *Shopping for a Better World: A Quick and Easy Guide to Socially Responsible Supermarket Shopping.* New York: Council on Economic Priorities, 1994.

Wittenberg, Ernest, and Elisabeth Wittenberg. *How to Win in Washington, DC: Very Practical Advice about Lobbying, the Grass Roots and the Media..* Cambridge, MA.: Blackwell, 1989.

Wolpe, Bruce C. *Lobbying Congress: How the System Works.* Washington, DC: CQ Press, 1990.

Wurman, Richard Saul. *Information Anxiety.* New York: Bantam Books, 1989.

Yankelovich, Daniel. *Coming to Public Judgment: Making Democracy Work in a Complex World.* Syracuse, NY: Syracuse University Press, 1991.

Zimmerman, Joseph. *Participatory Democracy.* New York: Praeger, 1986.

Zisk, Betty. *Money, Media, and the Grass Roots: State Ballot Issues and the Electoral Process.* Newbury Park, CA: Sage Publications, 1987.

Index

Abortion, 16, 35, 60, 62, 169
Action alerts, 190–192
Administrative agencies
  appropriations for, 167–168, 170–171
  cost-benefit analysis by, 100–102,
    160
  deregulation and, 53–54, 236–237
  discretion of, 58–61
  federal *vs* state regulation and, 55–57
  implementation role of, 57–58
  information before, 170
  limits on action of, 60–61
  lobbying of, 152, 153–154, 159,
    168–174
  public opinion and, 171–172
  rulemaking by, 44–45, 168–169, 173
Administrative Procedure Act, 61
Adoption, 141–142
Advertising. *See* Issue advertising
Aetna Insurance Company, 4
Affirmative action, 238, 248
AFL-CIO, 186
Agriculture Department, 94, 107
AIDS, 82, 93, 105, 110, 169
Alar, 101–102, 112
Alcoholic beverage industry
  advertising by, 112
  ballot initiative and, 216, 221, 223

Alcoholic beverage industry
  (continued)
  charitable giving and, 211–212
  grassroots and, 209
Alliance for Energy Security, 207
Alliance for Jobs and Health, 264*n.1*
Allied Chemical, 124
Alzheimer's Association, 34
American Arts Alliance, 27
American Association for the
  Advancement of Science, 27
American Association of Retired
  Persons, 4, 27, 30, 31–32, 186,
  192–193, 241
American Automobile Association,
  31, 34
American Bankers' Association, 199
American Bar Association, 31
American Civil Liberties Union, 27,
  141
American Council on Science and
  Health, 97
American Legion, 27
American Library Association, 27
American Medical Association, 29,
  31, 39, 47, 186
Americans for Tax Reform, 141
Anecdotal information, 88–89, 162

279

About the Author

Barry R. Rubin is a member of the faculty of George Washington University's Graduate School of Political Management. He also practices law and serves as president of Strategic Solutions, which provides strategic counseling and training in issue advocacy. He is chairman of the board of directors of 20/20 Vision, a national grassroots peace and environmental organization. He earned a B.A. degree from Brandeis University and a J.D. from Harvard Law School.